LUCILLE B

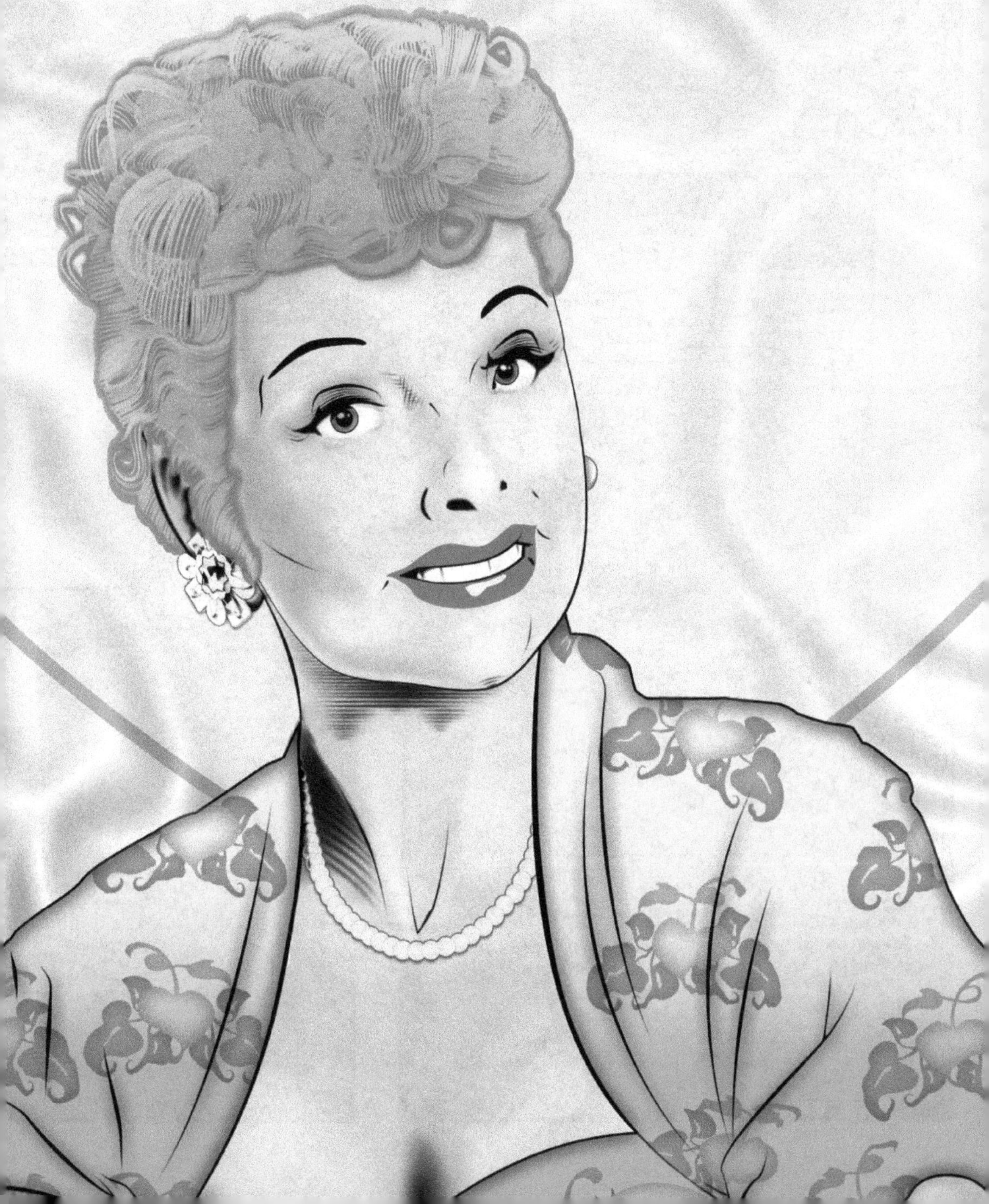

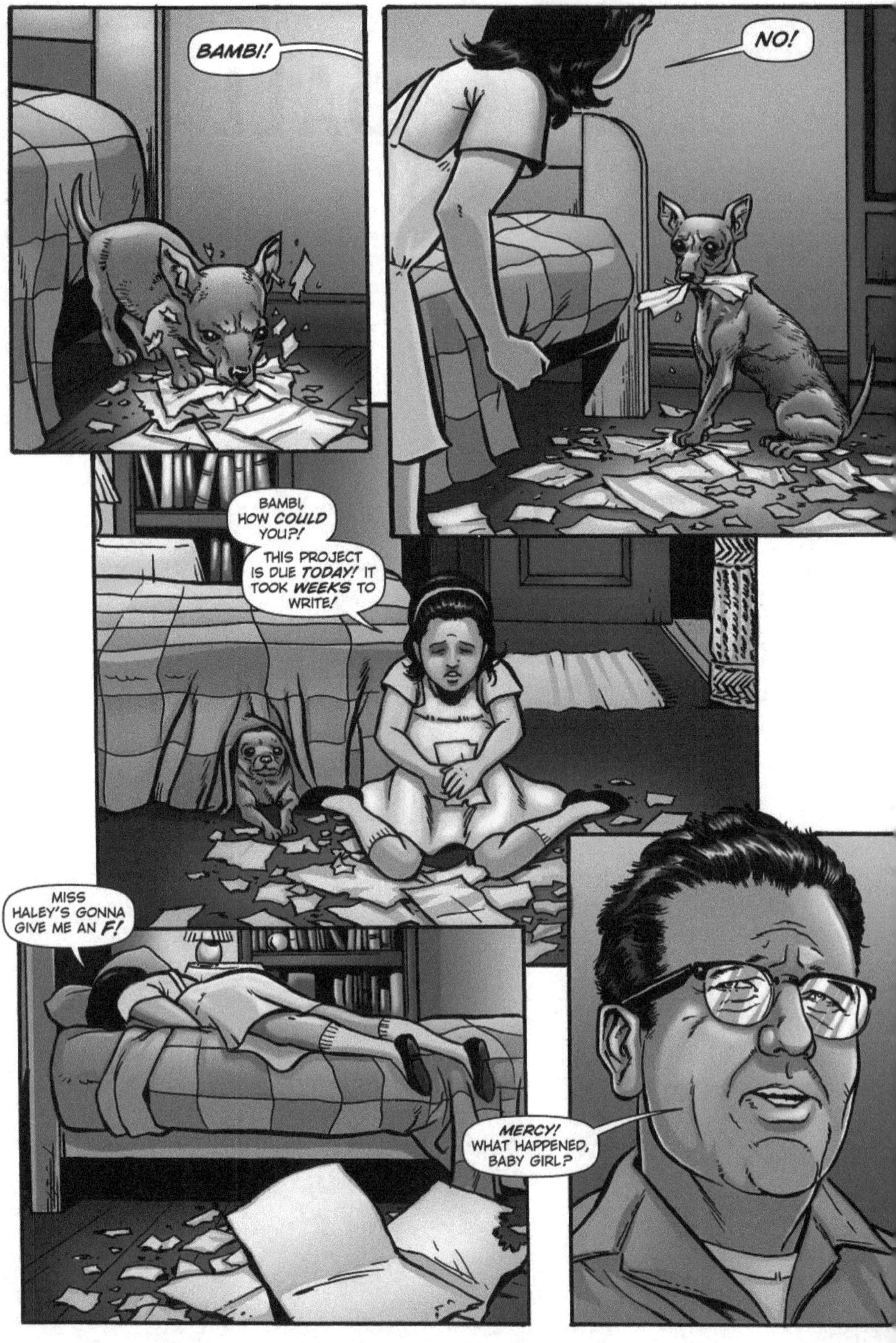
BAMBI!
NO!
BAMBI, HOW COULD YOU?!
THIS PROJECT IS DUE TODAY! IT TOOK WEEKS TO WRITE!
MISS HALEY'S GONNA GIVE ME AN F!
MERCY! WHAT HAPPENED, BABY GIRL?

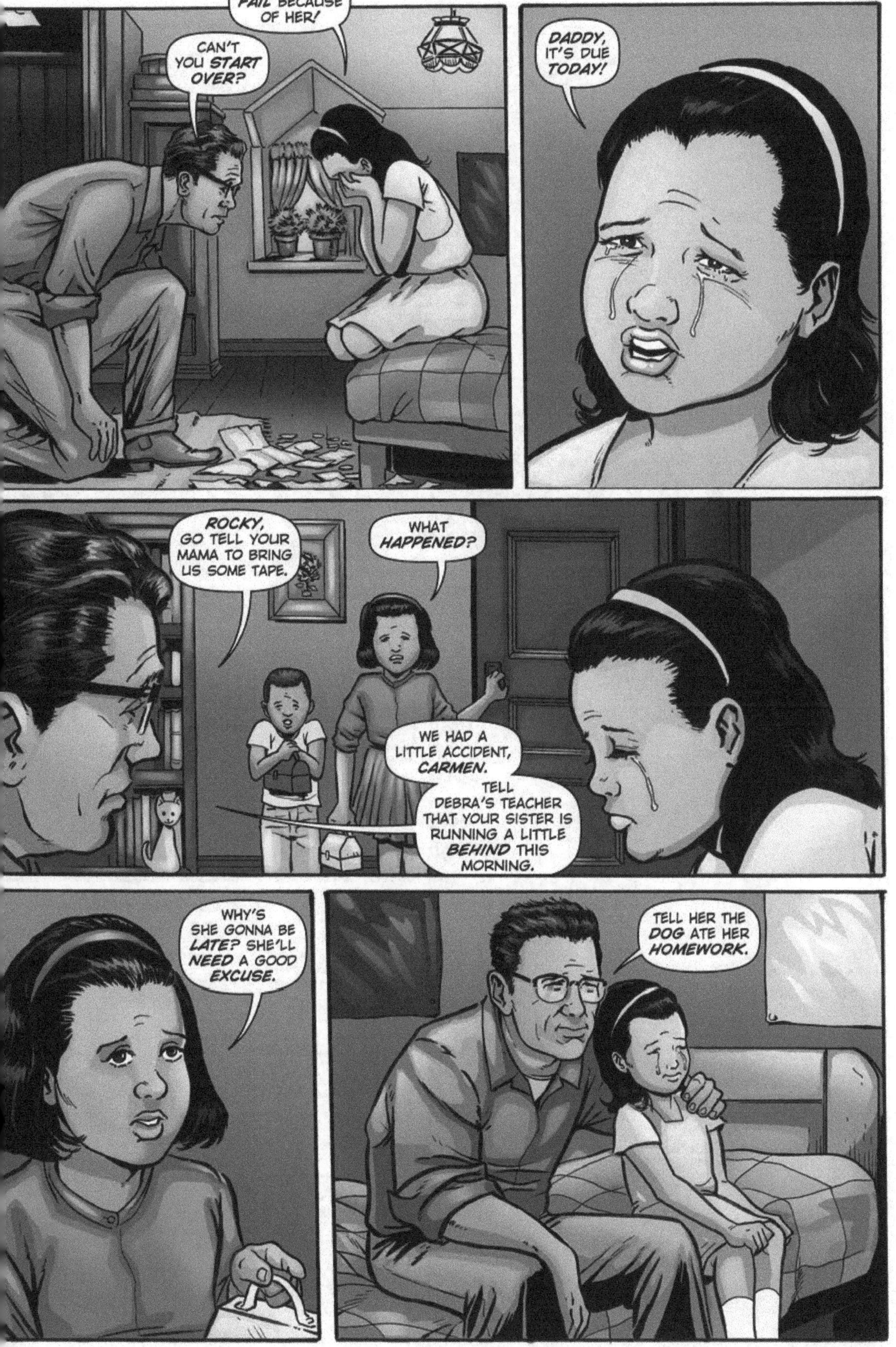
I'M GONNA FAIL BECAUSE OF HER!
CAN'T YOU START OVER?
DADDY, IT'S DUE TODAY!
ROCKY, GO TELL YOUR MAMA TO BRING US SOME TAPE.
WHAT HAPPENED?
WE HAD A LITTLE ACCIDENT, CARMEN.
TELL DEBRA'S TEACHER THAT YOUR SISTER IS RUNNING A LITTLE BEHIND THIS MORNING.
WHY'S SHE GONNA BE LATE? SHE'LL NEED A GOOD EXCUSE.
TELL HER THE DOG ATE HER HOMEWORK.

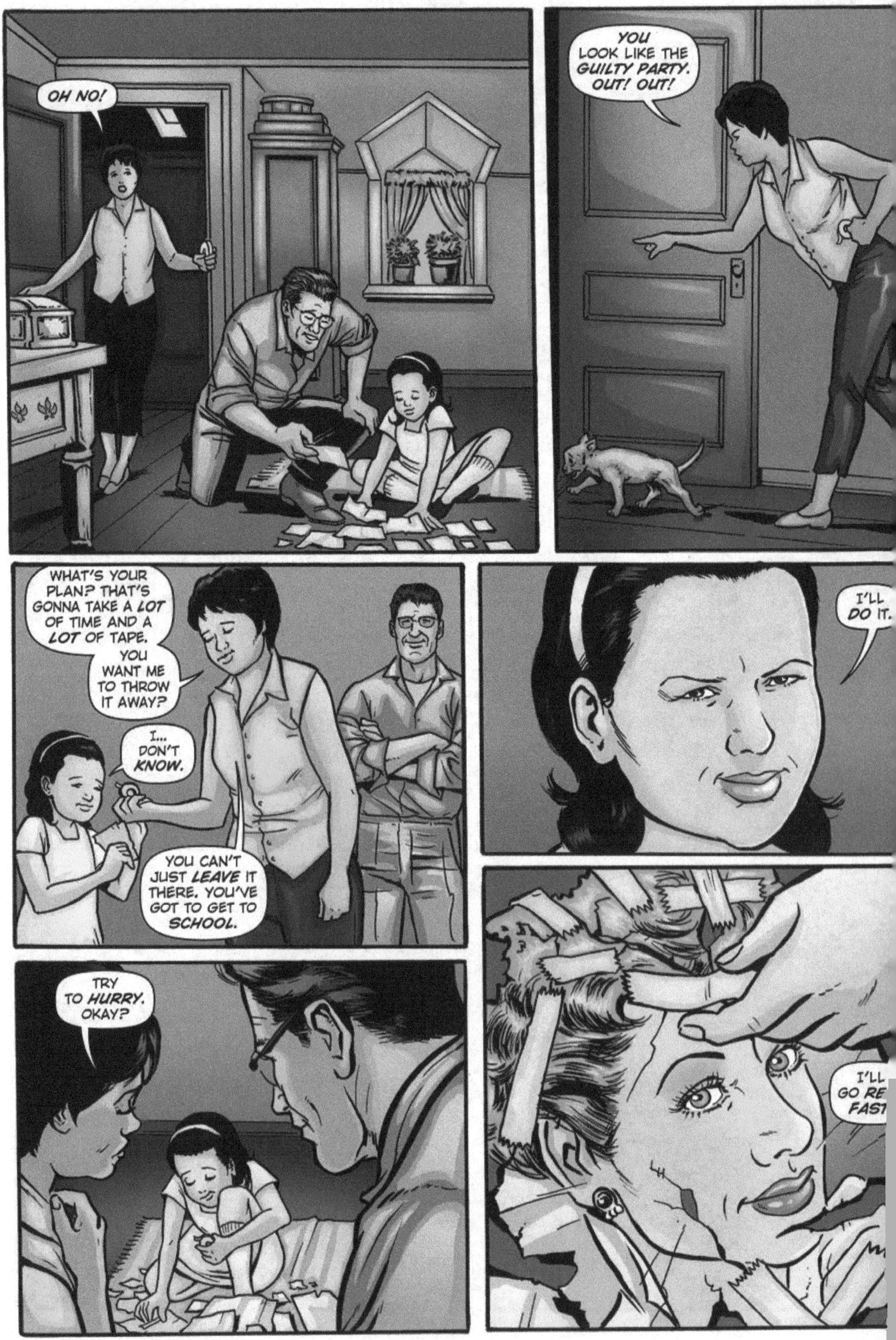
OH NO!
YOU LOOK LIKE THE GUILTY PARTY. OUT! OUT!
WHAT'S YOUR PLAN? THAT'S GONNA TAKE A LOT OF TIME AND A LOT OF TAPE.
YOU WANT ME TO THROW IT AWAY?
I... DON'T KNOW.
YOU CAN'T JUST LEAVE IT THERE. YOU'VE GOT TO GET TO SCHOOL.
I'LL DO IT.
TRY TO HURRY. OKAY?
I'LL GO RE FAST

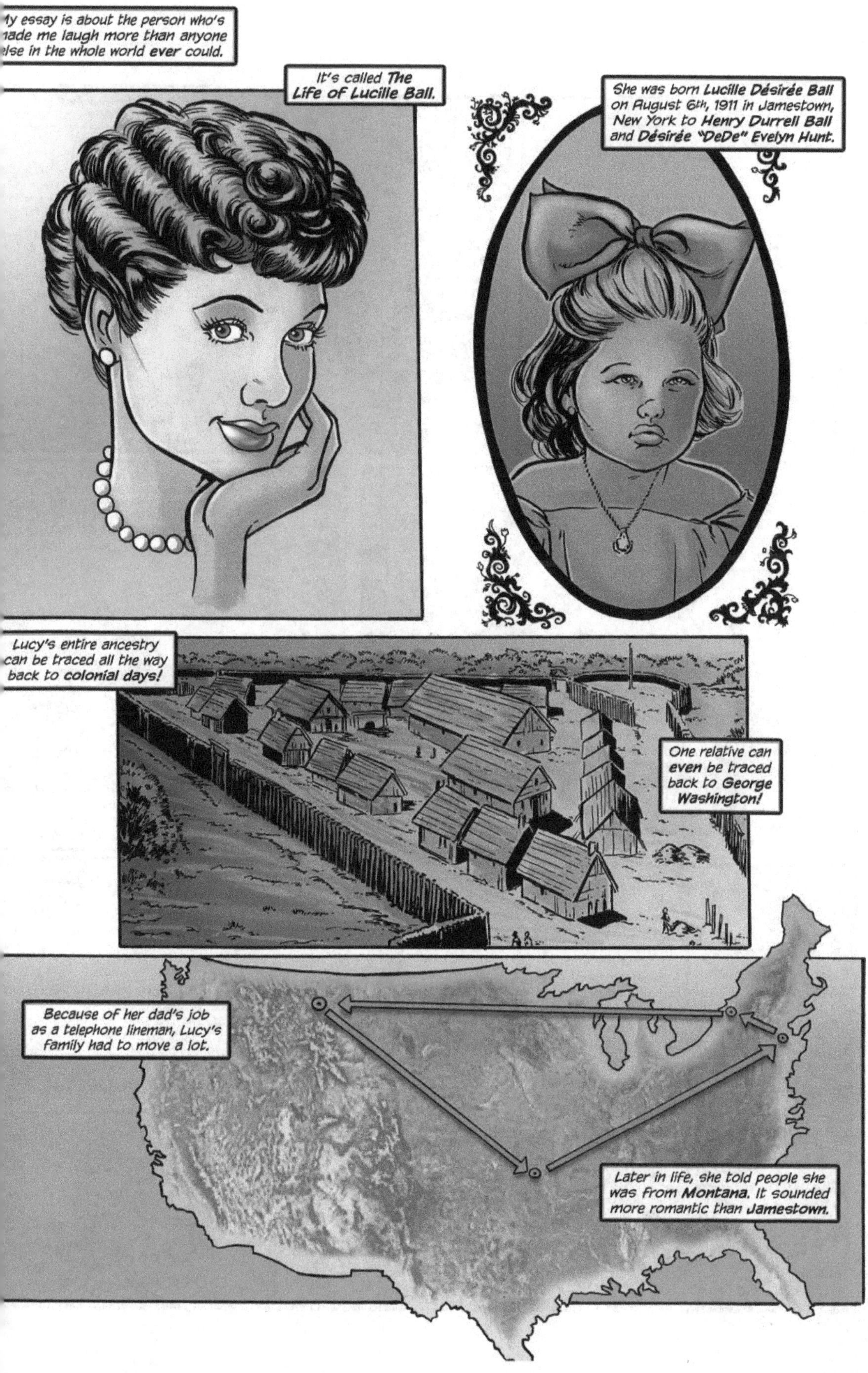

ly essay is about the person who's
nade me laugh more than anyone
else in the whole world ever could.
It's called The Life of Lucille Ball.
She was born Lucille Désirée Ball on August 6th, 1911 in Jamestown, New York to Henry Durrell Ball and Désirée "DeDe" Evelyn Hunt.
Lucy's entire ancestry can be traced all the way back to colonial days!
One relative can even be traced back to George Washington!
Because of her dad's job as a telephone lineman, Lucy's family had to move a lot.
Later in life, she told people she was from Montana. It sounded more romantic than Jamestown.

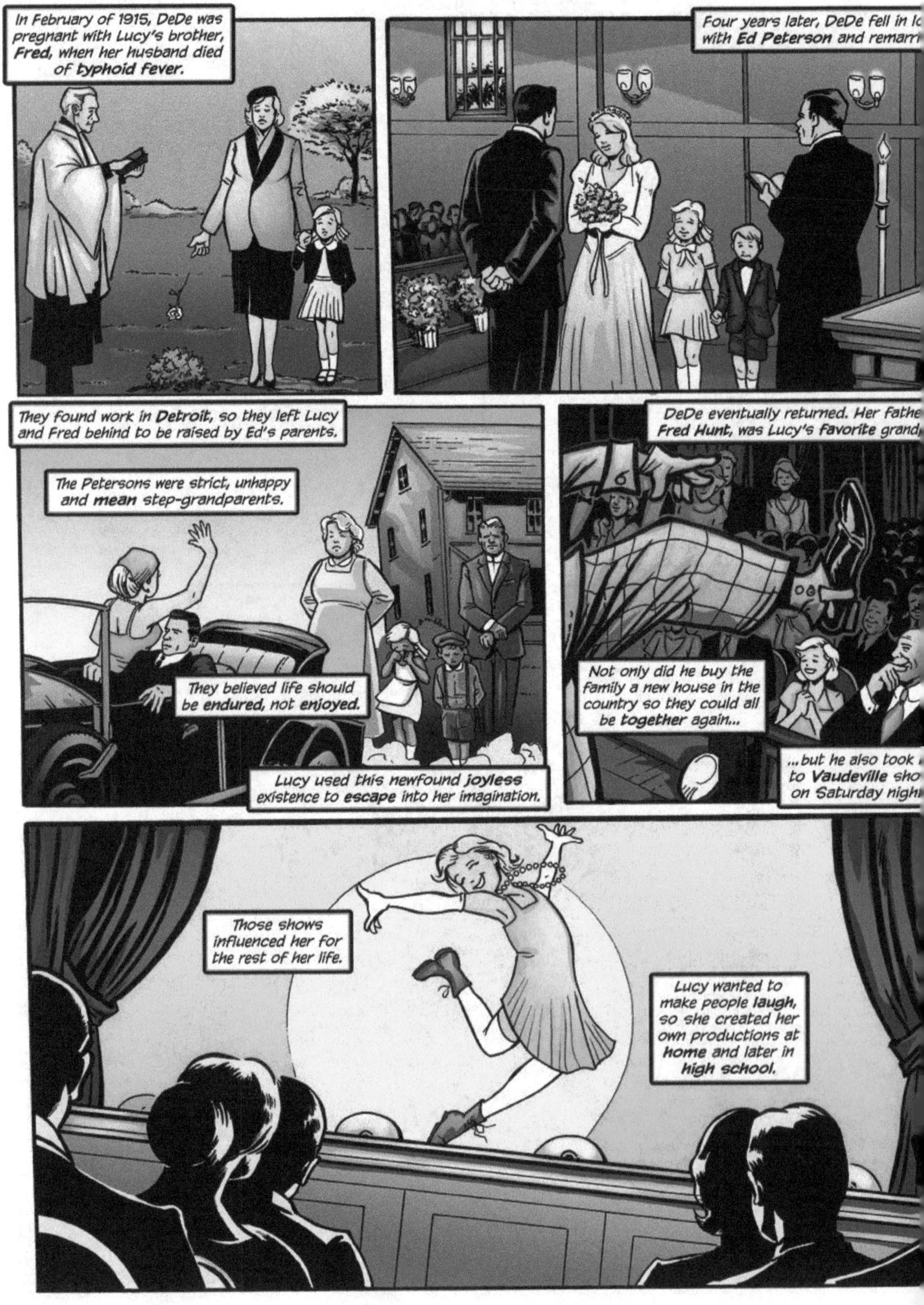
In February of 1915, DeDe was pregnant with Lucy's brother, Fred, when her husband died of typhoid fever.
Four years later, DeDe fell in lo
with Ed Peterson and remarr
They found work in Detroit, so they left Lucy and Fred behind to be raised by Ed's parents.
The Petersons were strict, unhappy and mean step-grandparents.
They believed life should be endured, not enjoyed.
Lucy used this newfound joyless existence to escape into her imagination.
DeDe eventually returned. Her fathe
Fred Hunt, was Lucy's favorite grand
Not only did he buy the family a new house in the country so they could all be together again...
...but he also took
to Vaudeville sho
on Saturday nigh
Those shows influenced her for the rest of her life.
Lucy wanted to make people laugh, so she created her own productions at home and later in high school.

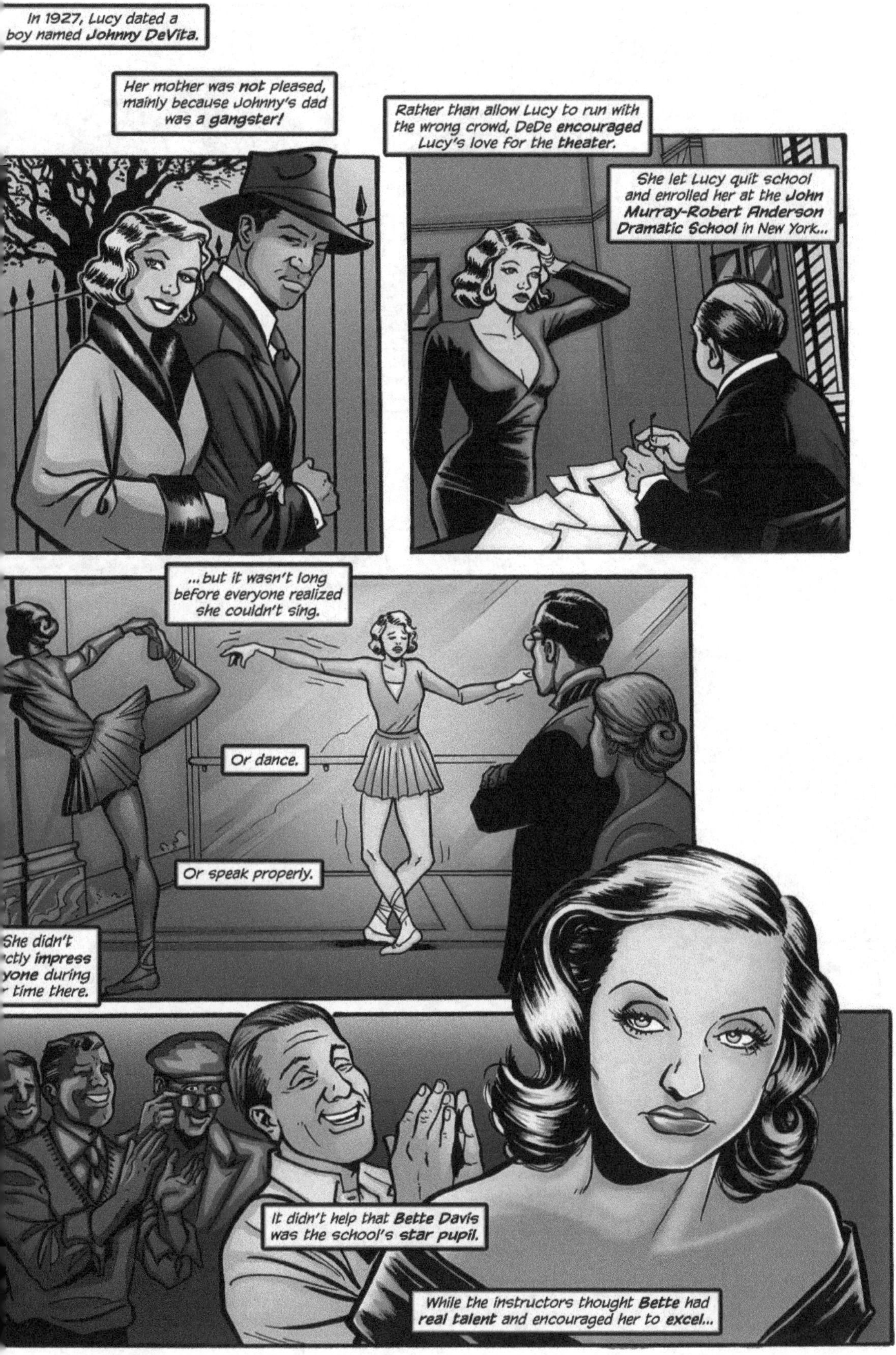
In 1927, Lucy dated a boy named Johnny DeVita.
Her mother was not pleased, mainly because Johnny's dad was a gangster!
Rather than allow Lucy to run with the wrong crowd, DeDe encouraged Lucy's love for the theater.
She let Lucy quit school and enrolled her at the John Murray-Robert Anderson Dramatic School in New York...
...but it wasn't long before everyone realized she couldn't sing.
Or dance.
Or speak properly.
She didn't ctly impress yone during time there.
It didn't help that Bette Davis was the school's star pupil.
While the instructors thought Bette had real talent and encouraged her to excel...

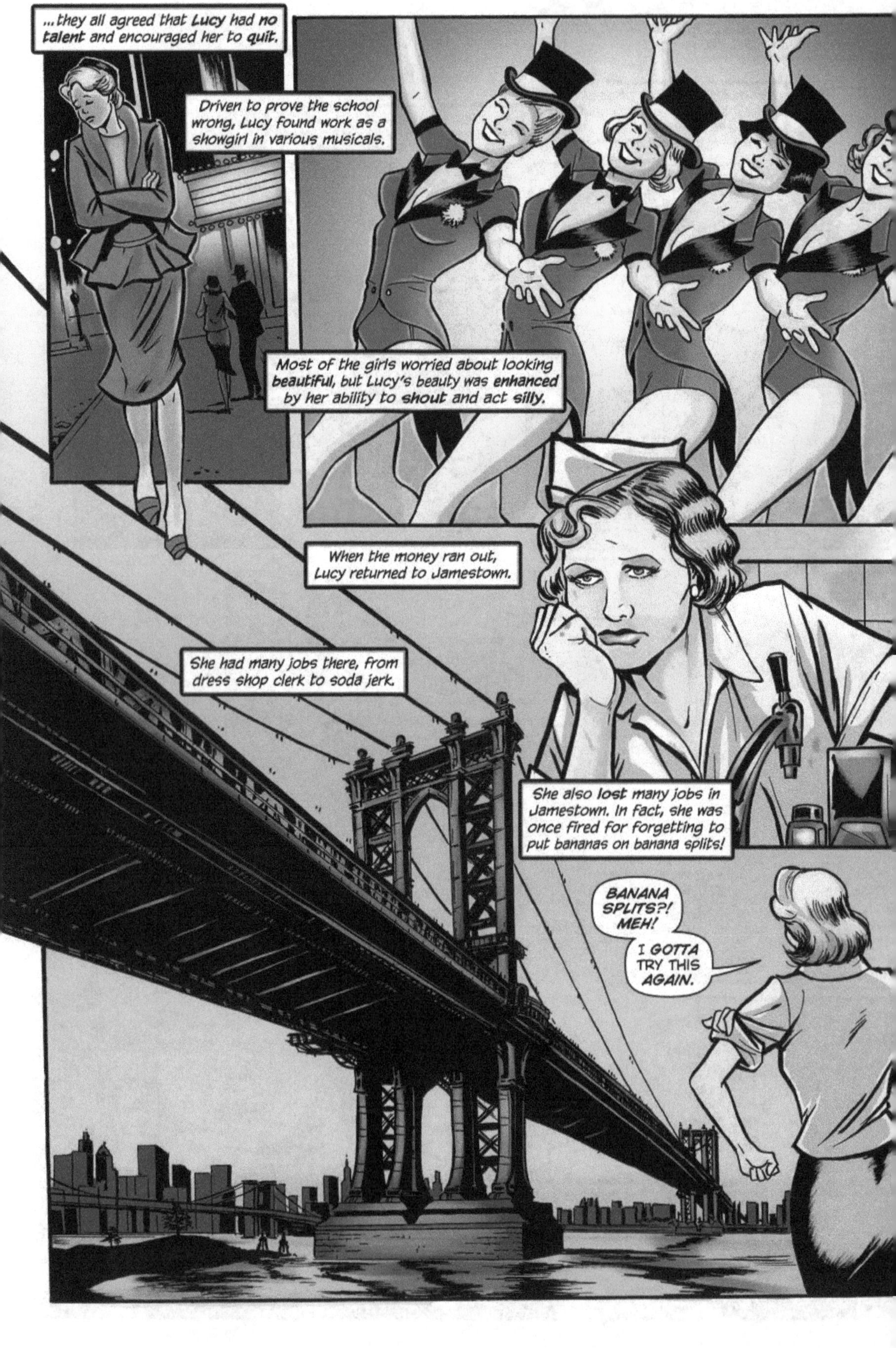

...they all agreed that Lucy had no talent and encouraged her to quit.
Driven to prove the school wrong, Lucy found work as a showgirl in various musicals.
Most of the girls worried about looking beautiful, but Lucy's beauty was enhanced by her ability to shout and act silly.
When the money ran out, Lucy returned to Jamestown.
She had many jobs there, from dress shop clerk to soda jerk.
She also lost many jobs in Jamestown. In fact, she was once fired for forgetting to put bananas on banana splits!
BANANA SPLITS?! MEH!
I GOTTA TRY THIS AGAIN.

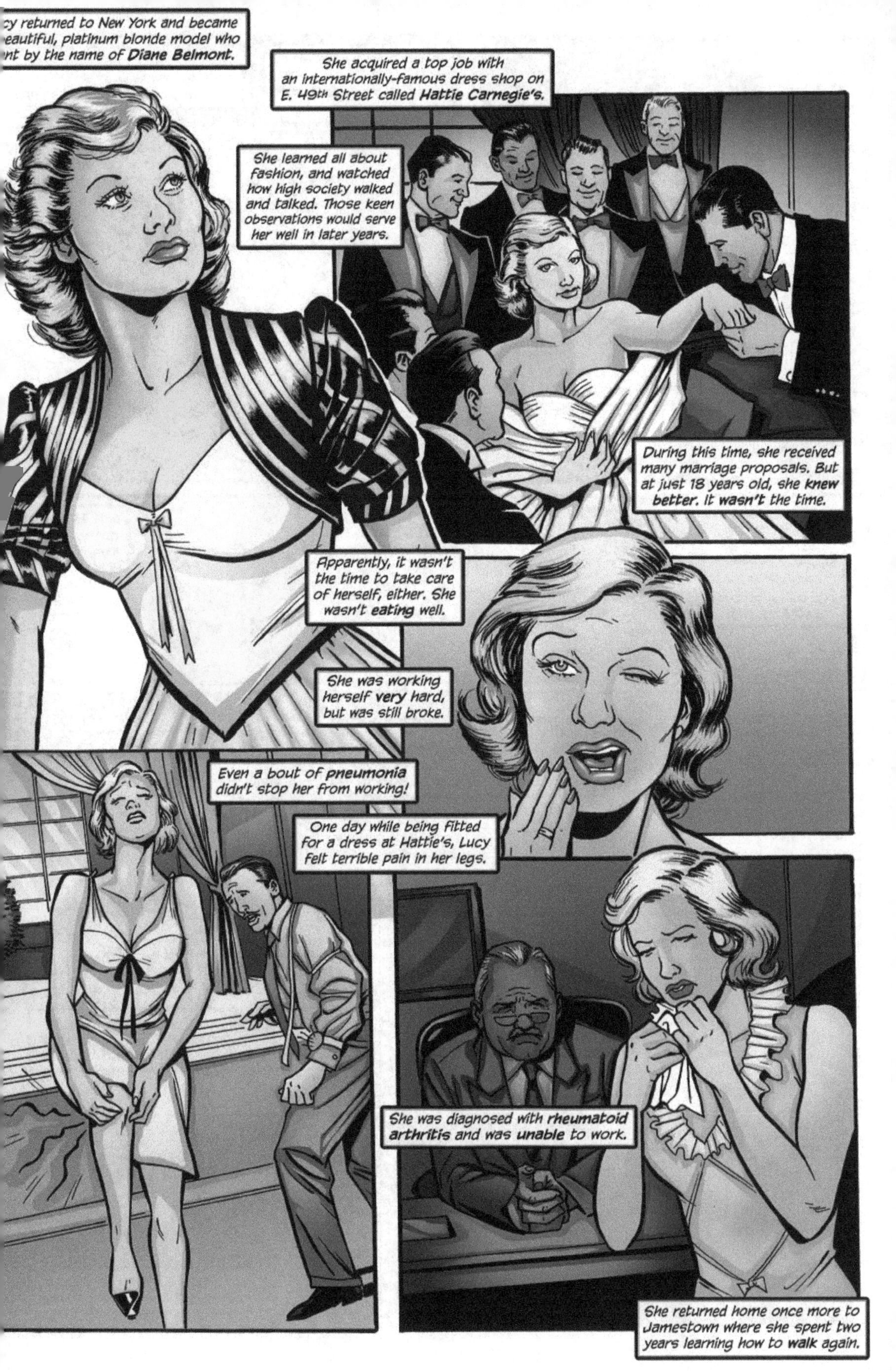
cy returned to New York and became
eautiful, platinum blonde model who
nt by the name of Diane Belmont.
She acquired a top job with an internationally-famous dress shop on E. 49th Street called Hattie Carnegie's.
She learned all about fashion, and watched how high society walked and talked. Those keen observations would serve her well in later years.
During this time, she received many marriage proposals. But at just 18 years old, she knew better. It wasn't the time.
Apparently, it wasn't the time to take care of herself, either. She wasn't eating well.
She was working herself very hard, but was still broke.
Even a bout of pneumonia didn't stop her from working!
One day while being fitted for a dress at Hattie's, Lucy felt terrible pain in her legs.
She was diagnosed with rheumatoid arthritis and was unable to work.
She returned home once more to Jamestown where she spent two years learning how to walk again.

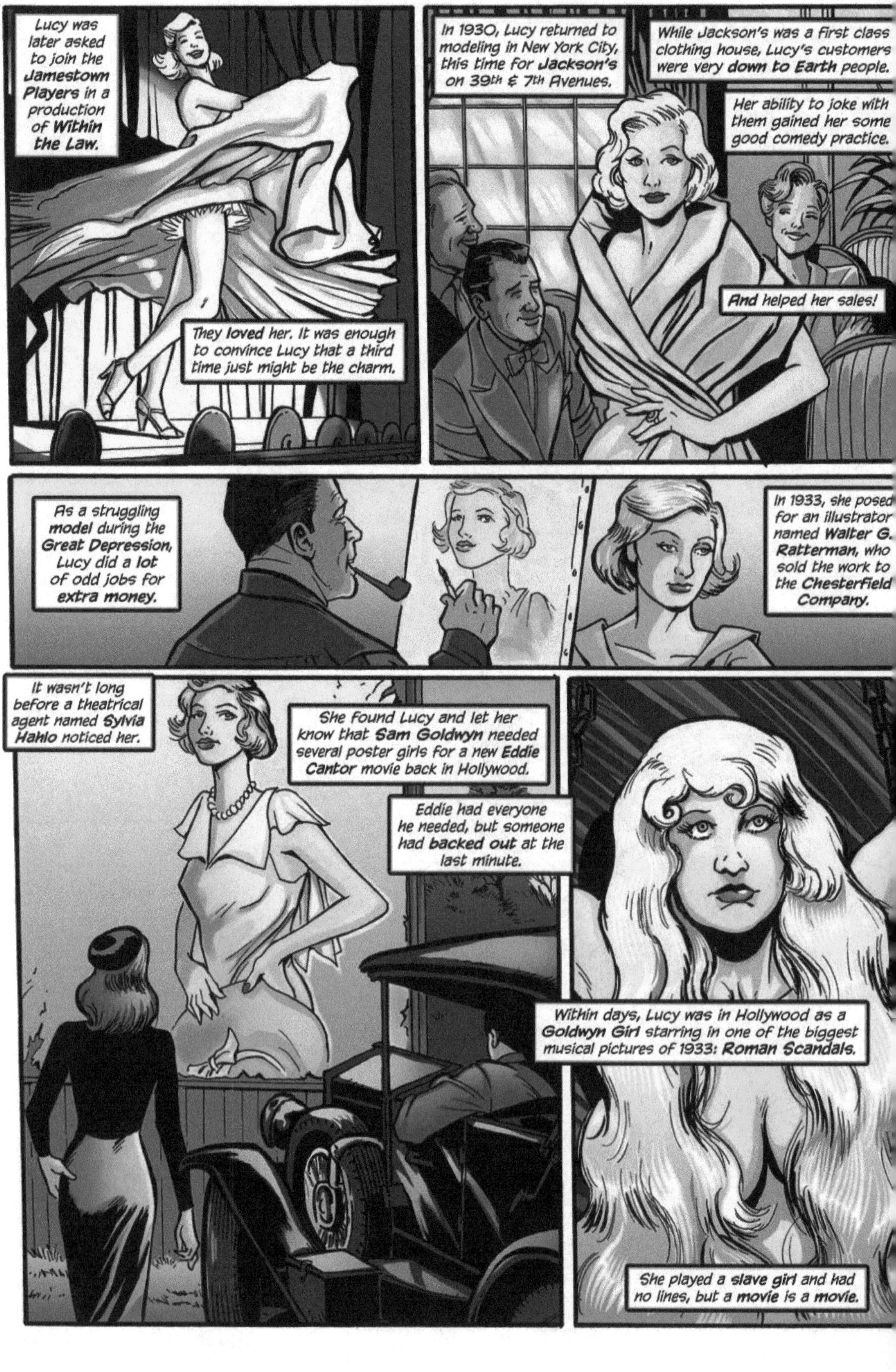
Lucy was later asked to join the Jamestown Players in a production of Within the Law.
They loved her. It was enough to convince Lucy that a third time just might be the charm.
In 1930, Lucy returned to modeling in New York City, this time for Jackson's on 39th & 7th Avenues.
While Jackson's was a first class clothing house, Lucy's customers were very down to Earth people.
Her ability to joke with them gained her some good comedy practice.
And helped her sales!
As a struggling model during the Great Depression, Lucy did a lot of odd jobs for extra money.
In 1933, she posed for an illustrator named Walter G. Ratterman, who sold the work to the Chesterfield Company.
It wasn't long before a theatrical agent named Sylvia Hahlo noticed her.
She found Lucy and let her know that Sam Goldwyn needed several poster girls for a new Eddie Cantor movie back in Hollywood.
Eddie had everyone he needed, but someone had backed out at the last minute.
Within days, Lucy was in Hollywood as a Goldwyn Girl starring in one of the biggest musical pictures of 1933: Roman Scandals.
She played a slave girl and had no lines, but a movie is a movie.

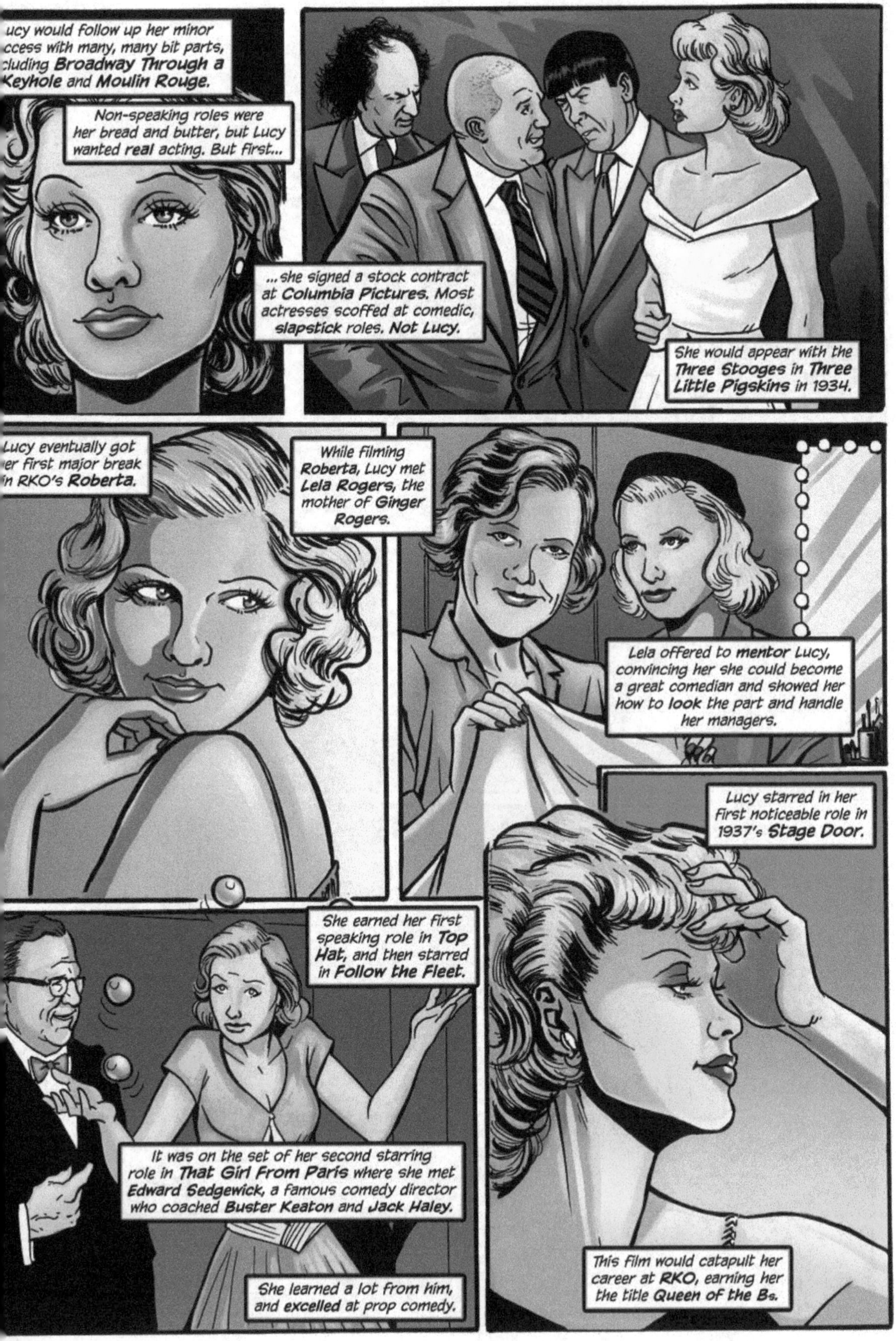

ucy would follow up her minor ccess with many, many bit parts, cluding Broadway Through a Keyhole and Moulin Rouge.
Non-speaking roles were her bread and butter, but Lucy wanted real acting. But first...
...she signed a stock contract at Columbia Pictures. Most actresses scoffed at comedic, slapstick roles. Not Lucy.
She would appear with the Three Stooges in Three Little Pigskins in 1934.
Lucy eventually got er first major break in RKO's Roberta.
While filming Roberta, Lucy met Lela Rogers, the mother of Ginger Rogers.
Lela offered to mentor Lucy, convincing her she could become a great comedian and showed her how to look the part and handle her managers.
Lucy starred in her first noticeable role in 1937's Stage Door.
She earned her first speaking role in Top Hat, and then starred in Follow the Fleet.
It was on the set of her second starring role in That Girl From Paris where she met Edward Sedgewick, a famous comedy director who coached Buster Keaton and Jack Haley.
She learned a lot from him, and excelled at prop comedy.
This film would catapult her career at RKO, earning her the title Queen of the Bs.

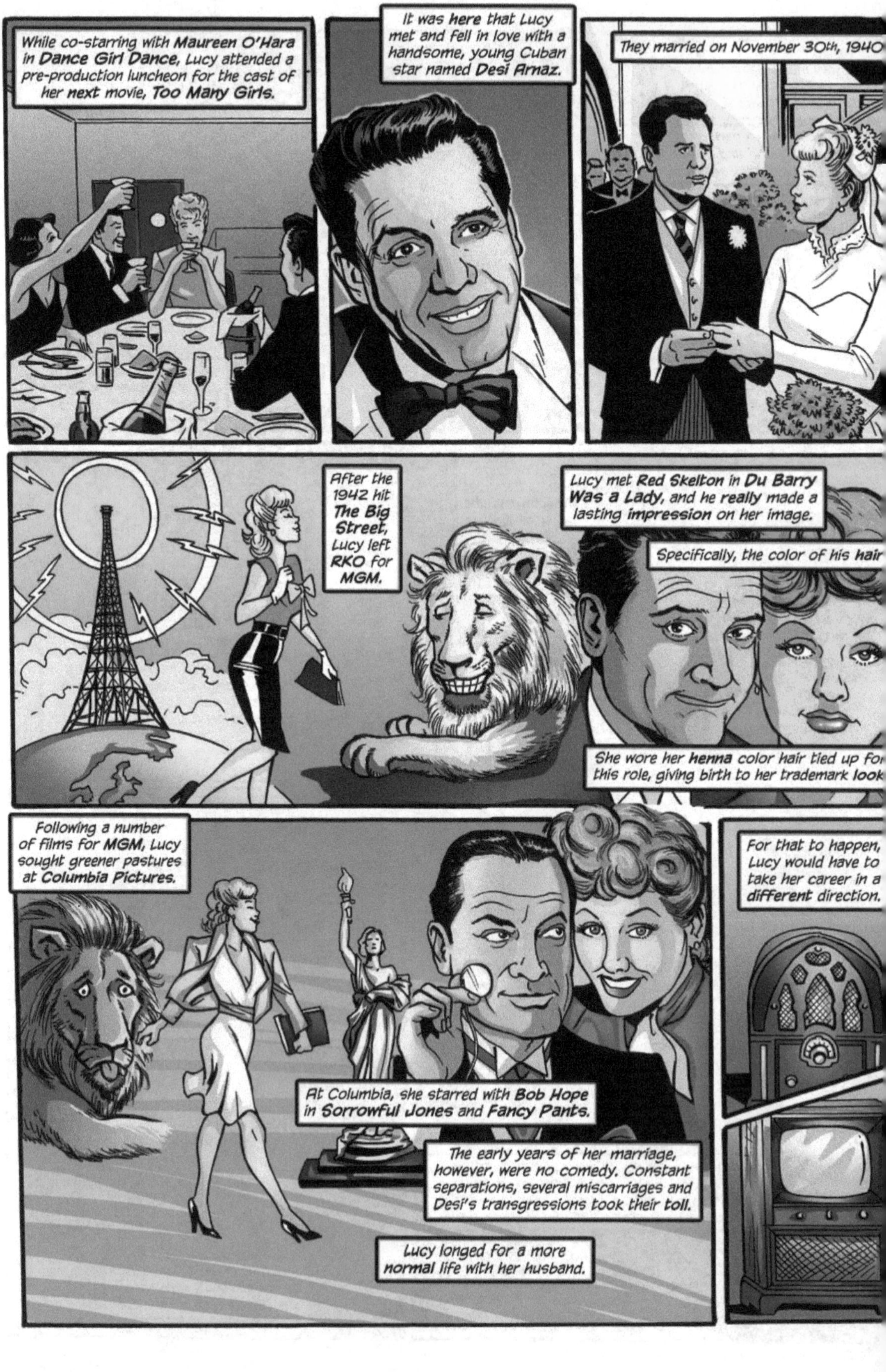
While co-starring with Maureen O'Hara in Dance Girl Dance, Lucy attended a pre-production luncheon for the cast of her next movie, Too Many Girls.
It was here that Lucy met and fell in love with a handsome, young Cuban star named Desi Arnaz.
They married on November 30th, 1940
After the 1942 hit The Big Street, Lucy left RKO for MGM.
Lucy met Red Skelton in Du Barry Was a Lady, and he really made a lasting impression on her image.
Specifically, the color of his hair
She wore her henna color hair tied up for this role, giving birth to her trademark look
Following a number of films for MGM, Lucy sought greener pastures at Columbia Pictures.
At Columbia, she starred with Bob Hope in Sorrowful Jones and Fancy Pants.
The early years of her marriage, however, were no comedy. Constant separations, several miscarriages and Desi's transgressions took their toll.
Lucy longed for a more normal life with her husband.
For that to happen, Lucy would have to take her career in a different direction.

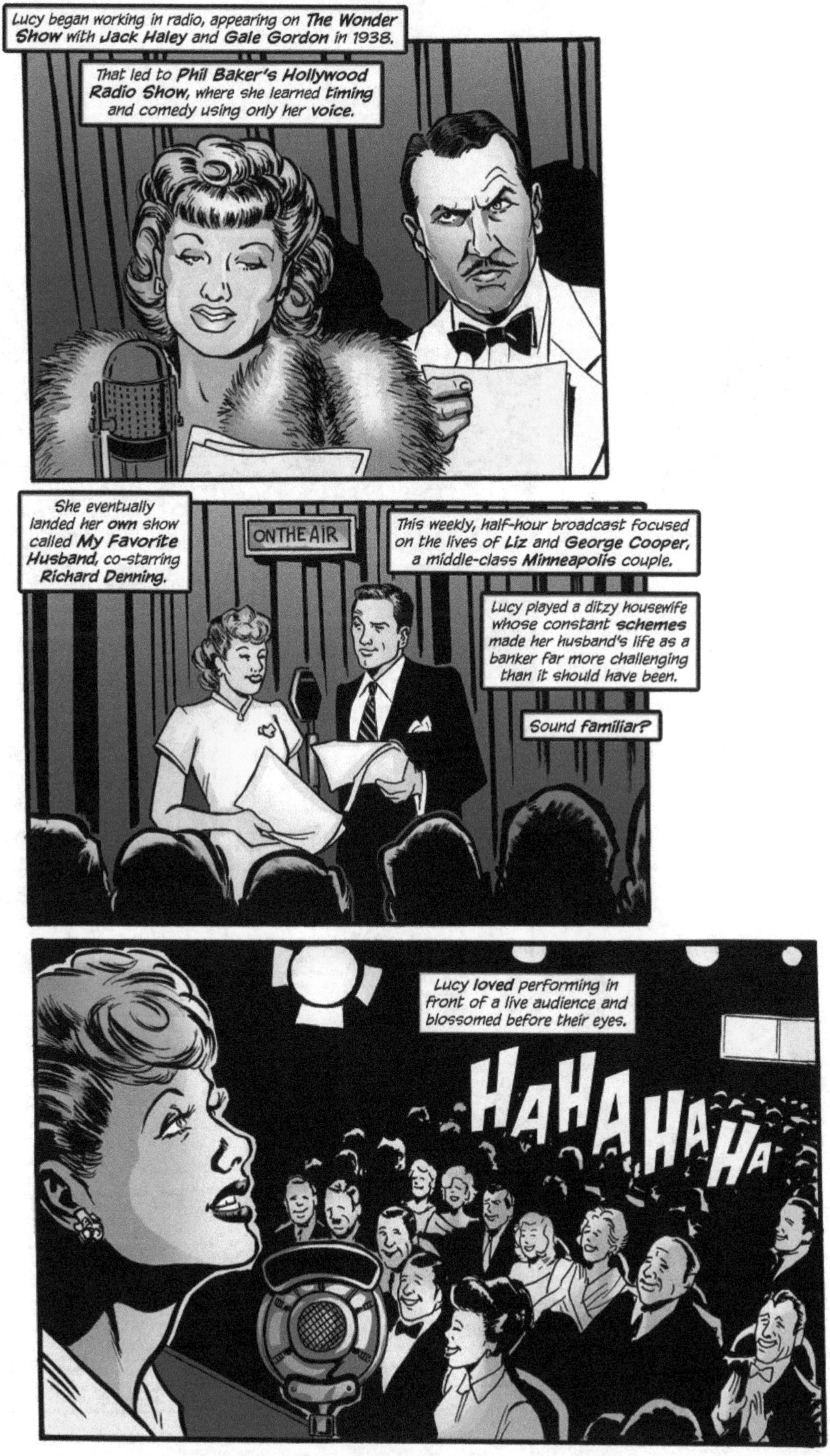
Lucy began working in radio, appearing on **The Wonder Show** with **Jack Haley** and **Gale Gordon** in 1938.
That led to **Phil Baker's Hollywood Radio Show**, where she learned **timing** and comedy using only her **voice.**
She eventually landed her **own** show called **My Favorite Husband**, co-starring **Richard Denning.**
ON THE AIR
This weekly, half-hour broadcast focused on the lives of **Liz** and **George Cooper**, a middle-class **Minneapolis** couple.
Lucy played a ditzy housewife whose constant **schemes** made her husband's life as a banker far more challenging than it should have been.
Sound **familiar?**
Lucy **loved** performing in front of a live audience and blossomed before their eyes.
HAHAHAHAHA

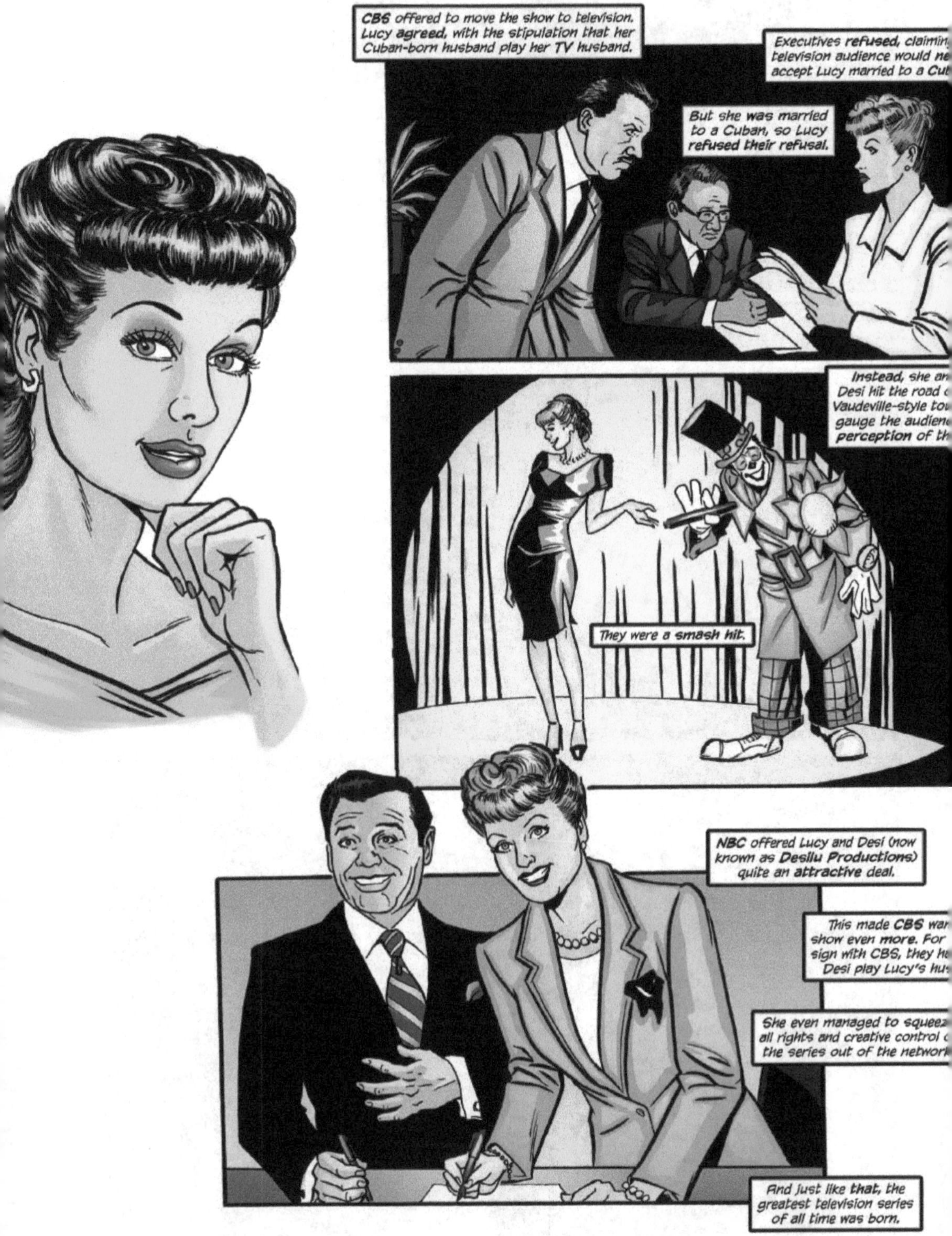

CBS offered to move the show to television. Lucy agreed, with the stipulation that her Cuban-born husband play her TV husband.
Executives refused, claimin television audience would ne accept Lucy married to a Cu
But she was married to a Cuban, so Lucy refused their refusal.
Instead, she an Desi hit the road Vaudeville-style to gauge the audien perception of th
They were a smash hit.
NBC offered Lucy and Desi (now known as Desilu Productions) quite an attractive deal.
This made CBS wa show even more. For sign with CBS, they h Desi play Lucy's hu
She even managed to squee all rights and creative control the series out of the networ
And just like that, the greatest television series of all time was born.

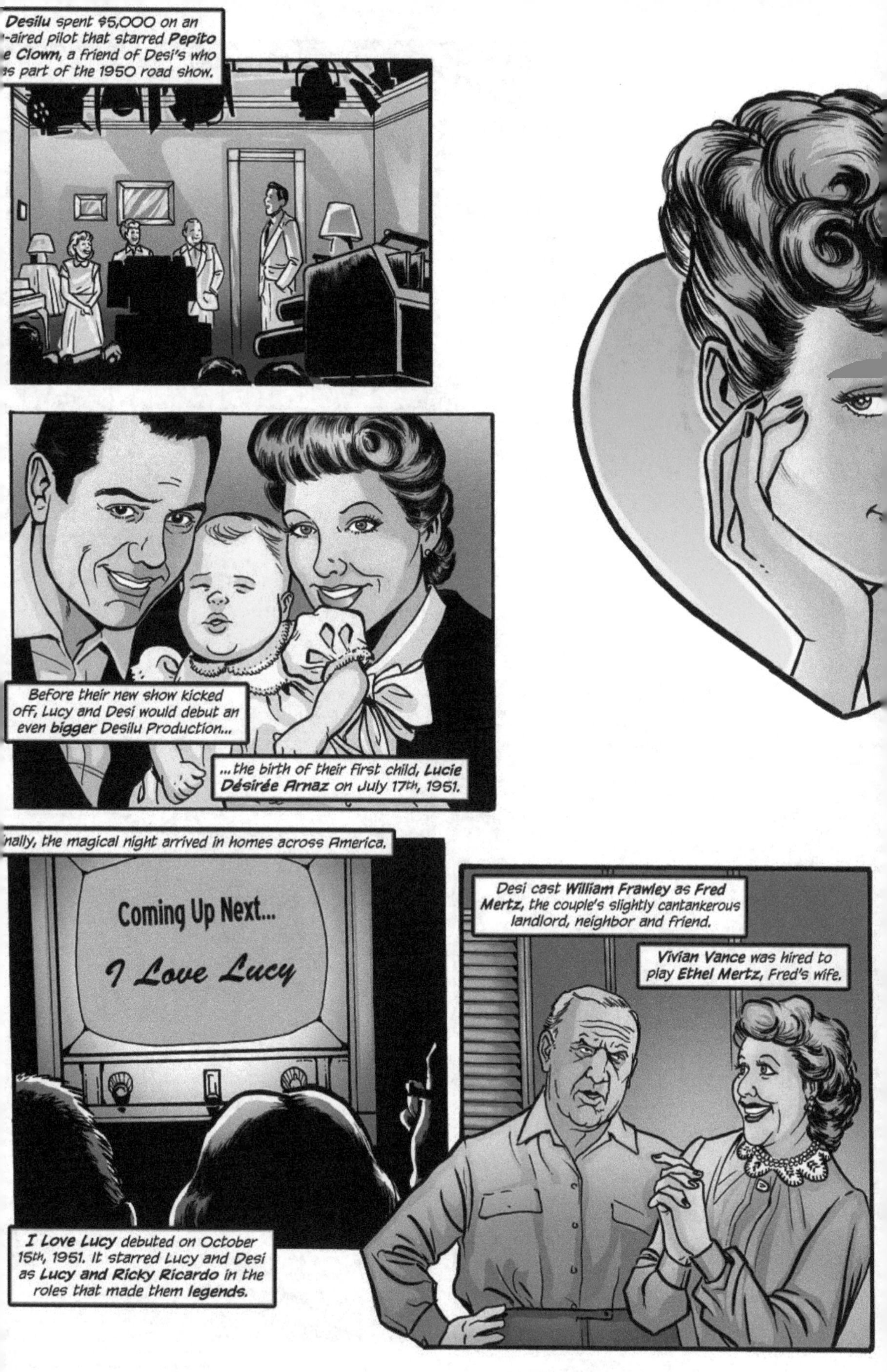
Desilu spent $5,000 on an
-aired pilot that starred Pepito
e Clown, a friend of Desi's who
s part of the 1950 road show.
Before their new show kicked off, Lucy and Desi would debut an even bigger Desilu Production...
...the birth of their first child, Lucie Désirée Arnaz on July 17th, 1951.
nally, the magical night arrived in homes across America.
Coming Up Next...
I Love Lucy
I Love Lucy debuted on October 15th, 1951. It starred Lucy and Desi as Lucy and Ricky Ricardo in the roles that made them legends.
Desi cast William Frawley as Fred Mertz, the couple's slightly cantankerous landlord, neighbor and friend.
Vivian Vance was hired to play Ethel Mertz, Fred's wife.

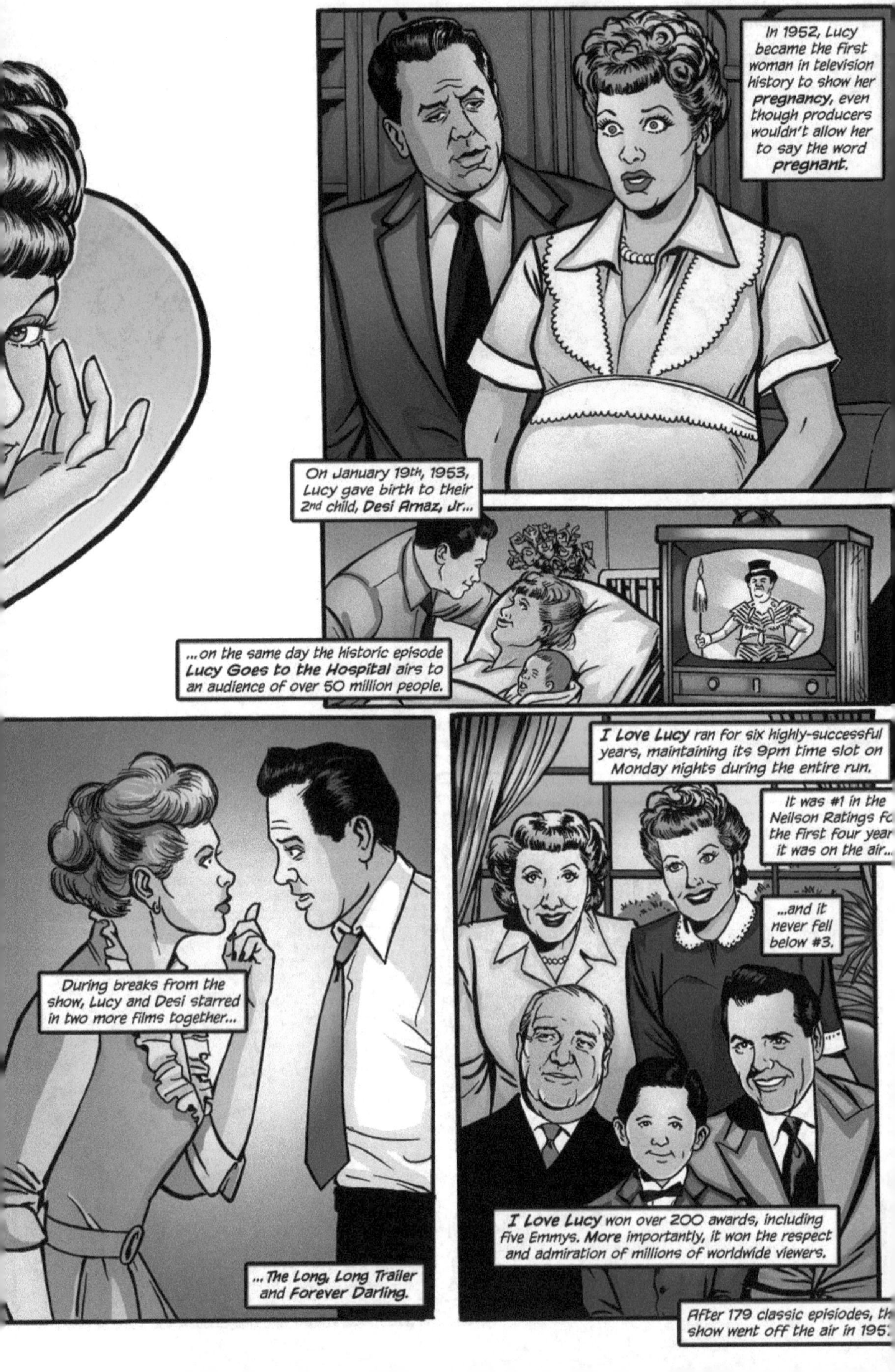

In 1952, Lucy became the first woman in television history to show her pregnancy, even though producers wouldn't allow her to say the word pregnant.
On January 19th, 1953, Lucy gave birth to their 2nd child, Desi Arnaz, Jr...
...on the same day the historic episode Lucy Goes to the Hospital airs to an audience of over 50 million people.
During breaks from the show, Lucy and Desi starred in two more films together...
...The Long, Long Trailer and Forever Darling.
I Love Lucy ran for six highly-successful years, maintaining its 9pm time slot on Monday nights during the entire run.
It was #1 in the Neilson Ratings fo the first four year it was on the air...
...and it never fell below #3.
I Love Lucy won over 200 awards, including five Emmys. More importantly, it won the respect and admiration of millions of worldwide viewers.
After 179 classic episodes, th show went off the air in 195

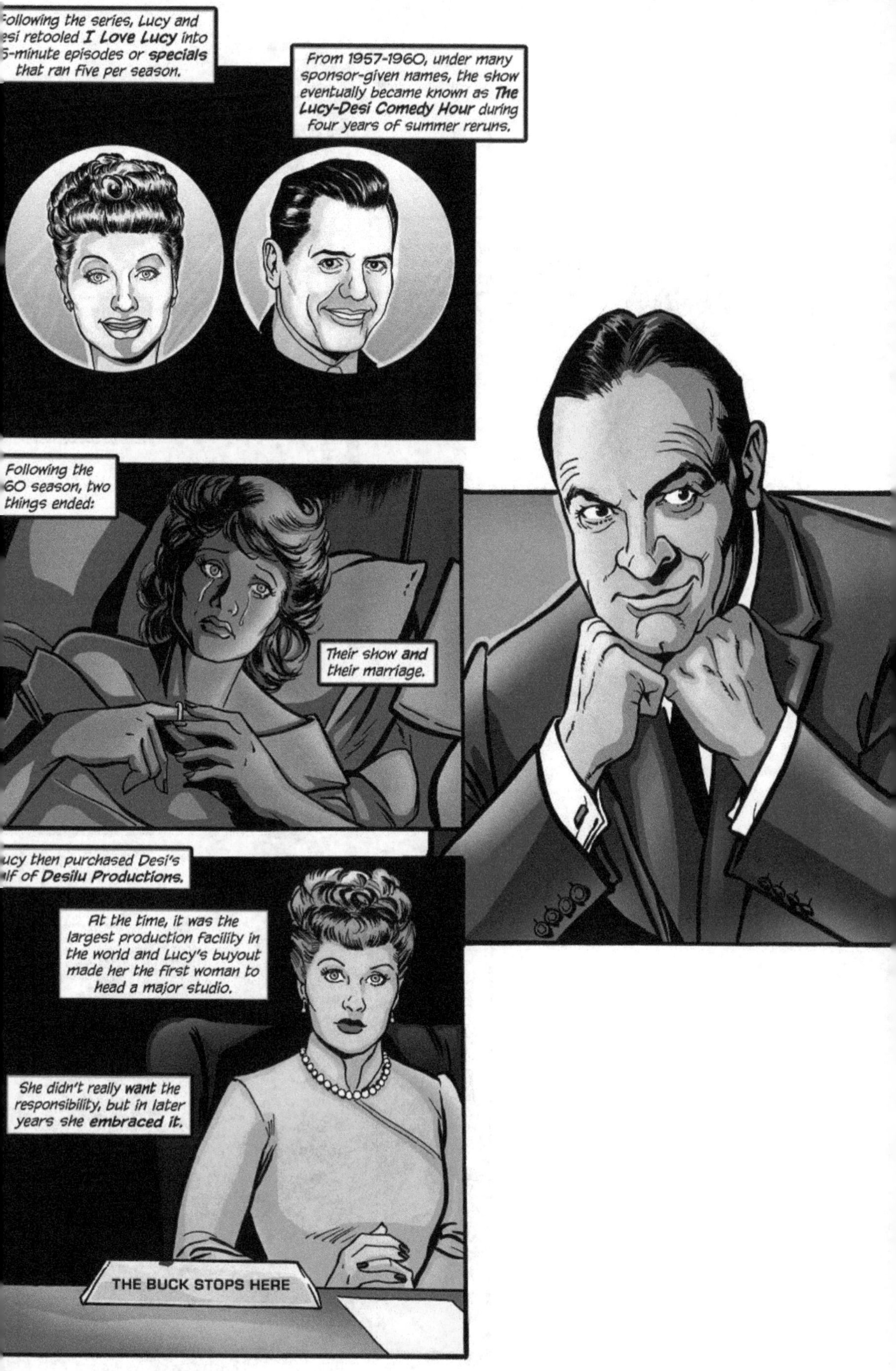

Following the series, Lucy and Desi retooled I Love Lucy into 6-minute episodes or specials that ran five per season.
From 1957-1960, under many sponsor-given names, the show eventually became known as The Lucy-Desi Comedy Hour during four years of summer reruns.
Following the 60 season, two things ended:
Their show and their marriage.
ucy then purchased Desi's alf of Desilu Productions.
At the time, it was the largest production facility in the world and Lucy's buyout made her the first woman to head a major studio.
She didn't really want the responsibility, but in later years she embraced it.
THE BUCK STOPS HERE

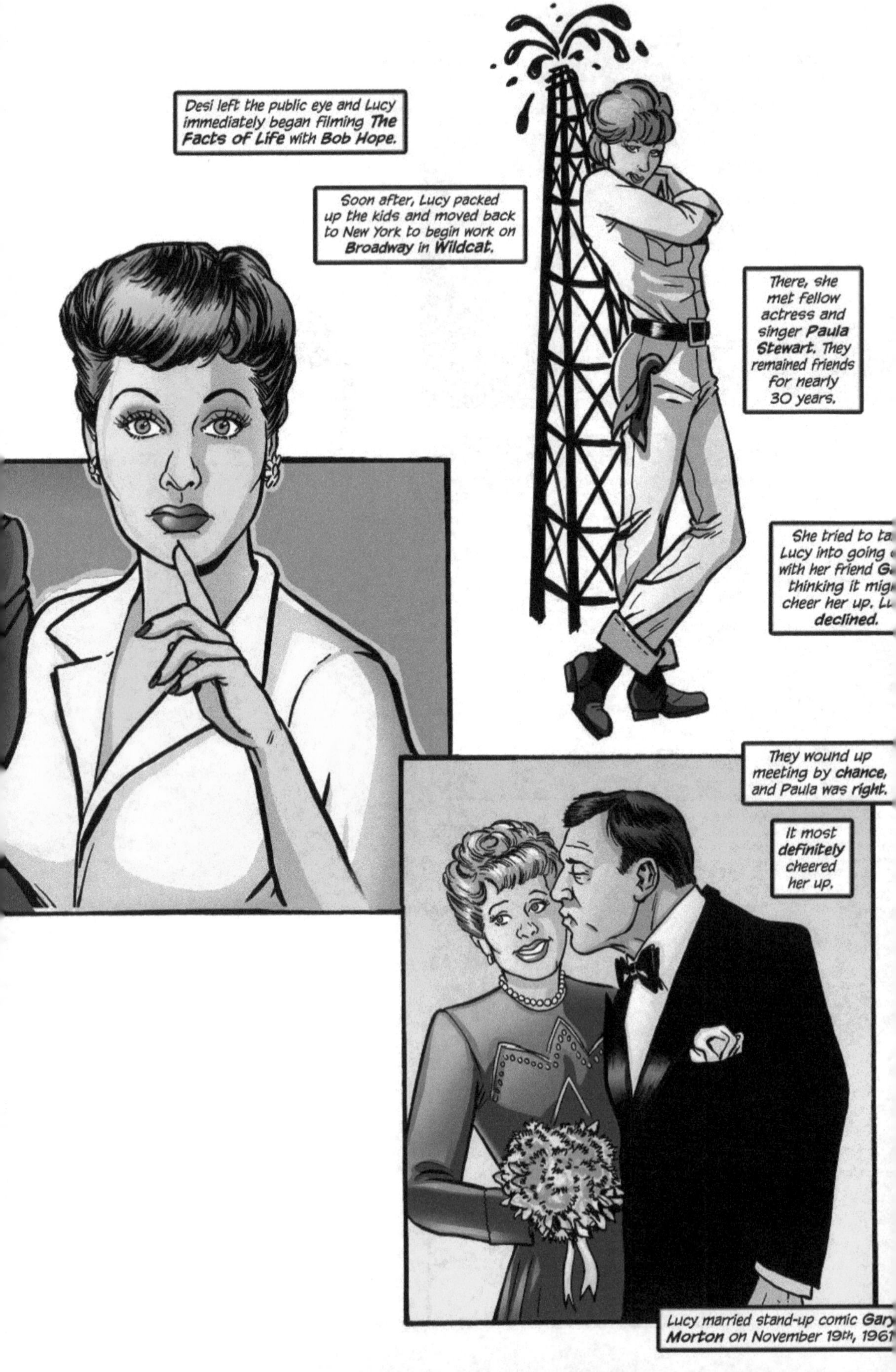
Desi left the public eye and Lucy immediately began filming The Facts of Life with Bob Hope.
Soon after, Lucy packed up the kids and moved back to New York to begin work on Broadway in Wildcat.
There, she met fellow actress and singer Paula Stewart. They remained friends for nearly 30 years.
She tried to ta
Lucy into going
with her friend G
thinking it mig
cheer her up. Lu
declined.
They wound up meeting by chance, and Paula was right.
It most definitely cheered her up.
Lucy married stand-up comic Gary
Morton on November 19th, 1961

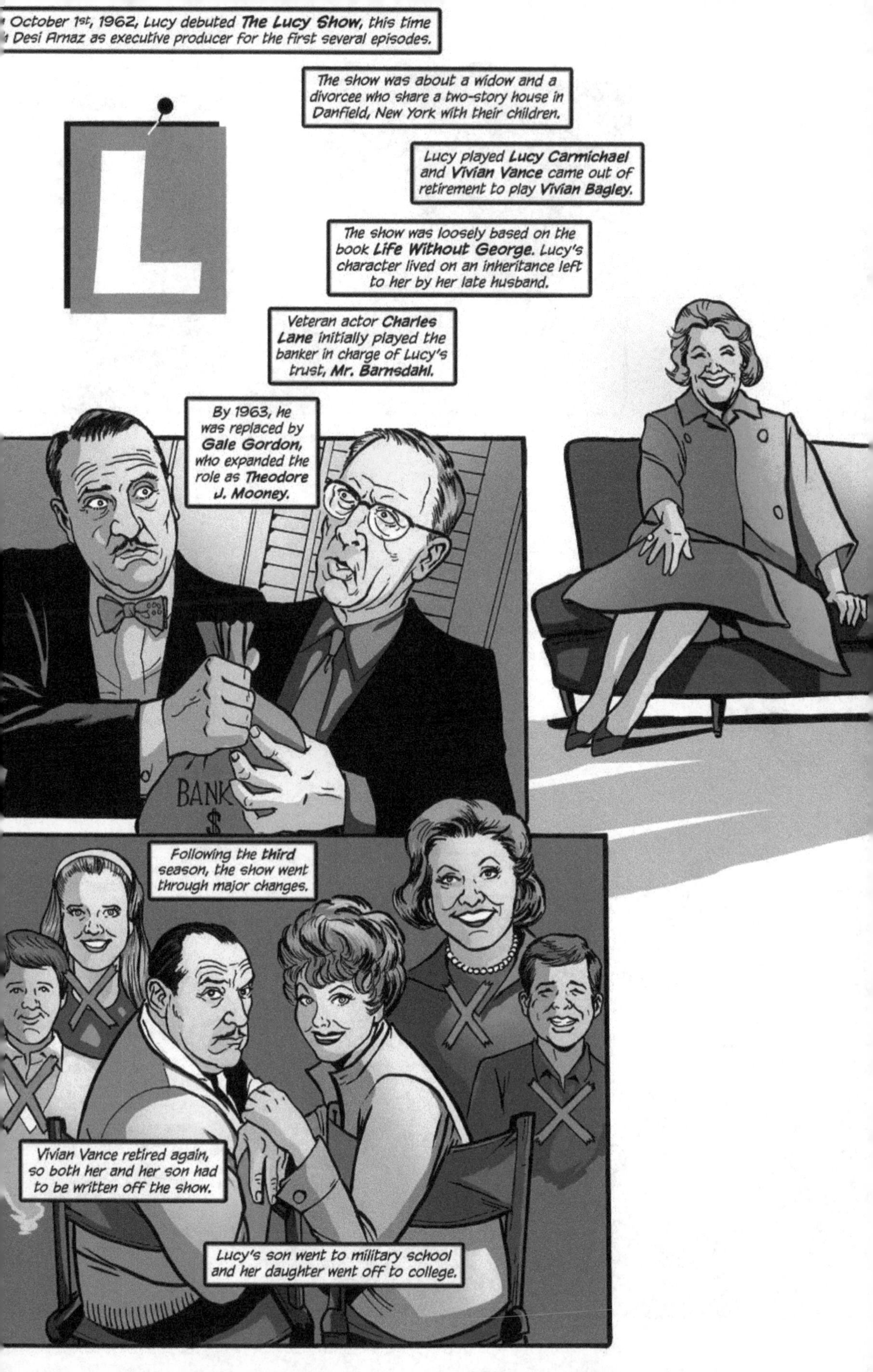
October 1st, 1962, Lucy debuted The Lucy Show, this time
Desi Arnaz as executive producer for the first several episodes.
The show was about a widow and a divorcee who share a two-story house in Danfield, New York with their children.
L
Lucy played Lucy Carmichael and Vivian Vance came out of retirement to play Vivian Bagley.
The show was loosely based on the book Life Without George. Lucy's character lived on an inheritance left to her by her late husband.
Veteran actor Charles Lane initially played the banker in charge of Lucy's trust, Mr. Barnsdahl.
By 1963, he was replaced by Gale Gordon, who expanded the role as Theodore J. Mooney.
BANK $
Following the third season, the show went through major changes.
Vivian Vance retired again, so both her and her son had to be written off the show.
Lucy's son went to military school and her daughter went off to college.

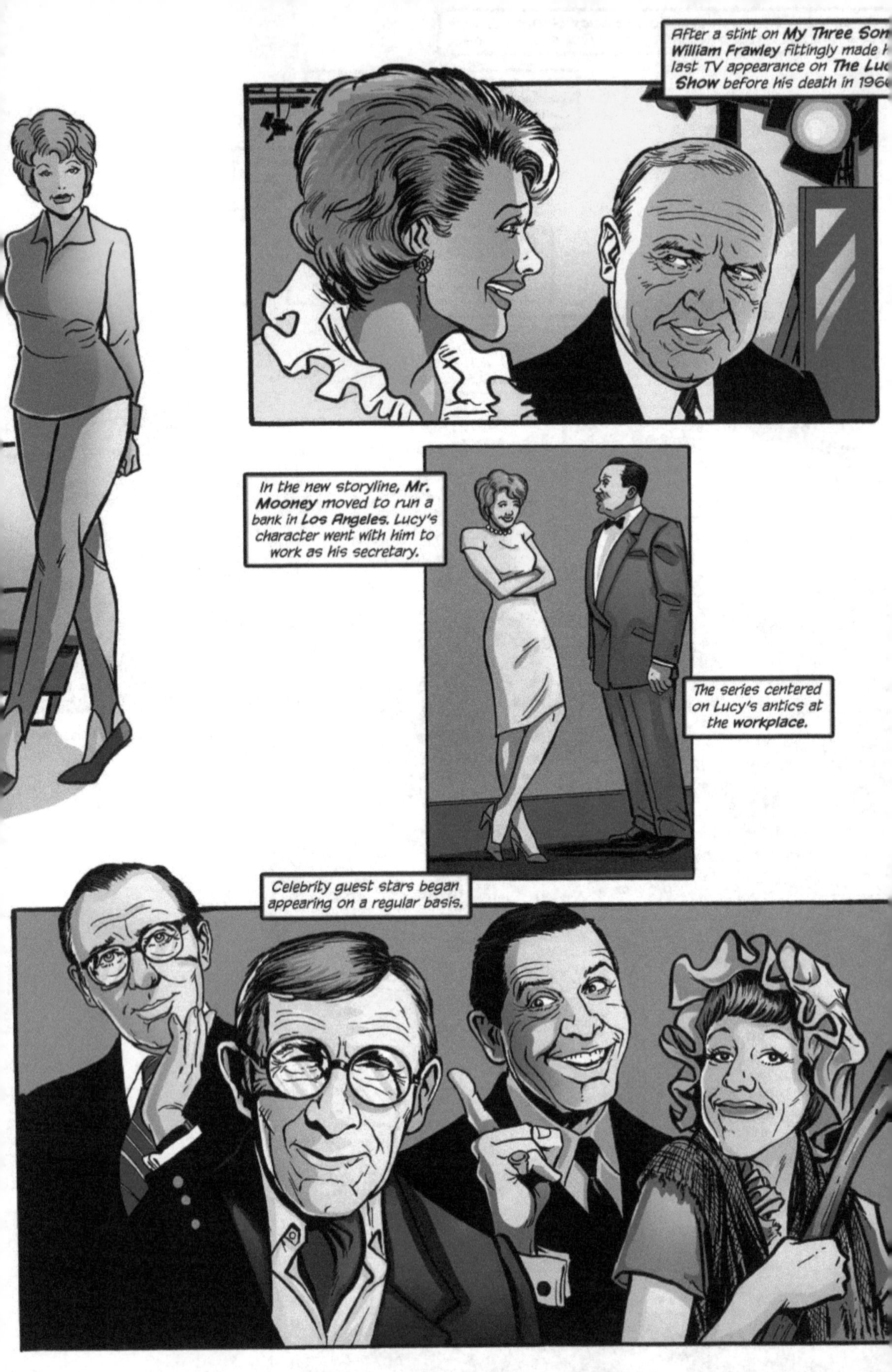
After a stint on My Three Son
William Frawley fittingly made
last TV appearance on The Lu
Show before his death in 196
In the new storyline, Mr. Mooney moved to run a bank in Los Angeles. Lucy's character went with him to work as his secretary.
The series centered on Lucy's antics at the workplace.
Celebrity guest stars began appearing on a regular basis.

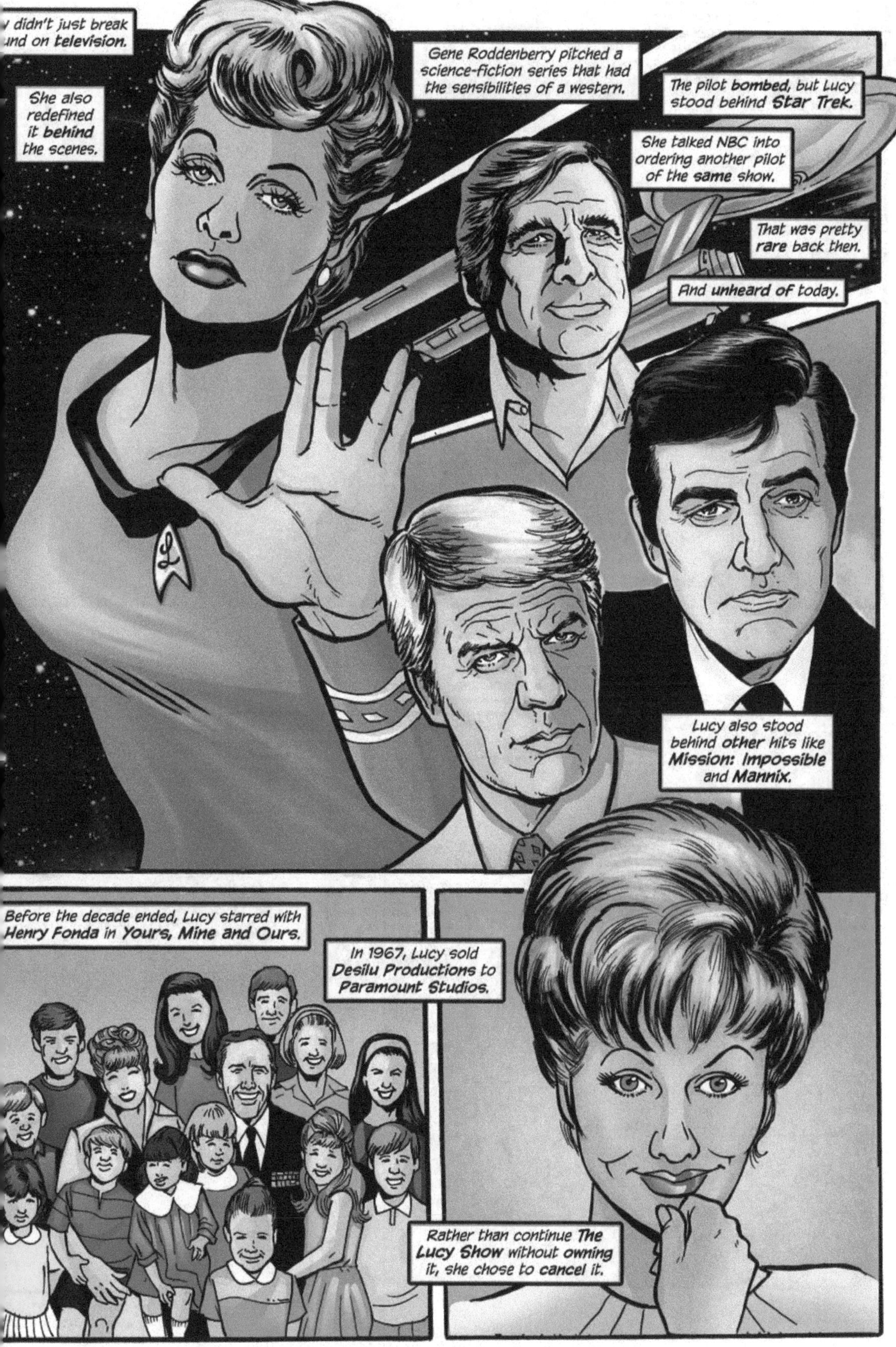
y didn't just break
und on television.
She also redefined it behind the scenes.
Gene Roddenberry pitched a science-fiction series that had the sensibilities of a western.
The pilot bombed, but Lucy stood behind Star Trek.
She talked NBC into ordering another pilot of the same show.
That was pretty rare back then.
And unheard of today.
Lucy also stood behind other hits like Mission: Impossible and Mannix.
Before the decade ended, Lucy starred with Henry Fonda in Yours, Mine and Ours.
In 1967, Lucy sold Desilu Productions to Paramount Studios.
Rather than continue The Lucy Show without owning it, she chose to cancel it.

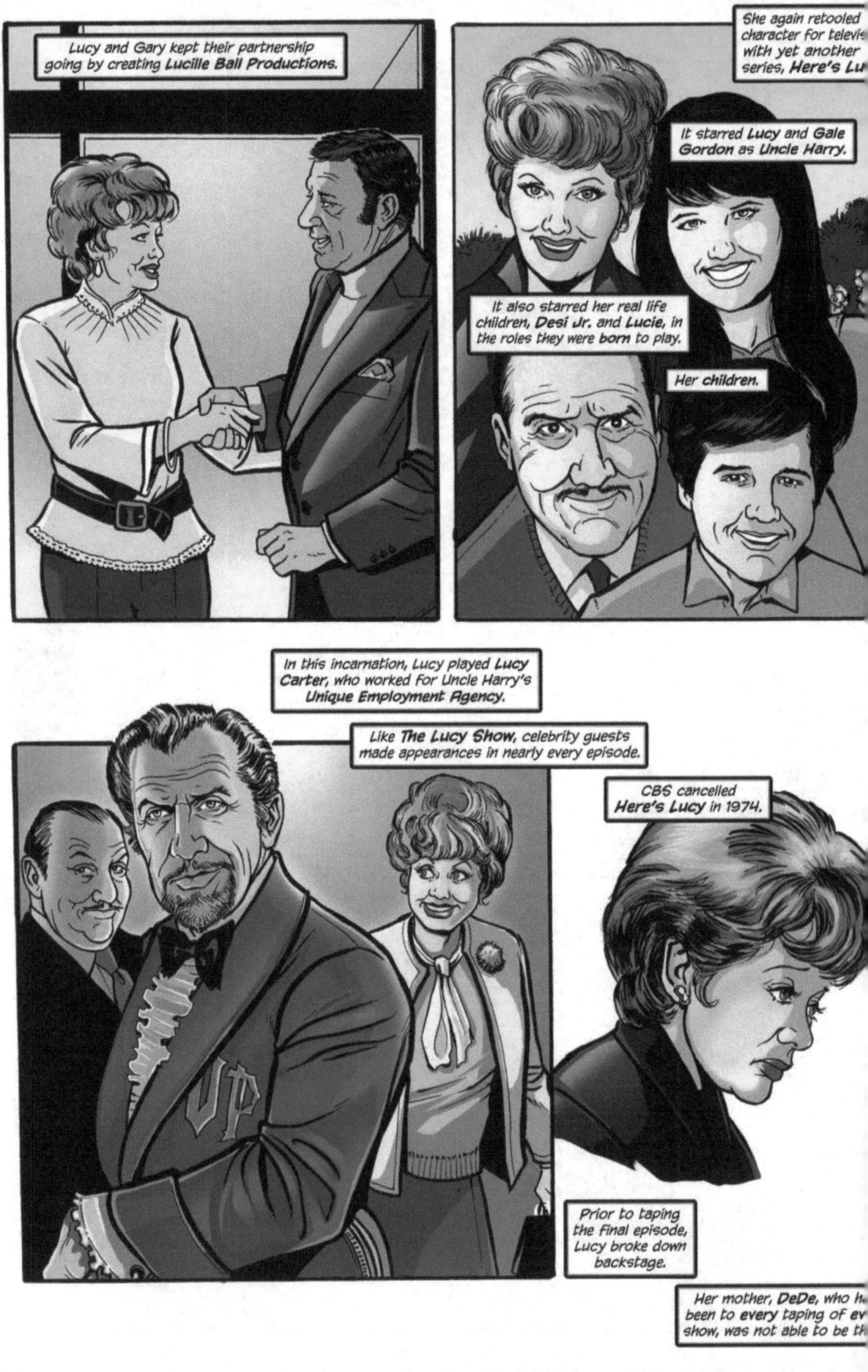

Lucy and Gary kept their partnership going by creating Lucille Ball Productions.
She again retooled character for televis with yet another series, Here's Lu
It starred Lucy and Gale Gordon as Uncle Harry.
It also starred her real life children, Desi Jr. and Lucie, in the roles they were born to play.
Her children.
In this incarnation, Lucy played Lucy Carter, who worked for Uncle Harry's Unique Employment Agency.
Like The Lucy Show, celebrity guests made appearances in nearly every episode.
CBS cancelled Here's Lucy in 1974.
Prior to taping the final episode, Lucy broke down backstage.
Her mother, DeDe, who h been to every taping of ev show, was not able to be th

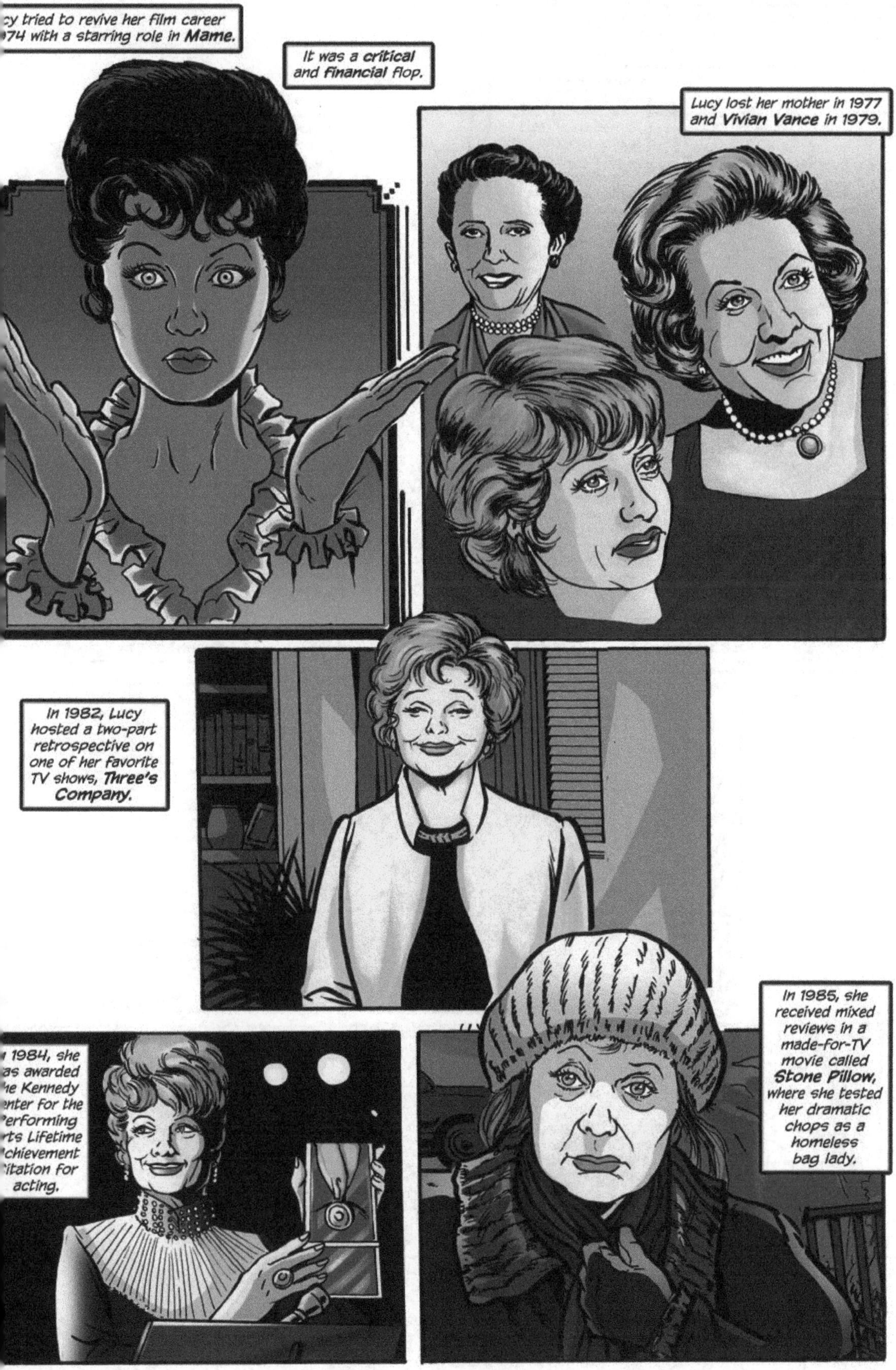

cy tried to revive her film career
974 with a starring role in Mame.
It was a critical and financial flop.
Lucy lost her mother in 1977 and Vivian Vance in 1979.
In 1982, Lucy hosted a two-part retrospective on one of her favorite TV shows, Three's Company.
1984, she as awarded he Kennedy enter for the Performing rts Lifetime chievement itation for acting.
In 1985, she received mixed reviews in a made-for-TV movie called Stone Pillow, where she tested her dramatic chops as a homeless bag lady.

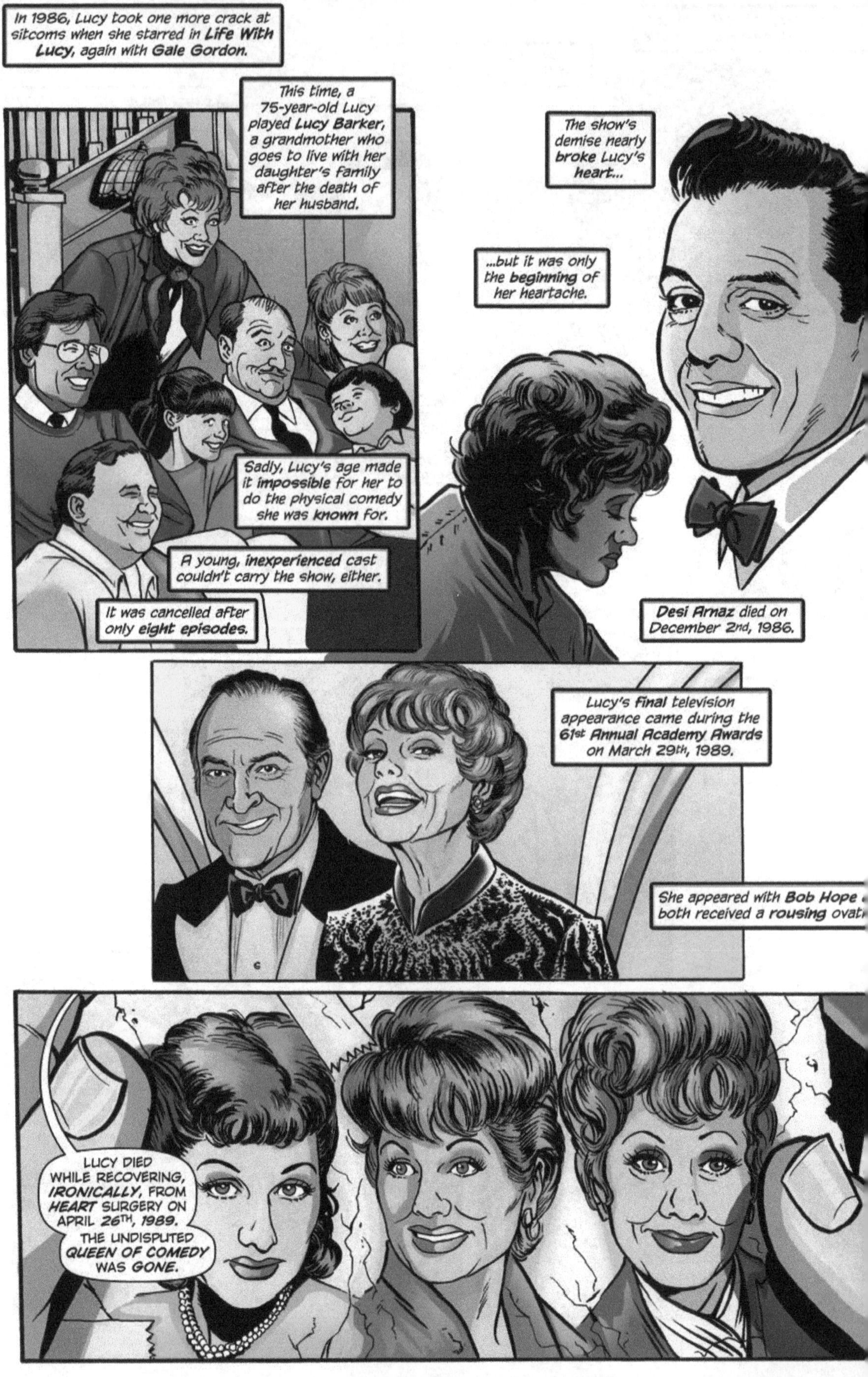
In 1986, Lucy took one more crack at sitcoms when she starred in **Life With Lucy**, again with **Gale Gordon**.
This time, a 75-year-old Lucy played **Lucy Barker**, a grandmother who goes to live with her daughter's family after the death of her husband.
Sadly, Lucy's age made it **impossible** for her to do the physical comedy she was **known** for.
A young, **inexperienced** cast couldn't carry the show, either.
It was cancelled after only **eight episodes**.
The show's demise nearly **broke** Lucy's **heart**...
...but it was only the **beginning** of her heartache.
Desi Arnaz died on December 2nd, 1986.
Lucy's **final** television appearance came during the **61st Annual Academy Awards** on March 29th, 1989.
She appeared with **Bob Hope**
both received a **rousing**
LUCY DIED WHILE RECOVERING, ***IRONICALLY***, FROM ***HEART*** SURGERY ON APRIL 26TH, *1989*. THE UNDISPUTED ***QUEEN OF COMEDY*** WAS ***GONE***.

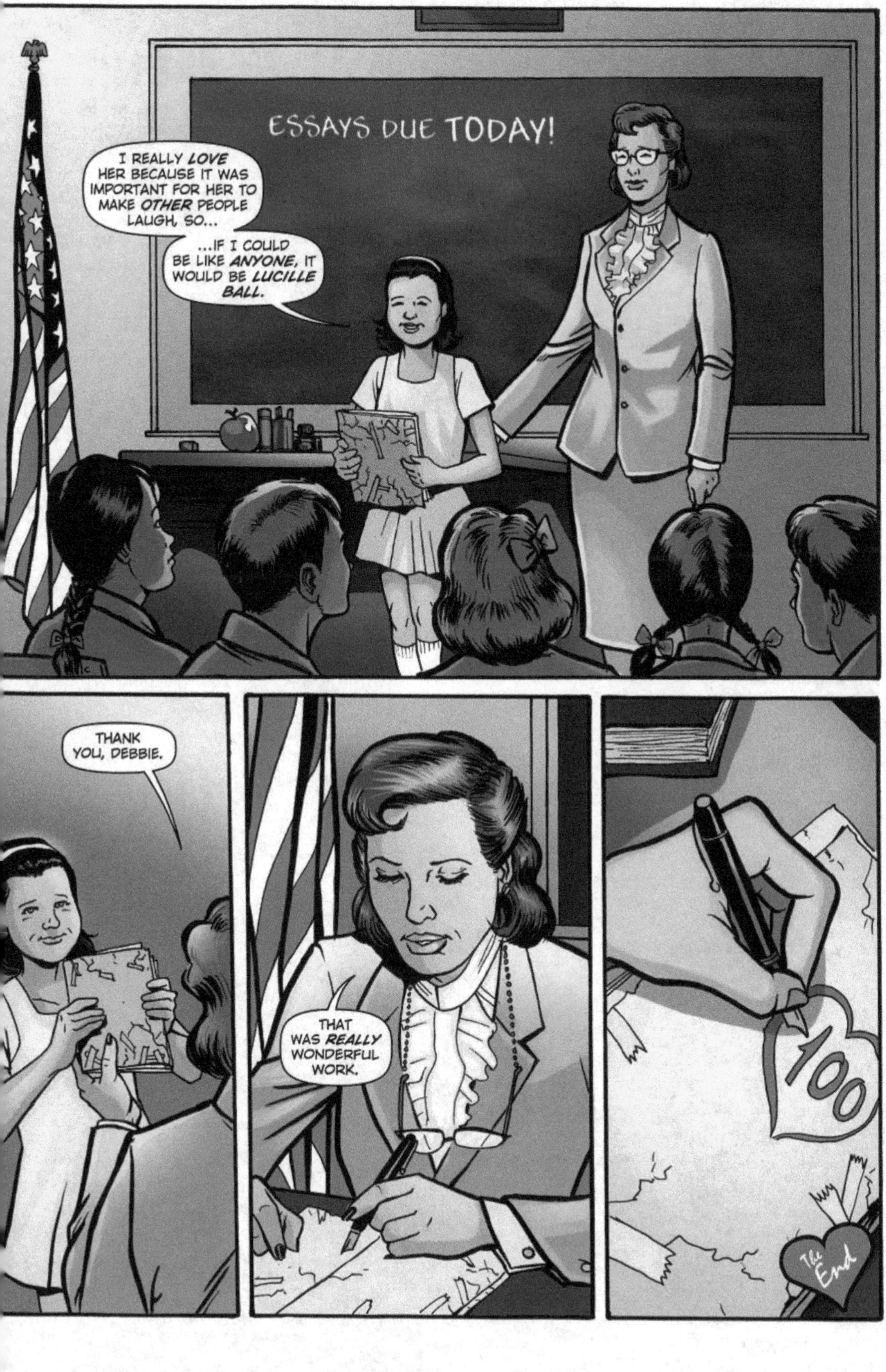
ESSAYS DUE TODAY!
I REALLY LOVE HER BECAUSE IT WAS IMPORTANT FOR HER TO MAKE OTHER PEOPLE LAUGH, SO...
...IF I COULD BE LIKE ANYONE, IT WOULD BE LUCILLE BALL.
THANK YOU, DEBBIE.
THAT WAS REALLY WONDERFUL WORK.
100
The End

BARBRA STREISAND

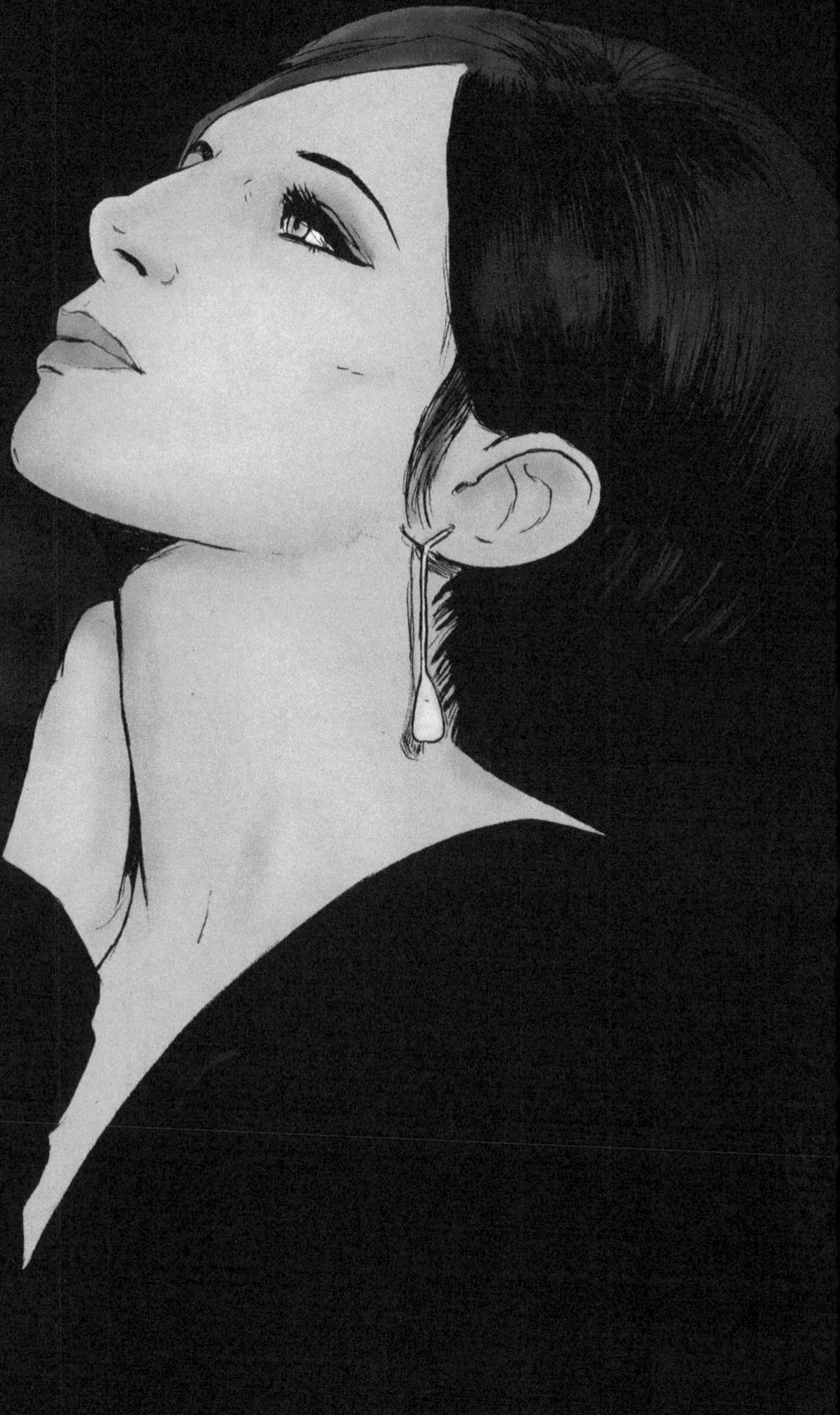

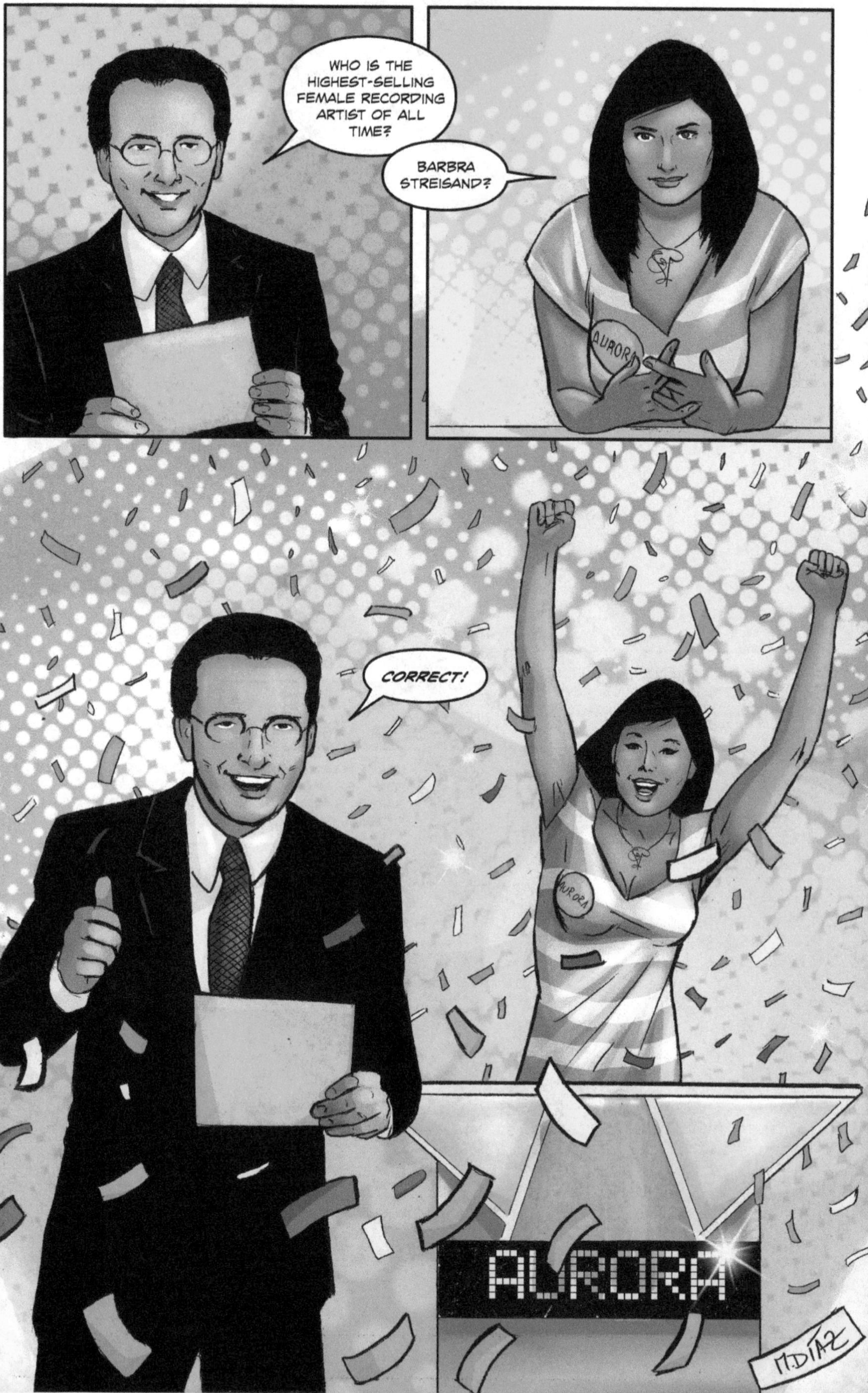
WHO IS THE HIGHEST-SELLING FEMALE RECORDING ARTIST OF ALL TIME?
BARBRA STREISAND?
AURORA
CORRECT!
AURORA
AURORA
M.DÍAZ

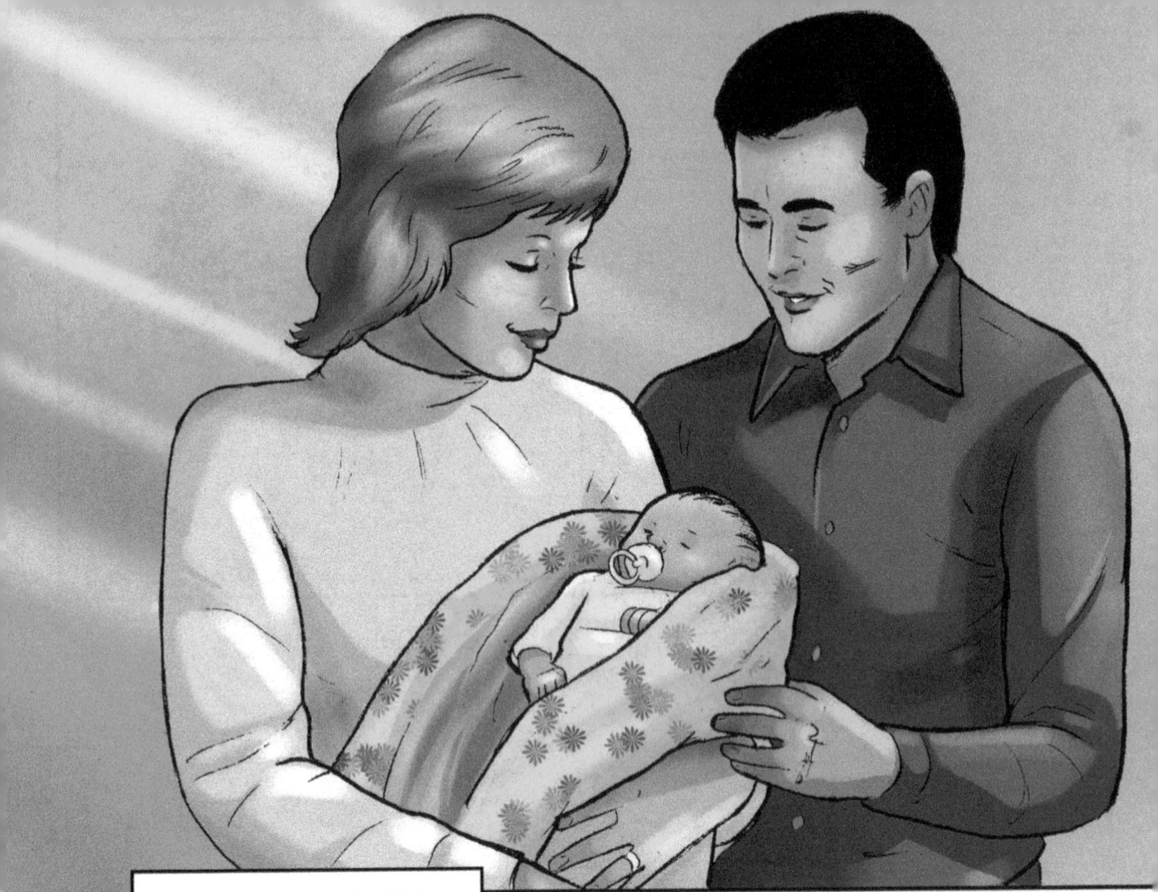

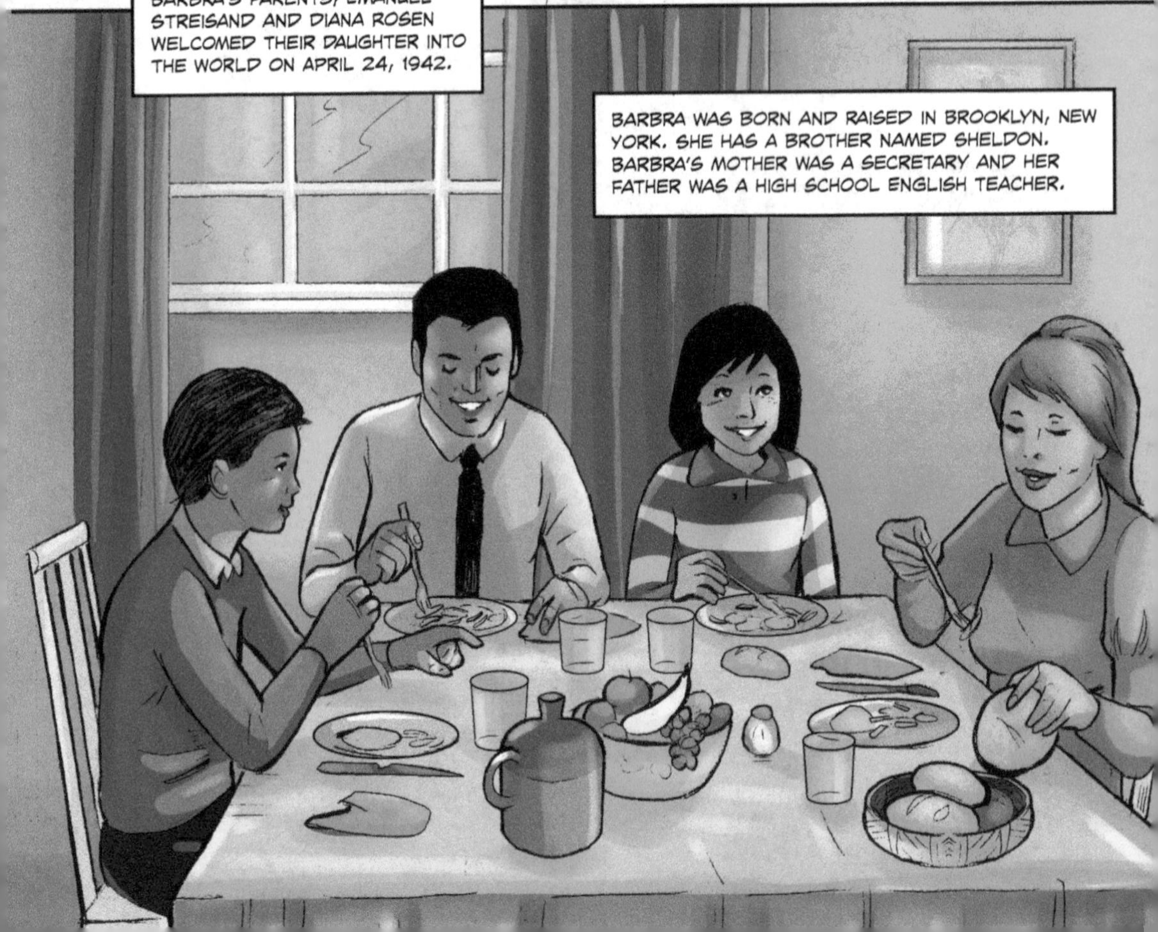
BARBRA'S PARENTS, EMANUEL STREISAND AND DIANA ROSEN WELCOMED THEIR DAUGHTER INTO THE WORLD ON APRIL 24, 1942.
BARBRA WAS BORN AND RAISED IN BROOKLYN, NEW YORK. SHE HAS A BROTHER NAMED SHELDON. BARBRA'S MOTHER WAS A SECRETARY AND HER FATHER WAS A HIGH SCHOOL ENGLISH TEACHER.

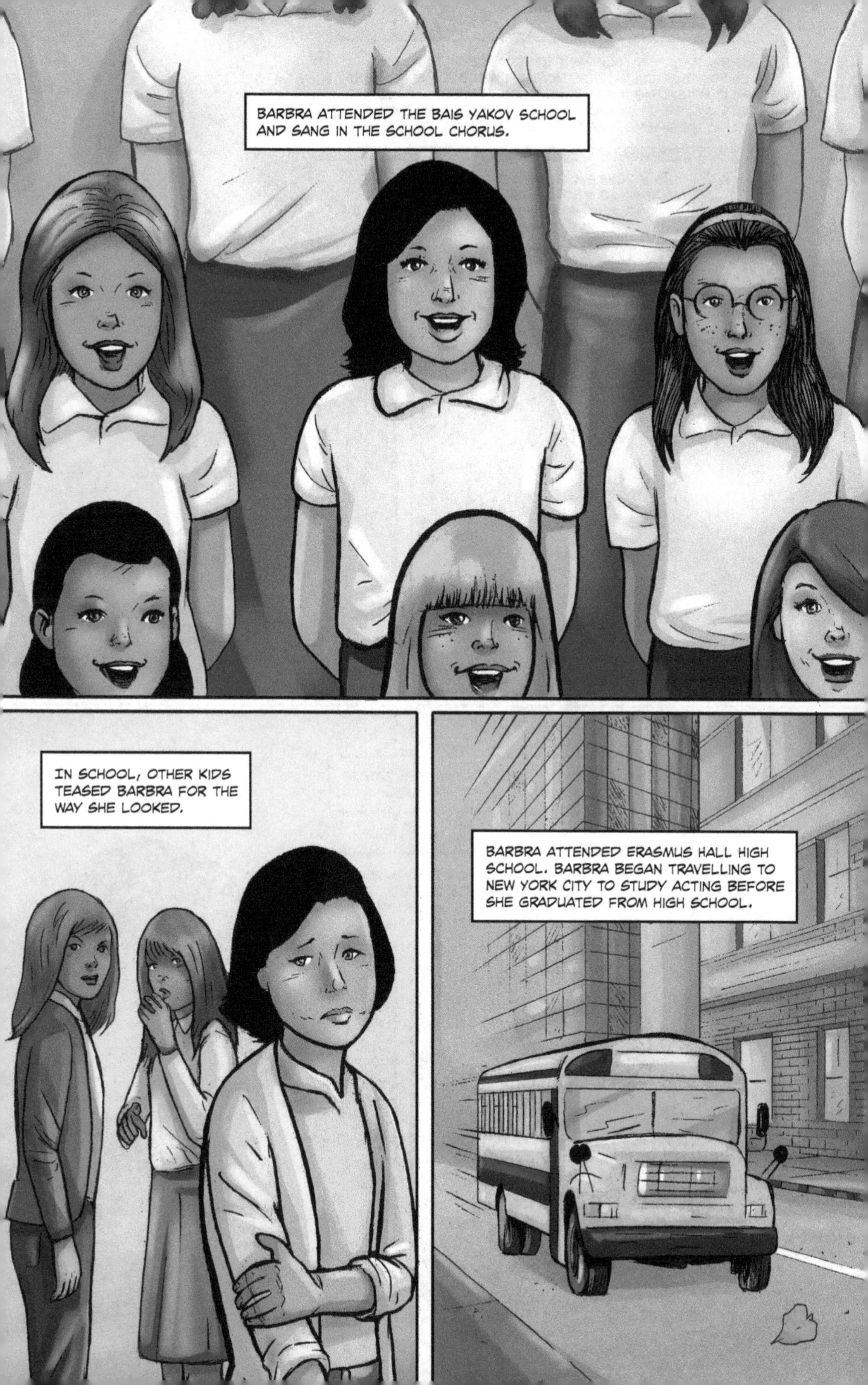
BARBRA ATTENDED THE BAIS YAKOV SCHOOL AND SANG IN THE SCHOOL CHORUS.
IN SCHOOL, OTHER KIDS TEASED BARBRA FOR THE WAY SHE LOOKED.
BARBRA ATTENDED ERASMUS HALL HIGH SCHOOL. BARBRA BEGAN TRAVELLING TO NEW YORK CITY TO STUDY ACTING BEFORE SHE GRADUATED FROM HIGH SCHOOL.

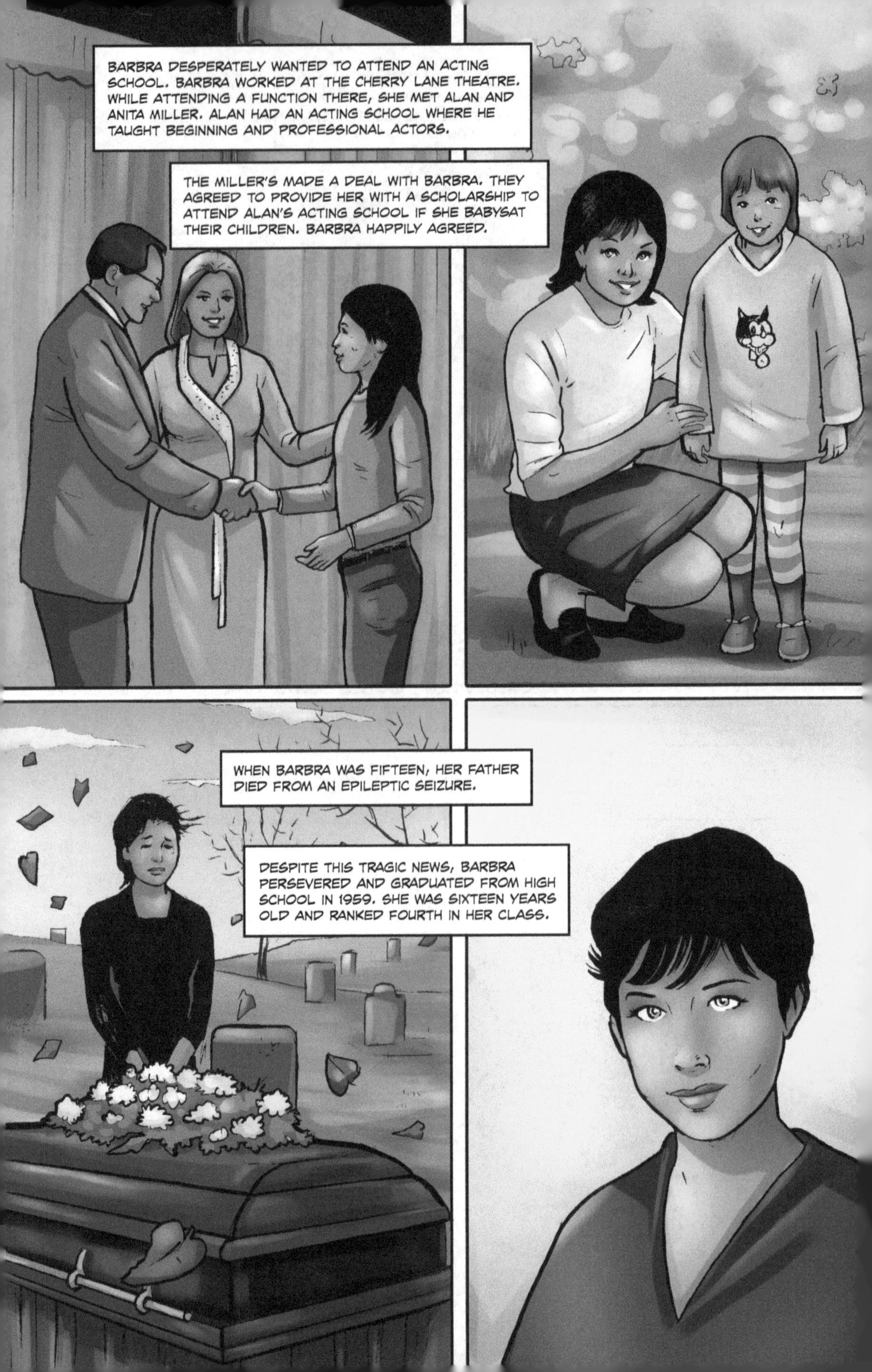
BARBRA DESPERATELY WANTED TO ATTEND AN ACTING SCHOOL. BARBRA WORKED AT THE CHERRY LANE THEATRE. WHILE ATTENDING A FUNCTION THERE, SHE MET ALAN AND ANITA MILLER. ALAN HAD AN ACTING SCHOOL WHERE HE TAUGHT BEGINNING AND PROFESSIONAL ACTORS.
THE MILLER'S MADE A DEAL WITH BARBRA. THEY AGREED TO PROVIDE HER WITH A SCHOLARSHIP TO ATTEND ALAN'S ACTING SCHOOL IF SHE BABYSAT THEIR CHILDREN. BARBRA HAPPILY AGREED.
WHEN BARBRA WAS FIFTEEN, HER FATHER DIED FROM AN EPILEPTIC SEIZURE.
DESPITE THIS TRAGIC NEWS, BARBRA PERSEVERED AND GRADUATED FROM HIGH SCHOOL IN 1959. SHE WAS SIXTEEN YEARS OLD AND RANKED FOURTH IN HER CLASS.

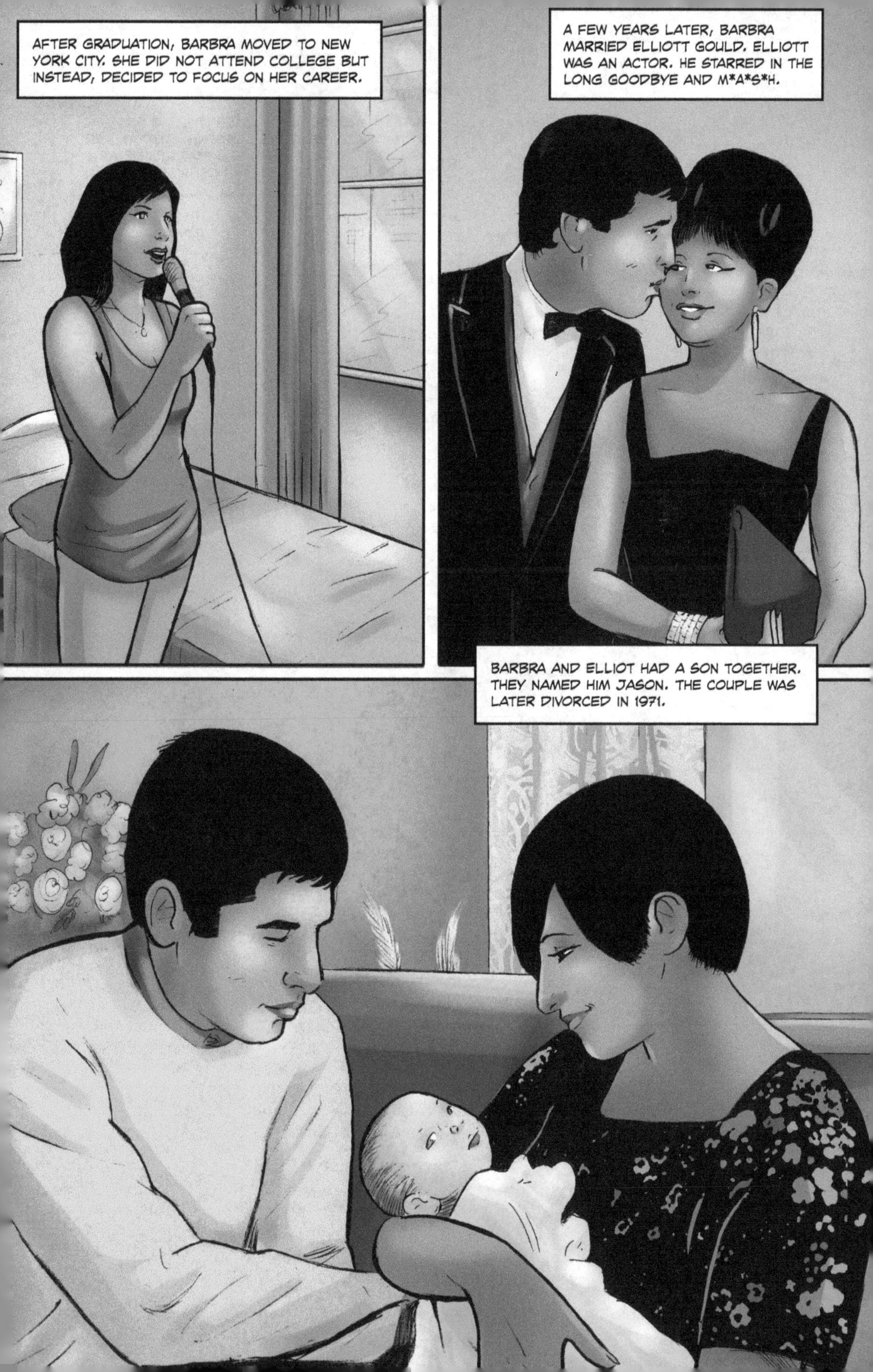
AFTER GRADUATION, BARBRA MOVED TO NEW YORK CITY. SHE DID NOT ATTEND COLLEGE BUT INSTEAD, DECIDED TO FOCUS ON HER CAREER.
A FEW YEARS LATER, BARBRA MARRIED ELLIOTT GOULD. ELLIOTT WAS AN ACTOR. HE STARRED IN THE LONG GOODBYE AND M*A*S*H.
BARBRA AND ELLIOT HAD A SON TOGETHER. THEY NAMED HIM JASON. THE COUPLE WAS LATER DIVORCED IN 1971.

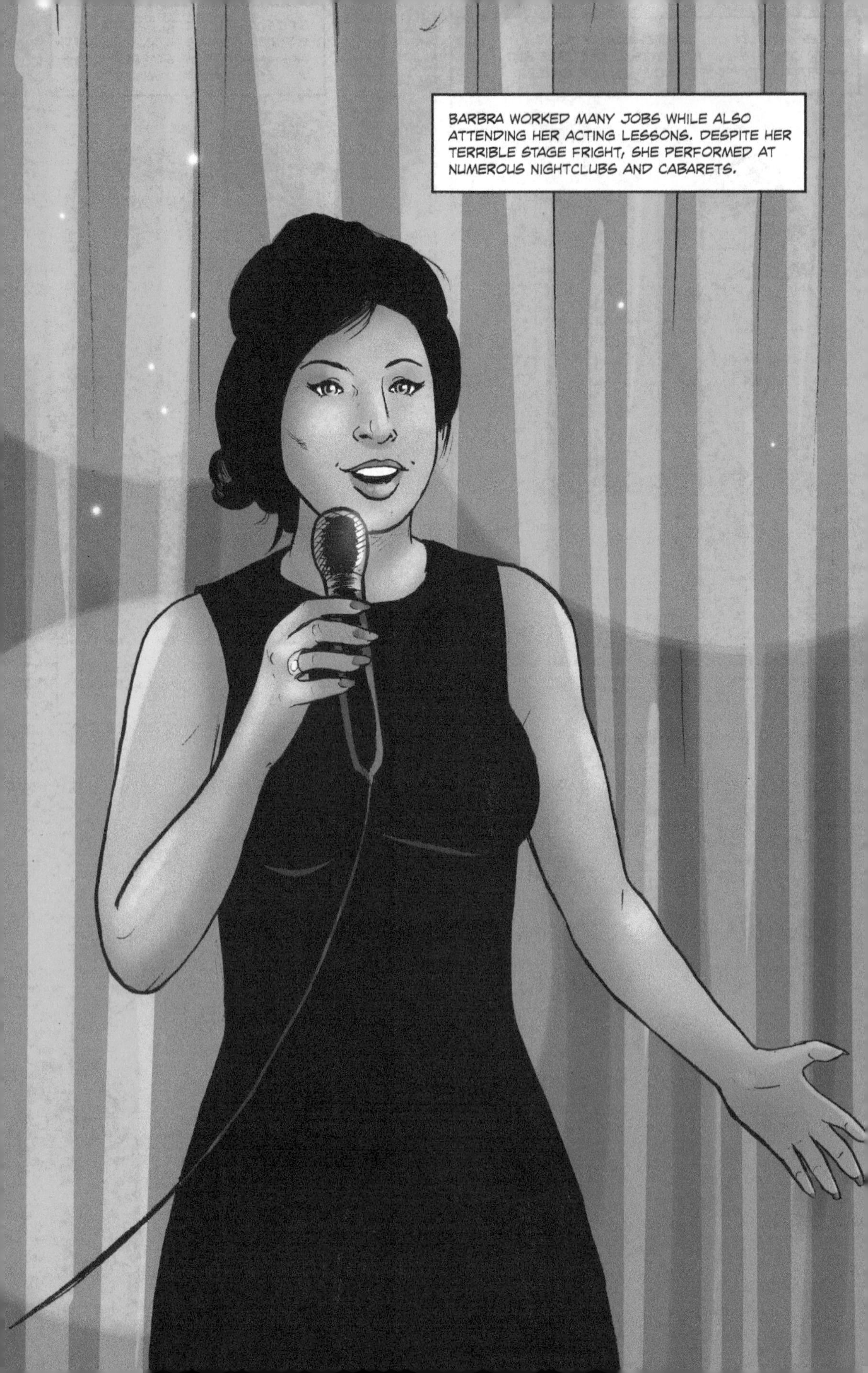
BARBRA WORKED MANY JOBS WHILE ALSO ATTENDING HER ACTING LESSONS. DESPITE HER TERRIBLE STAGE FRIGHT, SHE PERFORMED AT NUMEROUS NIGHTCLUBS AND CABARETS.

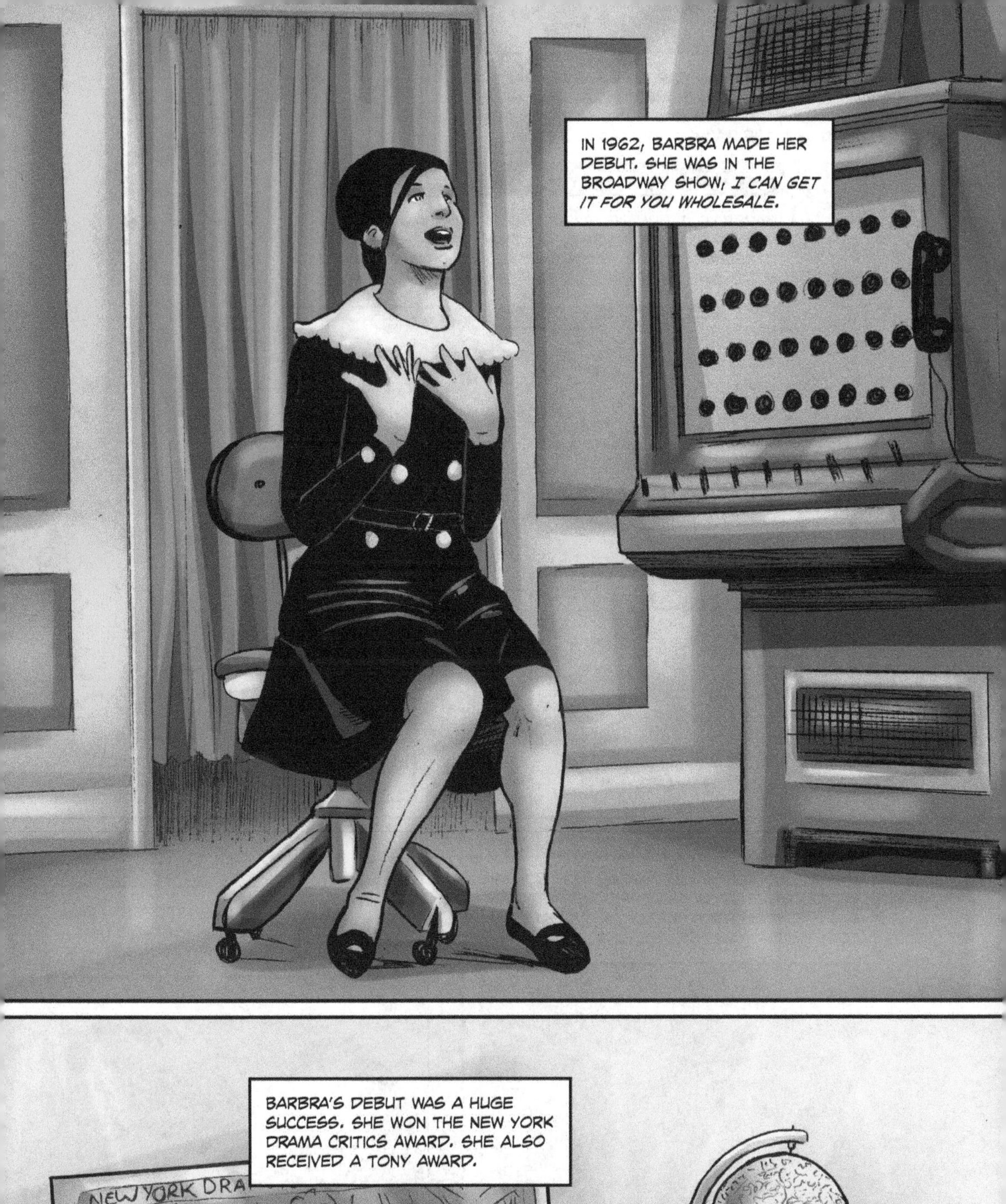
IN 1962, BARBRA MADE HER DEBUT. SHE WAS IN THE BROADWAY SHOW, *I CAN GET IT FOR YOU WHOLESALE.*

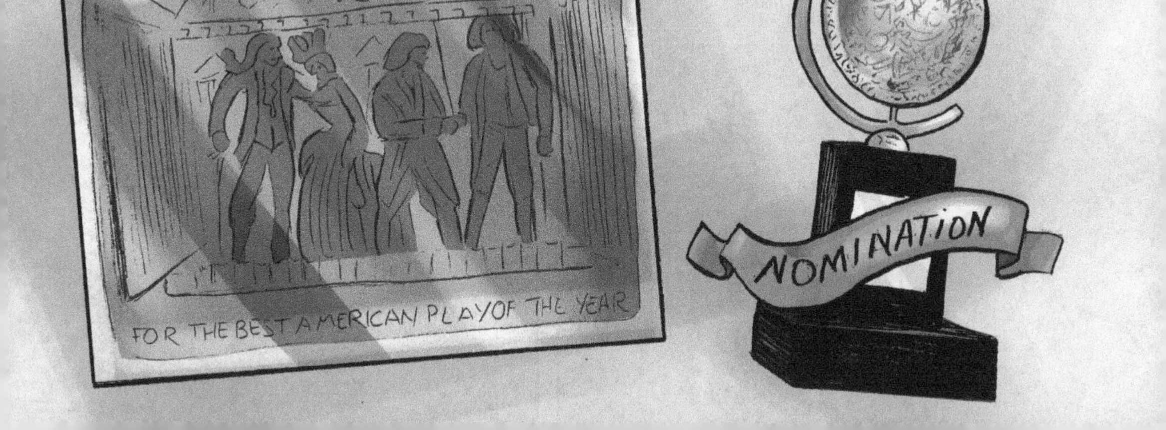
BARBRA'S DEBUT WAS A HUGE SUCCESS. SHE WON THE NEW YORK DRAMA CRITICS AWARD. SHE ALSO RECEIVED A TONY AWARD.
NEW YORK DRA
FOR THE BEST AMERICAN PLAY OF THE YEAR
NOMINATION

LATER THAT YEAR BARBRA SIGNED A RECORD DEAL WITH COLUMBIA RECORDS. THAT SAME YEAR, BARBRA RELEASED HER FIRST ALBUM TITLED, THE BARBRA STREISAND ALBUM.

BARBRA'S ALBUM RECEIVED TWO GRAMMY AWARDS AND IT ALSO BECAME A TOP 10 GOLD RECORD. THE BARBRA STREISAND ALBUM WAS NAMED ALBUM OF THE YEAR. THIS MADE HER THE YOUNGEST WINNER IN THAT CATEGORY!

BARBRA PREFERRED BROADWAY PERFORMANCES TO LIVE CONCERTS. IN 1964 SHE APPEARED IN FUNNY GIRL. THE SHOW PLAYED FOR TWO YEARS AND BARBRA WON A TONY AWARD FOR HER PERFORMANCE.

THE SONG "PEOPLE" FROM FUNNY GIRL BECAME HER FIRST TOP 10 SINGLE.

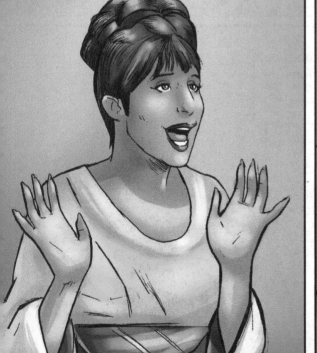

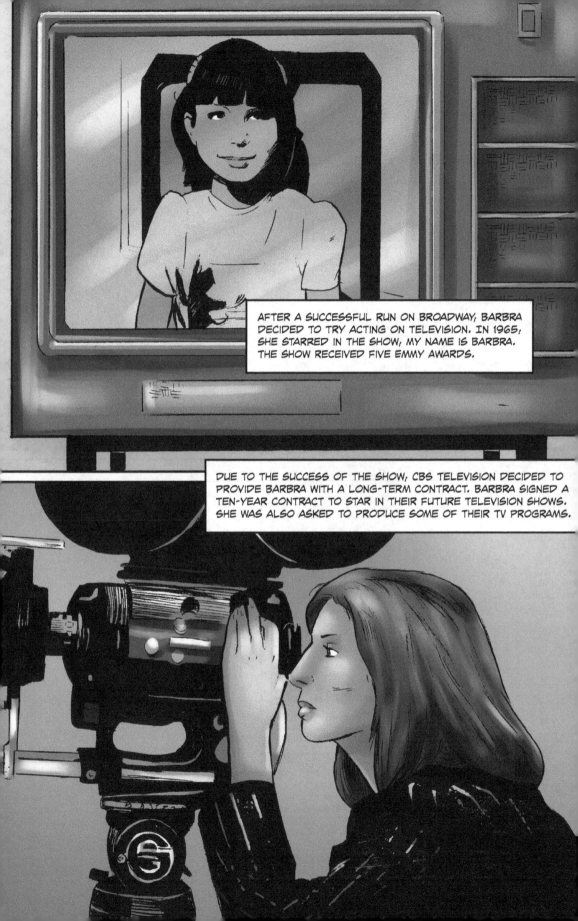

AFTER A SUCCESSFUL RUN ON BROADWAY, BARBRA DECIDED TO TRY ACTING ON TELEVISION. IN 1965, SHE STARRED IN THE SHOW, MY NAME IS BARBRA. THE SHOW RECEIVED FIVE EMMY AWARDS.

DUE TO THE SUCCESS OF THE SHOW, CBS TELEVISION DECIDED TO PROVIDE BARBRA WITH A LONG-TERM CONTRACT. BARBRA SIGNED A TEN-YEAR CONTRACT TO STAR IN THEIR FUTURE TELEVISION SHOWS. SHE WAS ALSO ASKED TO PRODUCE SOME OF THEIR TV PROGRAMS.

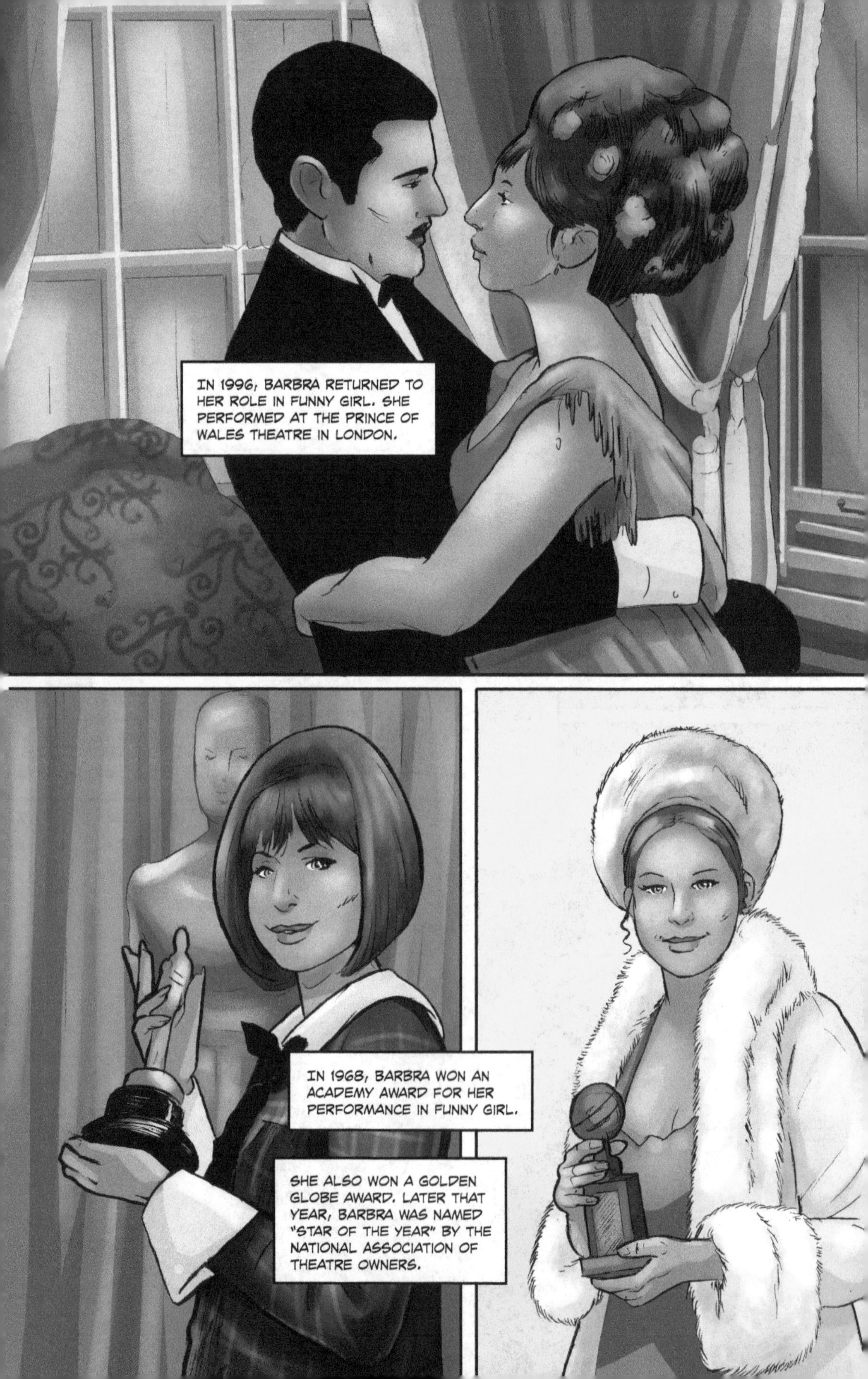
IN 1996, BARBRA RETURNED TO HER ROLE IN FUNNY GIRL. SHE PERFORMED AT THE PRINCE OF WALES THEATRE IN LONDON.
IN 1968, BARBRA WON AN ACADEMY AWARD FOR HER PERFORMANCE IN FUNNY GIRL.
SHE ALSO WON A GOLDEN GLOBE AWARD. LATER THAT YEAR, BARBRA WAS NAMED "STAR OF THE YEAR" BY THE NATIONAL ASSOCIATION OF THEATRE OWNERS.

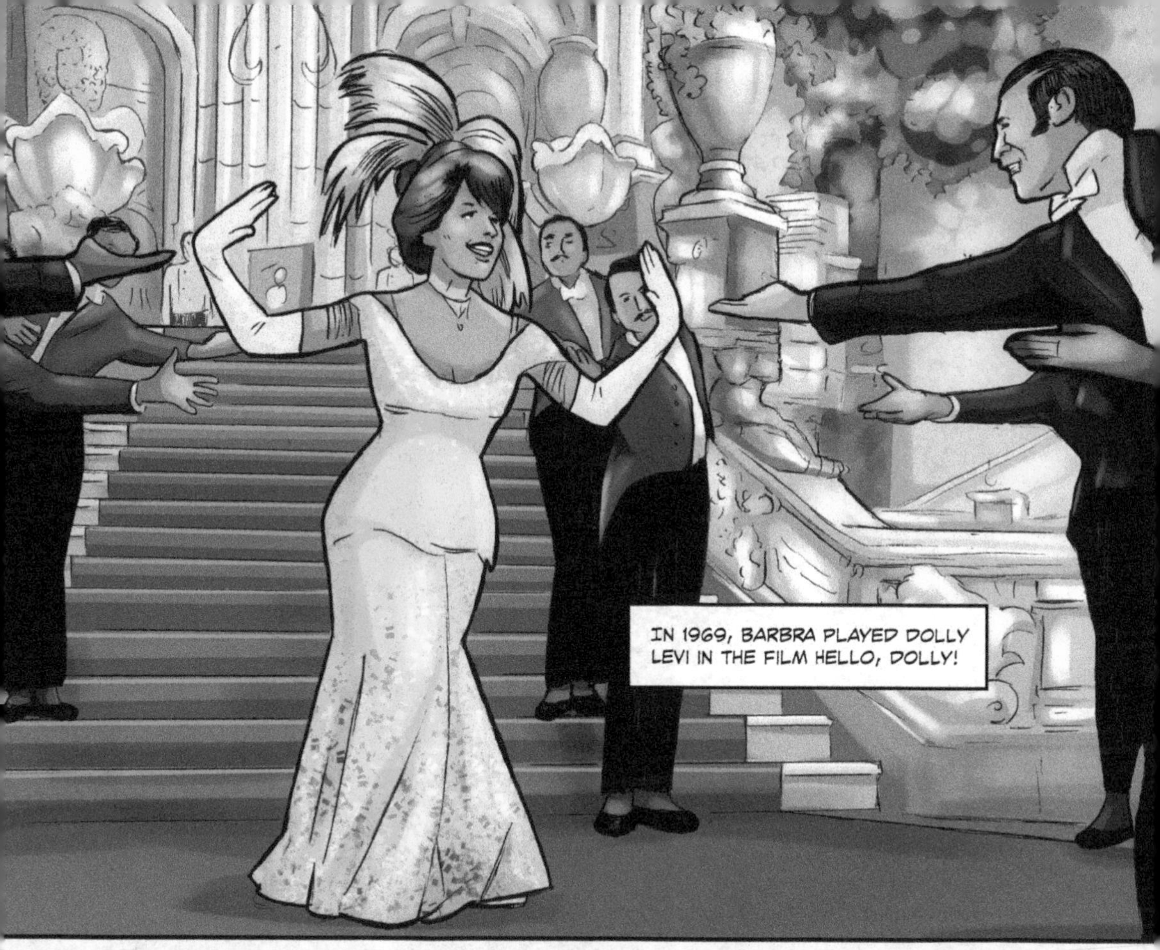
IN 1969, BARBRA PLAYED DOLLY LEVI IN THE FILM HELLO, DOLLY!

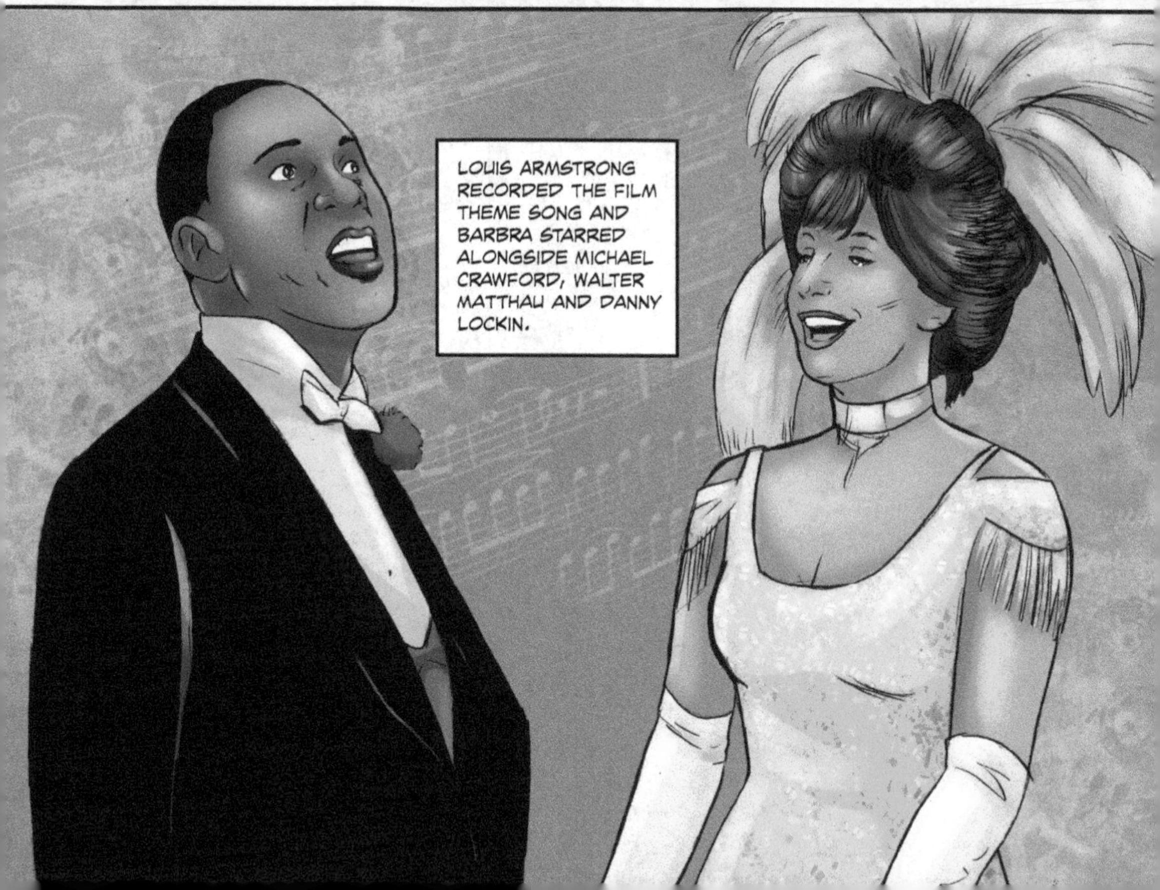
LOUIS ARMSTRONG RECORDED THE FILM THEME SONG AND BARBRA STARRED ALONGSIDE MICHAEL CRAWFORD, WALTER MATTHAU AND DANNY LOCKIN.

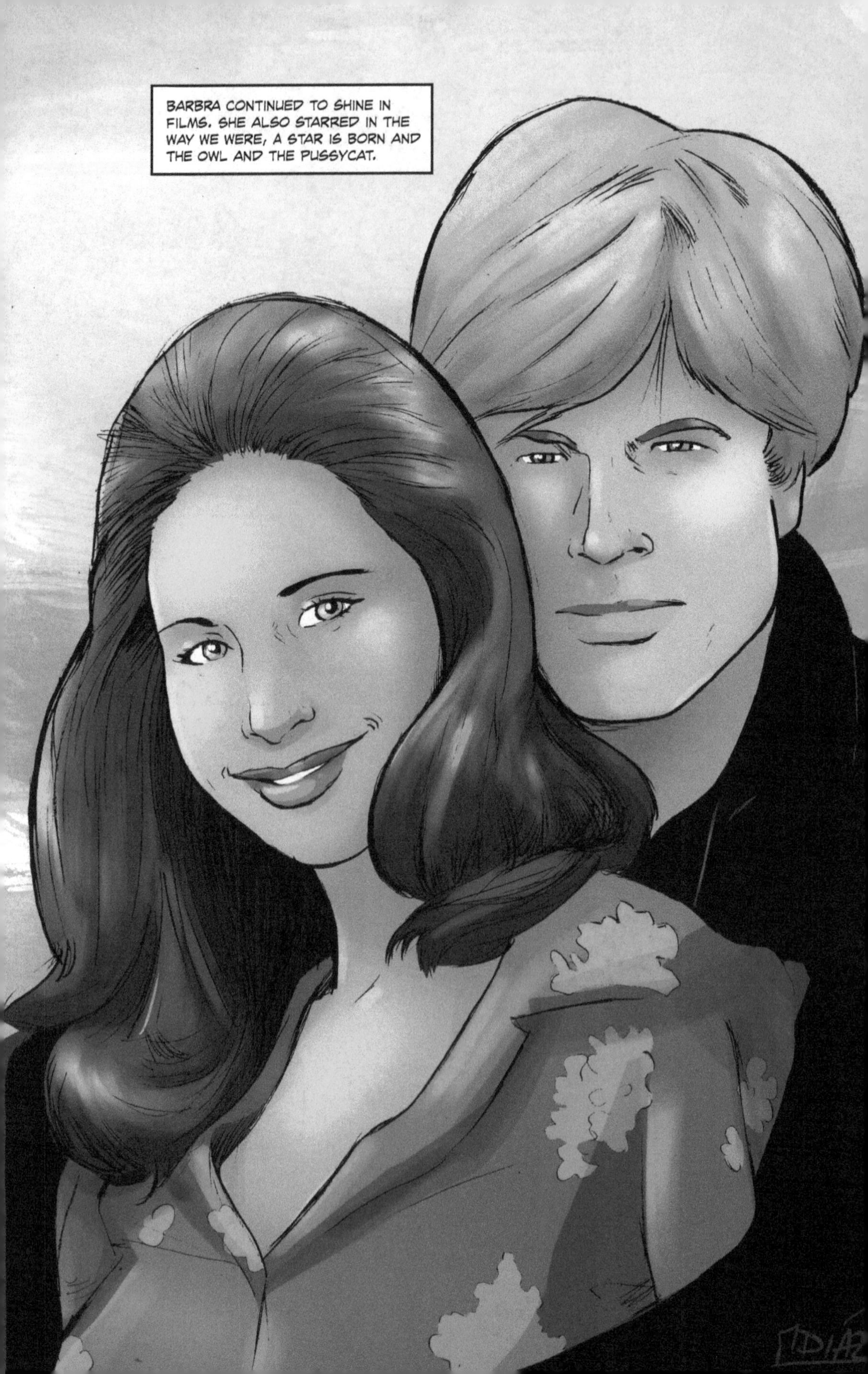
BARBRA CONTINUED TO SHINE IN FILMS. SHE ALSO STARRED IN THE WAY WE WERE, A STAR IS BORN AND THE OWL AND THE PUSSYCAT.

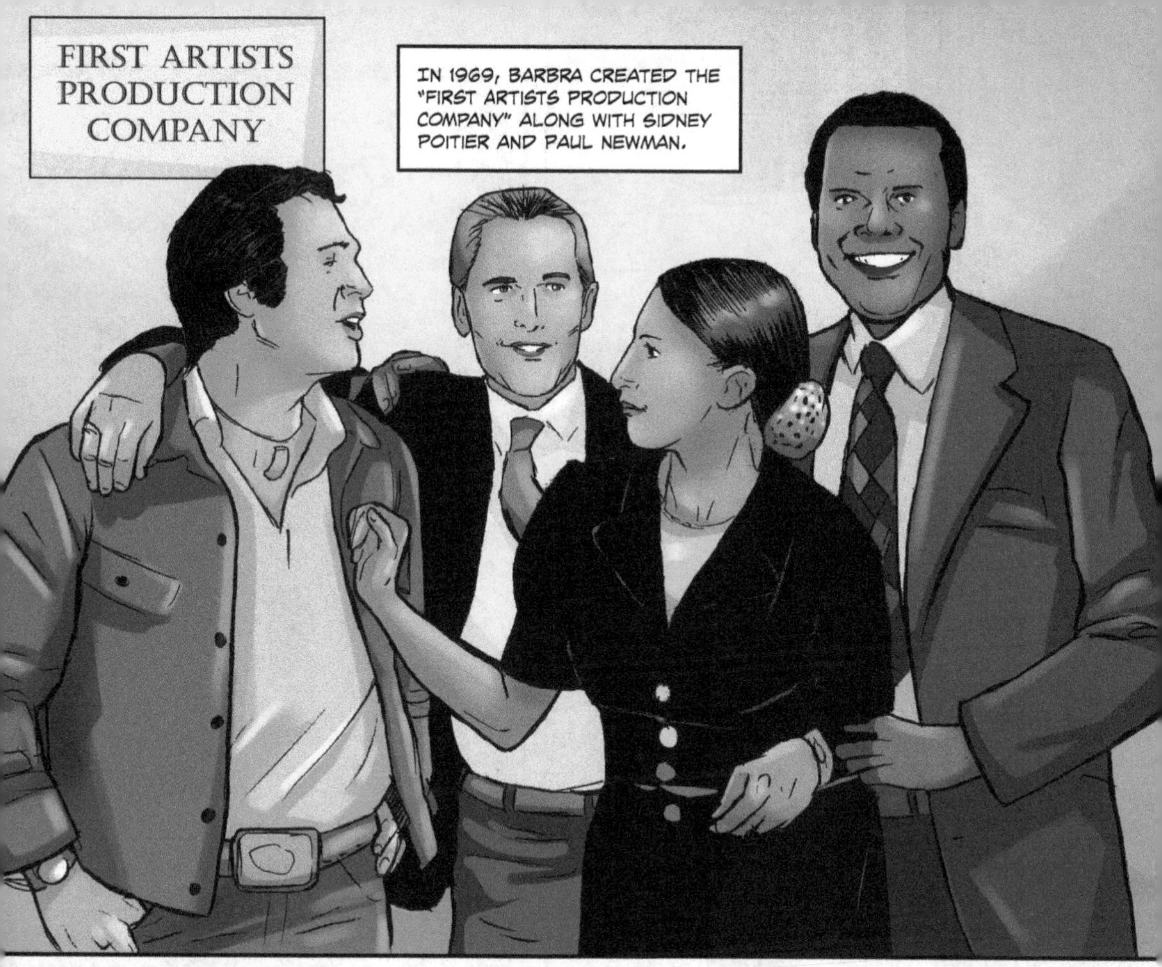
FIRST ARTISTS PRODUCTION COMPANY
IN 1969, BARBRA CREATED THE "FIRST ARTISTS PRODUCTION COMPANY" ALONG WITH SIDNEY POITIER AND PAUL NEWMAN.

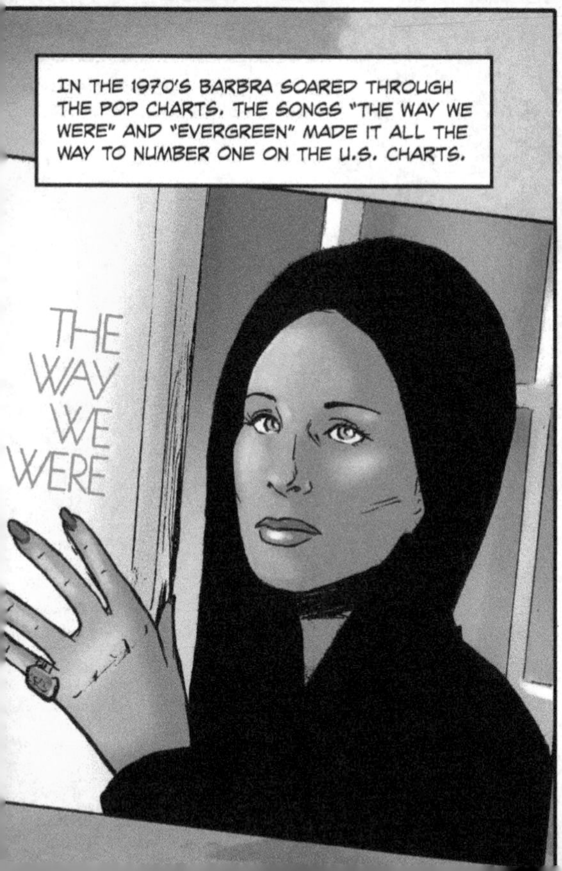
IN THE 1970'S BARBRA SOARED THROUGH THE POP CHARTS. THE SONGS "THE WAY WE WERE" AND "EVERGREEN" MADE IT ALL THE WAY TO NUMBER ONE ON THE U.S. CHARTS.
THE WAY WE WERE

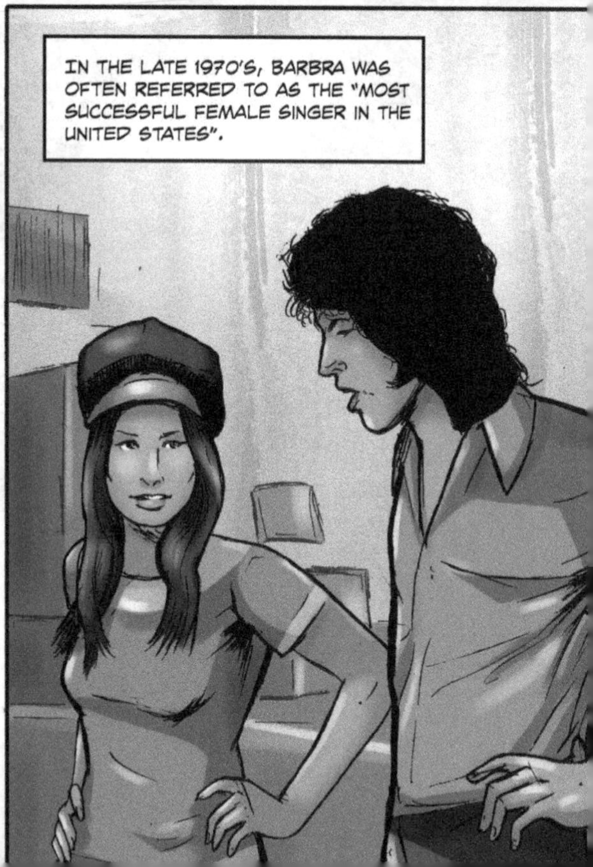
IN THE LATE 1970'S, BARBRA WAS OFTEN REFERRED TO AS THE "MOST SUCCESSFUL FEMALE SINGER IN THE UNITED STATES".

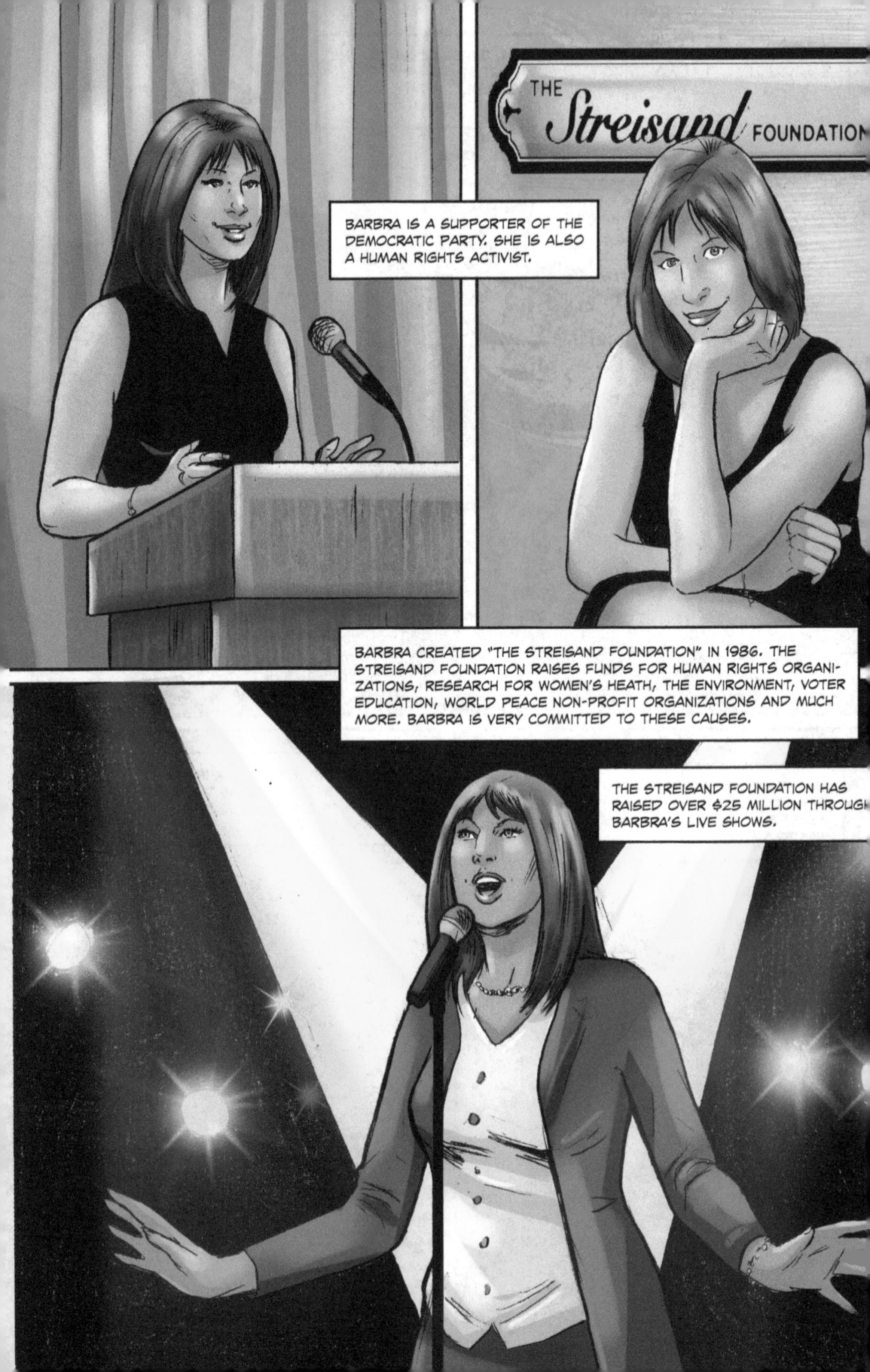

BARBRA IS A SUPPORTER OF THE DEMOCRATIC PARTY. SHE IS ALSO A HUMAN RIGHTS ACTIVIST.
THE Streisand FOUNDATION
BARBRA CREATED "THE STREISAND FOUNDATION" IN 1986. THE STREISAND FOUNDATION RAISES FUNDS FOR HUMAN RIGHTS ORGANIZATIONS, RESEARCH FOR WOMEN'S HEATH, THE ENVIRONMENT, VOTER EDUCATION, WORLD PEACE NON-PROFIT ORGANIZATIONS AND MUCH MORE. BARBRA IS VERY COMMITTED TO THESE CAUSES.
THE STREISAND FOUNDATION HAS RAISED OVER $25 MILLION THROUGH BARBRA'S LIVE SHOWS.

BARBRA IS THE ONLY FEMALE ARTIST TO HAVE RECEIVED BOTH A RECORDING ACADEMY LIFETIME ACHIEVEMENT AWARD AND THE AMERICAN FILM INSTITUTE AWARD. THE ONLY OTHER ARTIST TO DO SO WAS FRANK SINATRA.

ACADEMY AWARD WINNER

Evergreen

(Love Theme From "A Star Is Born")

OVER ONE MILLION COPIES SOLD

Words by PAUL WILLIAMS   Music by BARBRA STREISAND

BARBRA WAS ALSO THE FIRST WOMAN TO WIN AN ACADEMY AWARD FOR BEST SONG. SHE RECEIVED THIS AWARD FOR THE SONG "EVERGREEN" IN 1976.

BARBRA WAS THE FIRST WOMAN TO PRODUCE, WRITE AND STAR IN A MAJOR MOTION PICTURE. BARBRA ACHIEVED THIS TITLE THROUGH THE PRODUCTION OF YENTL IN 1983.

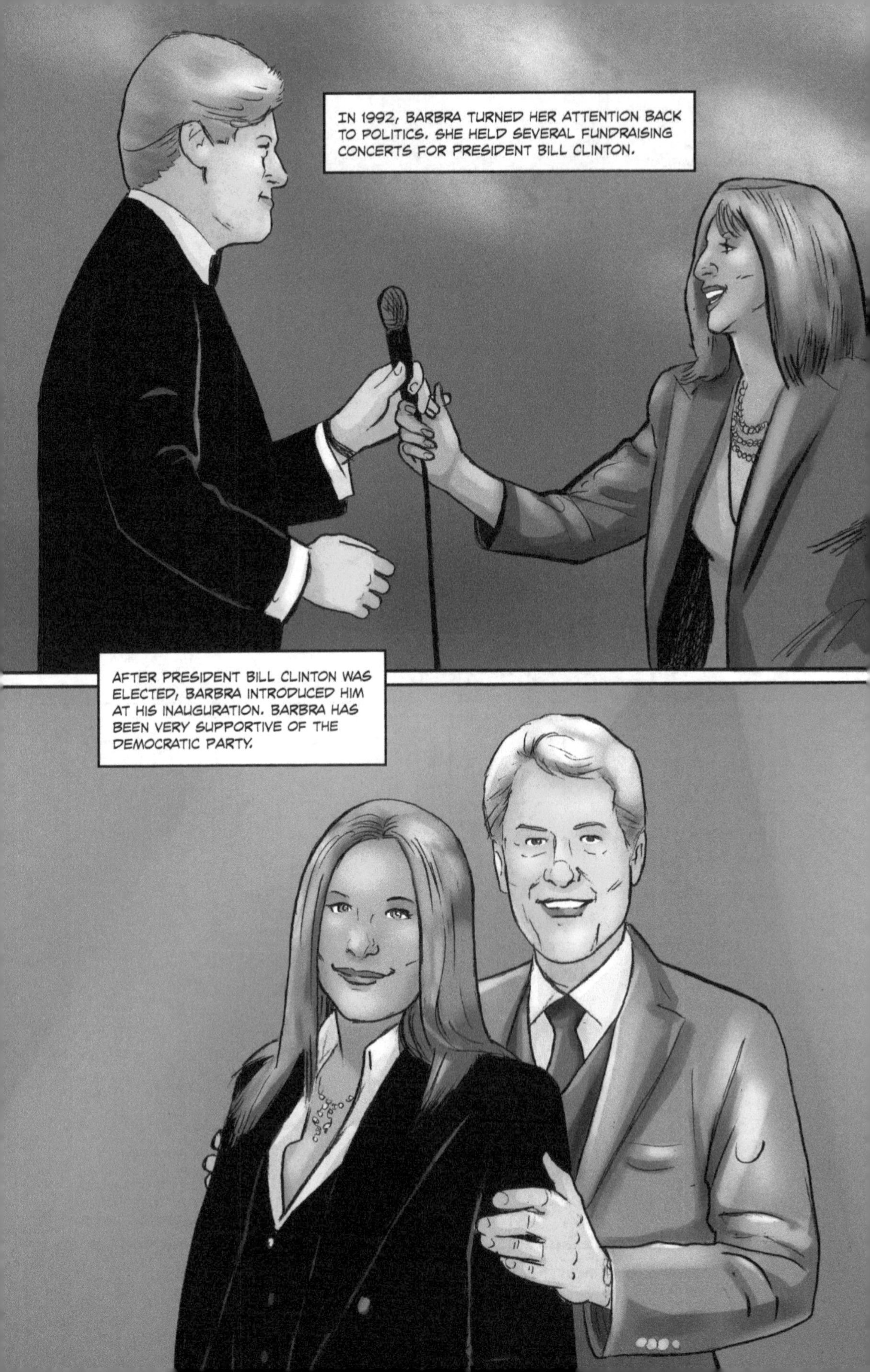
IN 1992, BARBRA TURNED HER ATTENTION BACK TO POLITICS. SHE HELD SEVERAL FUNDRAISING CONCERTS FOR PRESIDENT BILL CLINTON.
AFTER PRESIDENT BILL CLINTON WAS ELECTED, BARBRA INTRODUCED HIM AT HIS INAUGURATION. BARBRA HAS BEEN VERY SUPPORTIVE OF THE DEMOCRATIC PARTY.

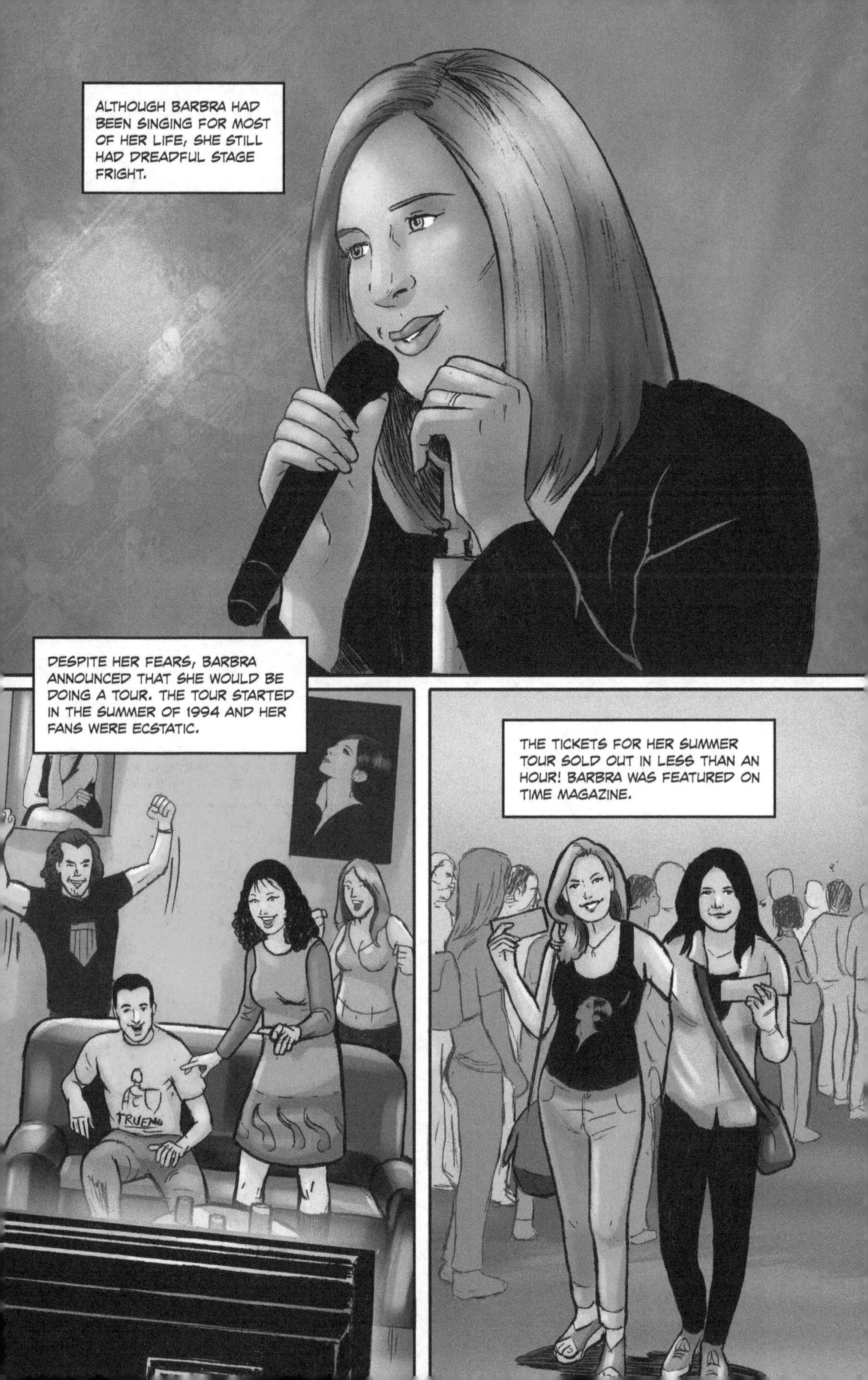
ALTHOUGH BARBRA HAD BEEN SINGING FOR MOST OF HER LIFE, SHE STILL HAD DREADFUL STAGE FRIGHT.
DESPITE HER FEARS, BARBRA ANNOUNCED THAT SHE WOULD BE DOING A TOUR. THE TOUR STARTED IN THE SUMMER OF 1994 AND HER FANS WERE ECSTATIC.
TRUENO
THE TICKETS FOR HER SUMMER TOUR SOLD OUT IN LESS THAN AN HOUR! BARBRA WAS FEATURED ON TIME MAGAZINE.

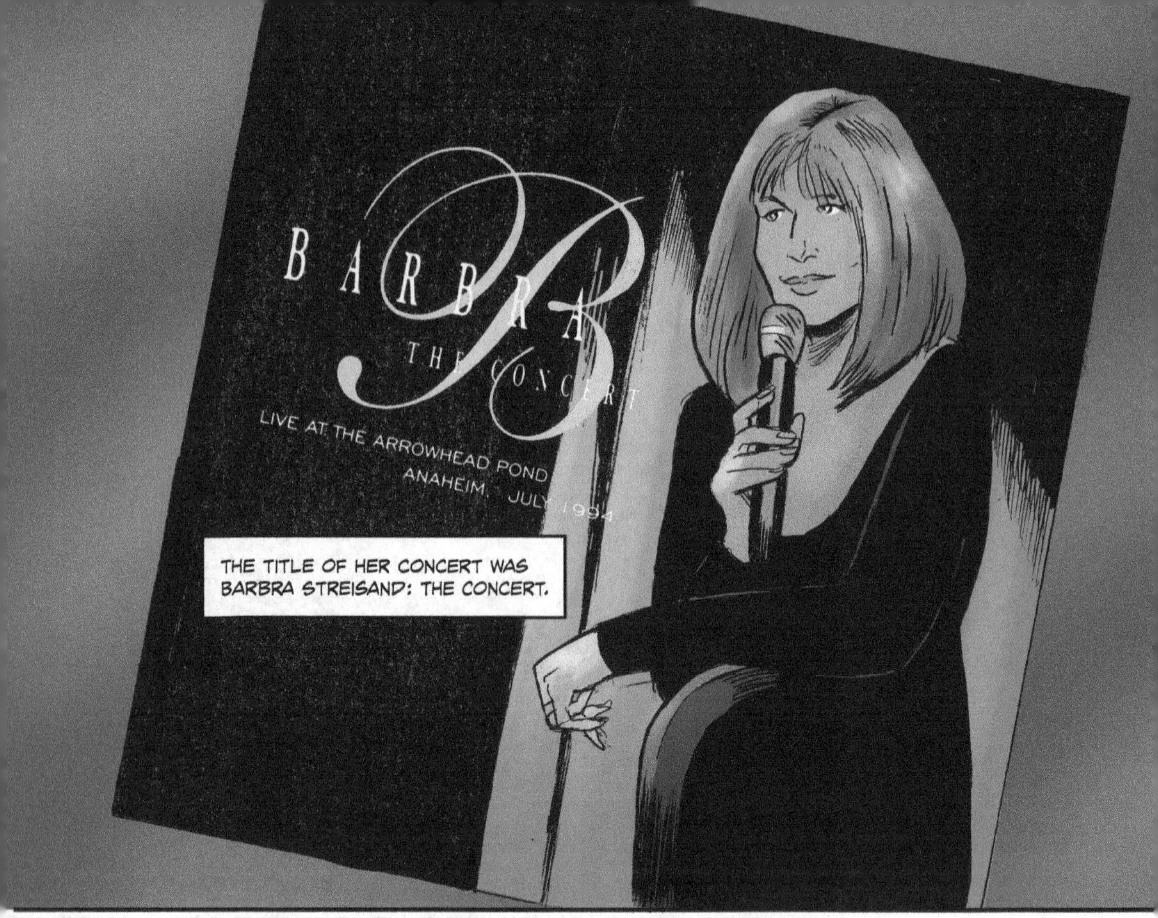
BARBRA
THE CONCERT
LIVE AT THE ARROWHEAD POND
ANAHEIM, JULY 1994
THE TITLE OF HER CONCERT WAS BARBRA STREISAND: THE CONCERT.

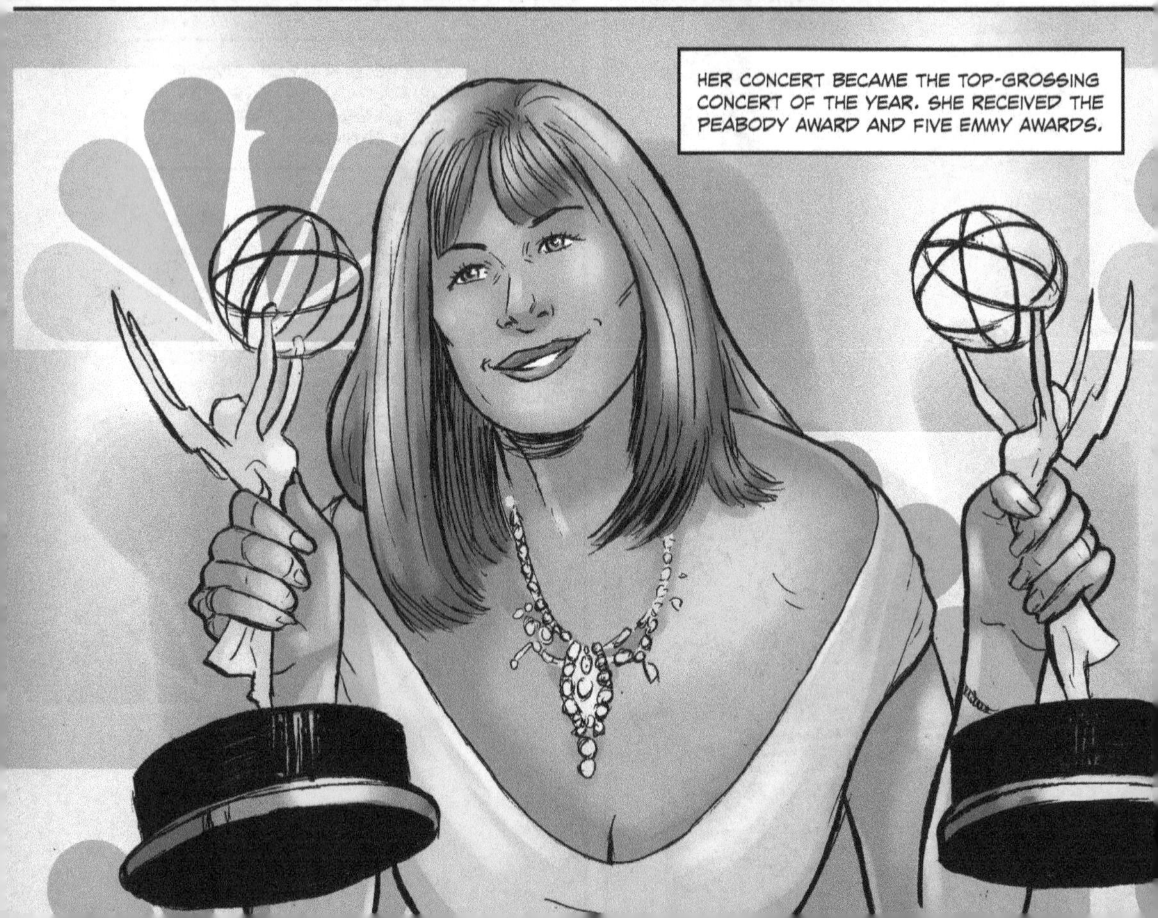
HER CONCERT BECAME THE TOP-GROSSING CONCERT OF THE YEAR. SHE RECEIVED THE PEABODY AWARD AND FIVE EMMY AWARDS.

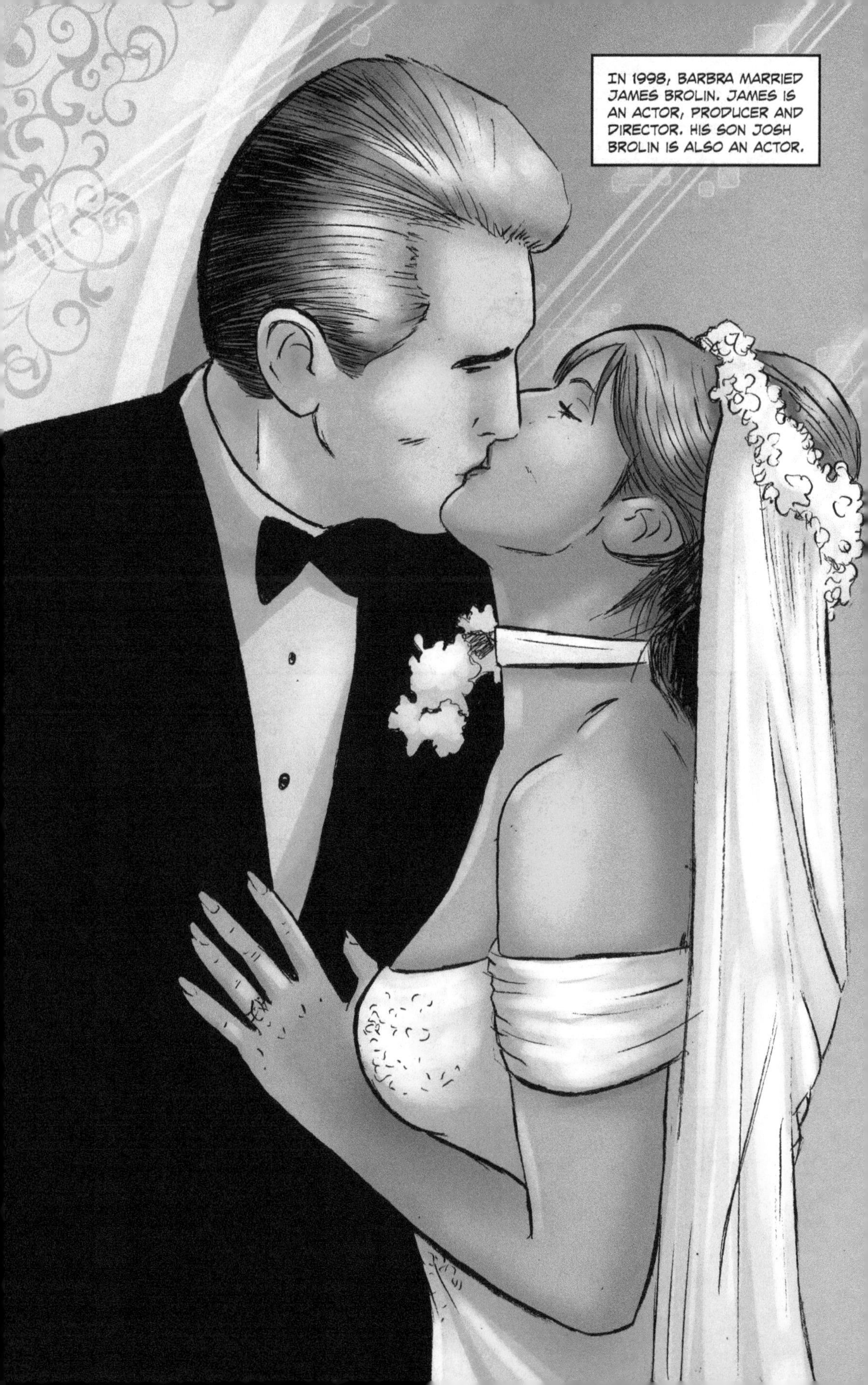
IN 1998, BARBRA MARRIED JAMES BROLIN. JAMES IS AN ACTOR, PRODUCER AND DIRECTOR. HIS SON JOSH BROLIN IS ALSO AN ACTOR.

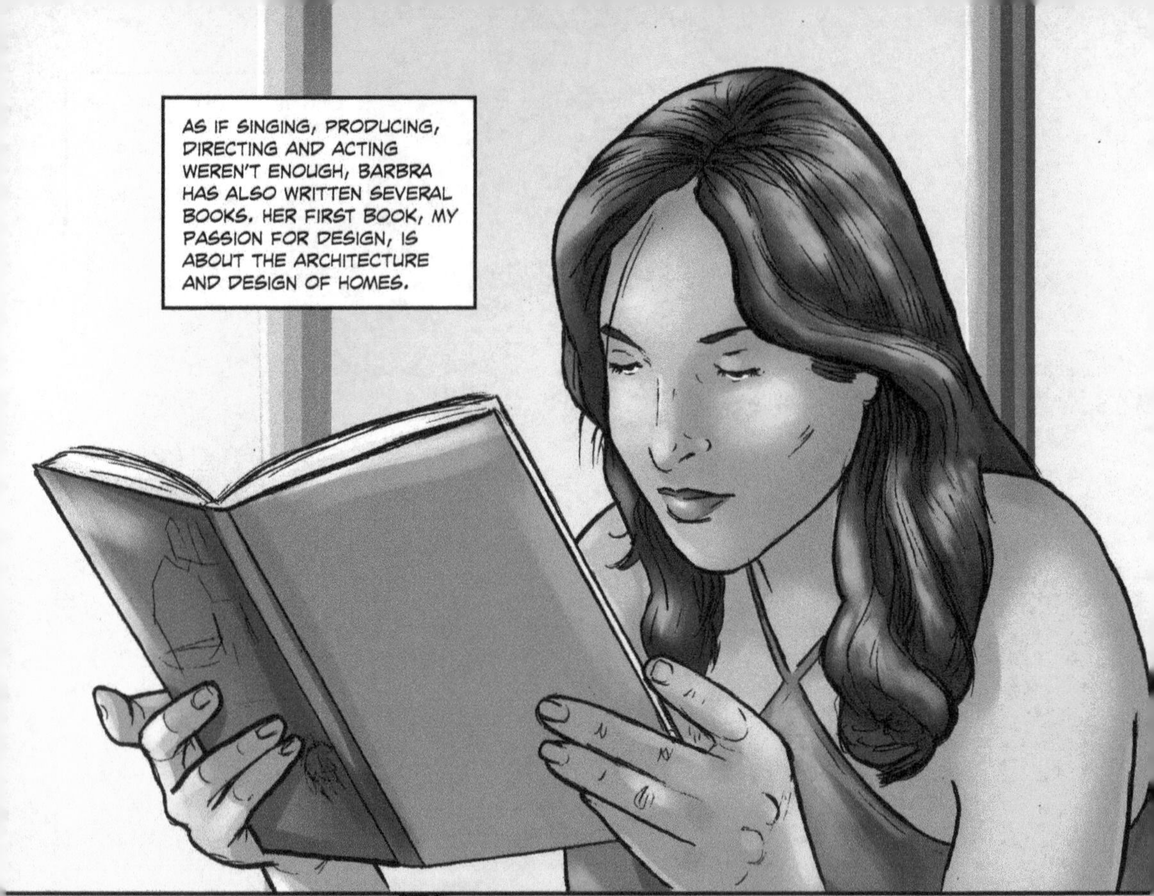
AS IF SINGING, PRODUCING, DIRECTING AND ACTING WEREN'T ENOUGH, BARBRA HAS ALSO WRITTEN SEVERAL BOOKS. HER FIRST BOOK, MY PASSION FOR DESIGN, IS ABOUT THE ARCHITECTURE AND DESIGN OF HOMES.

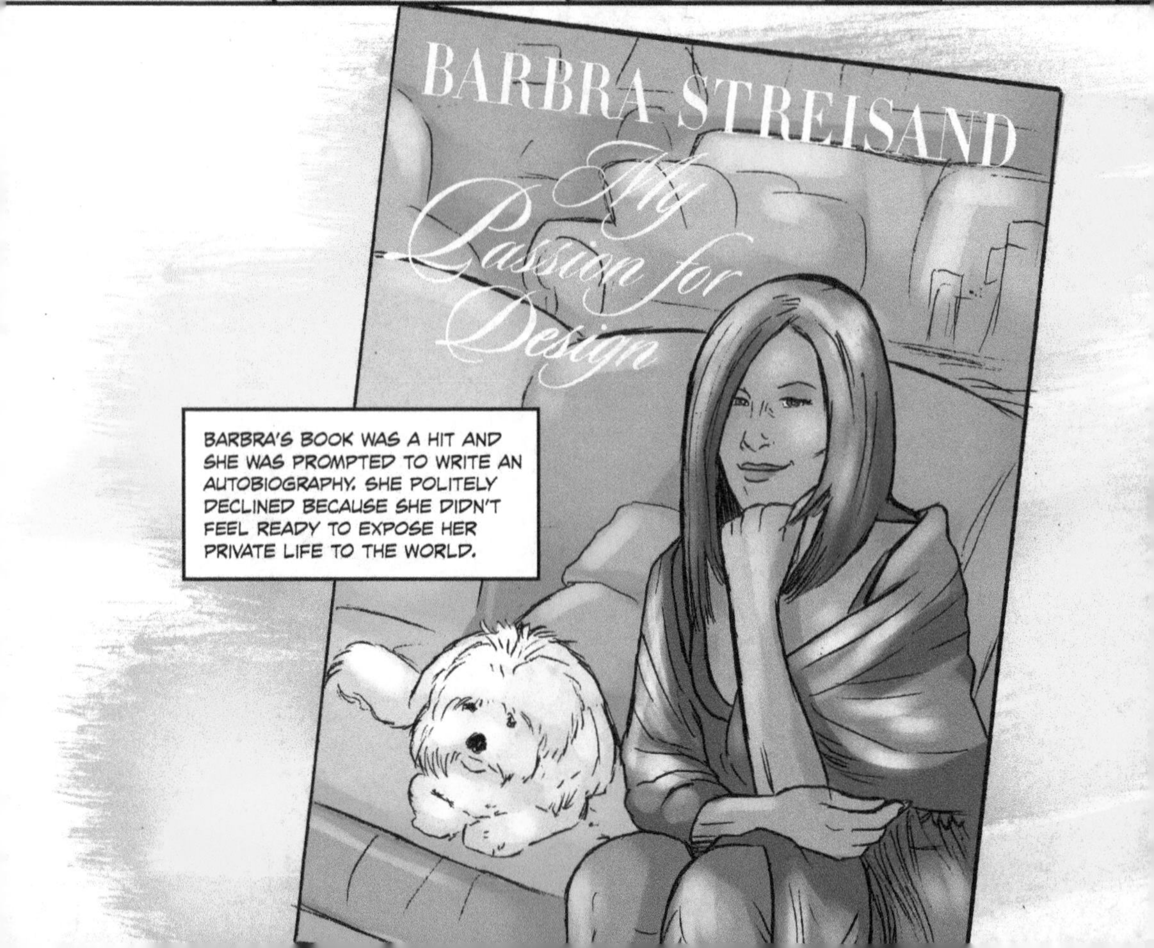
BARBRA STREISAND
My Passion for Design
BARBRA'S BOOK WAS A HIT AND SHE WAS PROMPTED TO WRITE AN AUTOBIOGRAPHY. SHE POLITELY DECLINED BECAUSE SHE DIDN'T FEEL READY TO EXPOSE HER PRIVATE LIFE TO THE WORLD.

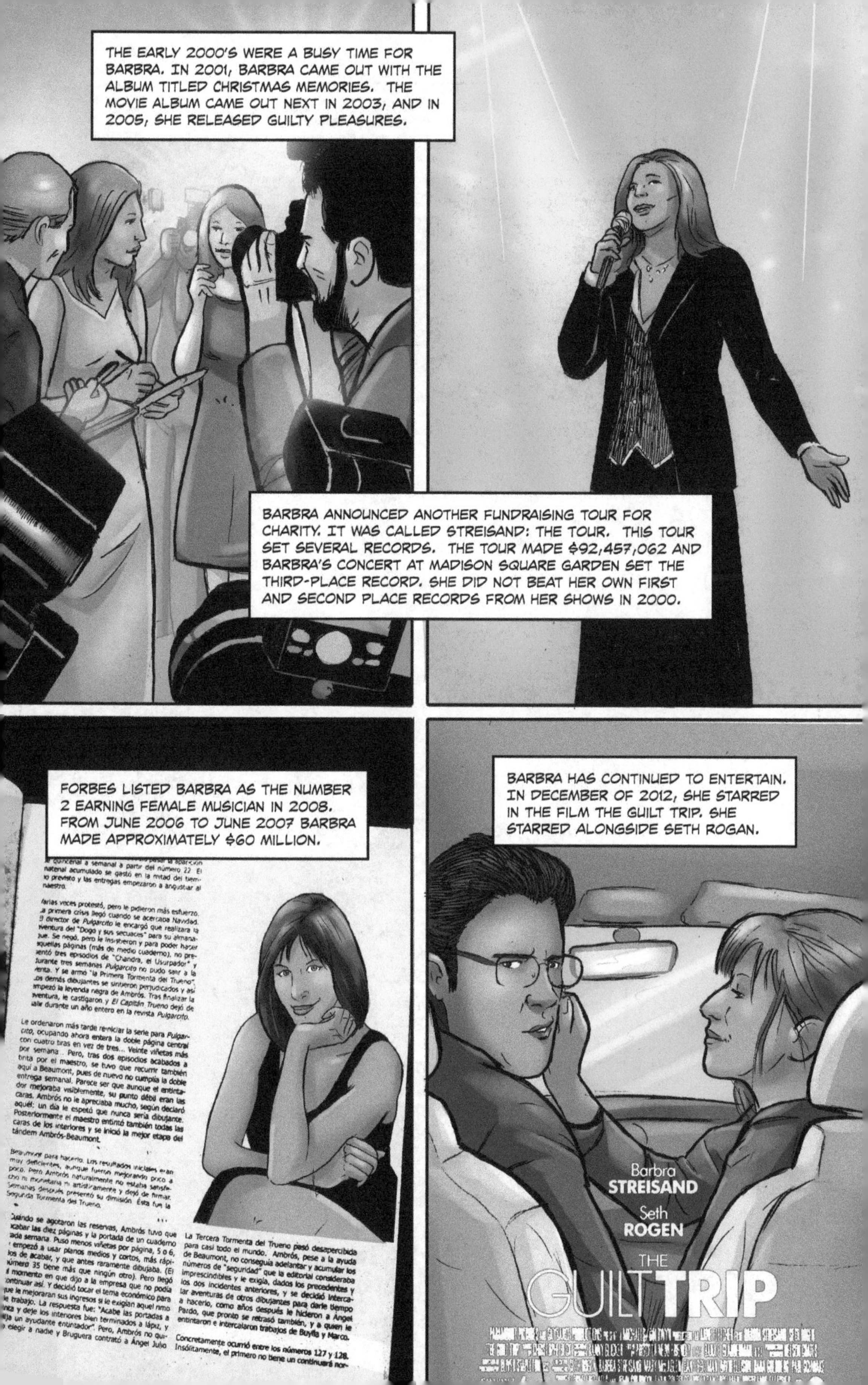
THE EARLY 2000'S WERE A BUSY TIME FOR BARBRA. IN 2001, BARBRA CAME OUT WITH THE ALBUM TITLED CHRISTMAS MEMORIES. THE MOVIE ALBUM CAME OUT NEXT IN 2003, AND IN 2005, SHE RELEASED GUILTY PLEASURES.
BARBRA ANNOUNCED ANOTHER FUNDRAISING TOUR FOR CHARITY. IT WAS CALLED STREISAND: THE TOUR. THIS TOUR SET SEVERAL RECORDS. THE TOUR MADE $92,457,062 AND BARBRA'S CONCERT AT MADISON SQUARE GARDEN SET THE THIRD-PLACE RECORD. SHE DID NOT BEAT HER OWN FIRST AND SECOND PLACE RECORDS FROM HER SHOWS IN 2000.
FORBES LISTED BARBRA AS THE NUMBER 2 EARNING FEMALE MUSICIAN IN 2008. FROM JUNE 2006 TO JUNE 2007 BARBRA MADE APPROXIMATELY $60 MILLION.
BARBRA HAS CONTINUED TO ENTERTAIN. IN DECEMBER OF 2012, SHE STARRED IN THE FILM THE GUILT TRIP. SHE STARRED ALONGSIDE SETH ROGAN.
Barbra
STREISAND
Seth
ROGEN
THE
GUILT TRIP

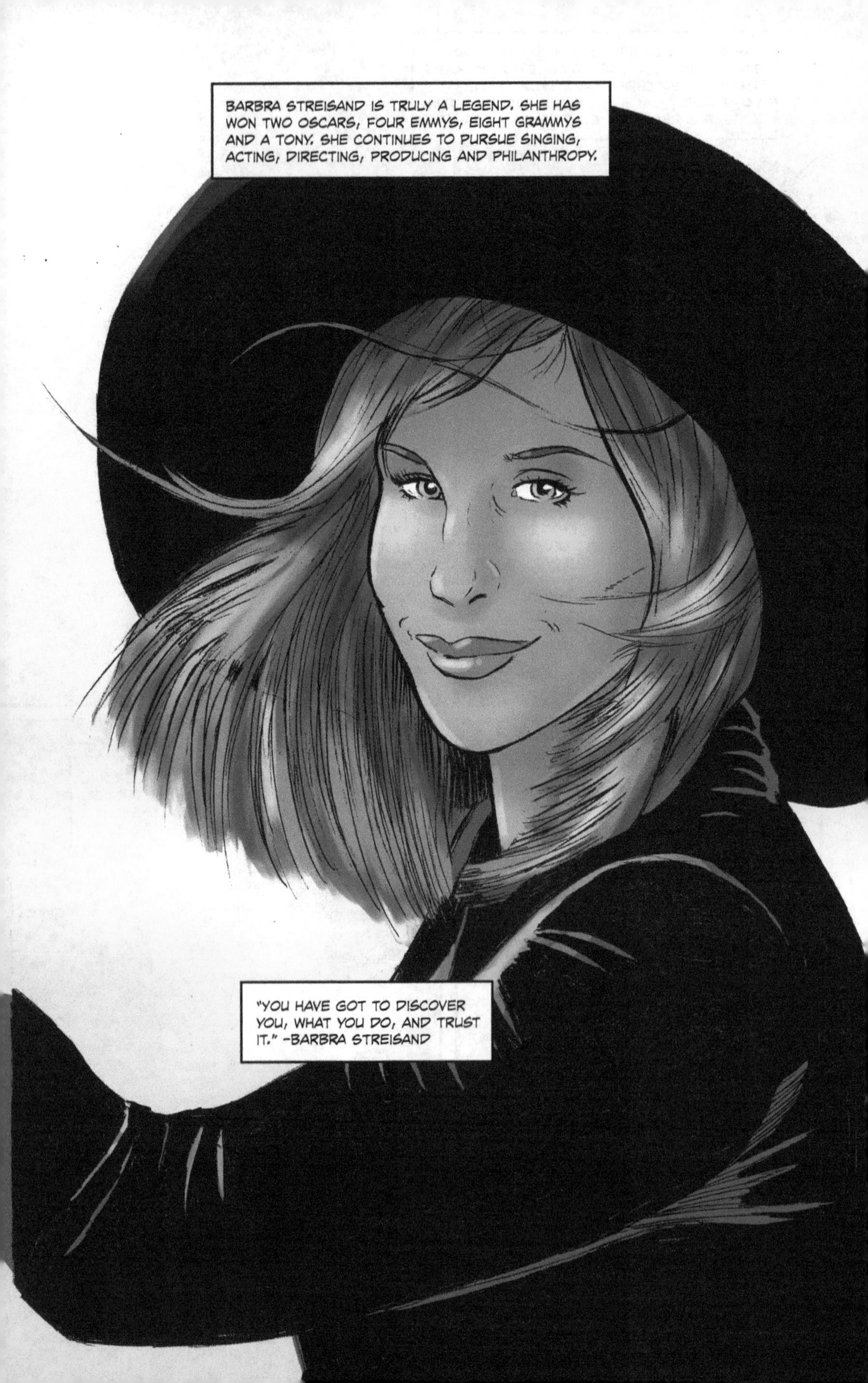
BARBRA STREISAND IS TRULY A LEGEND. SHE HAS WON TWO OSCARS, FOUR EMMYS, EIGHT GRAMMYS AND A TONY. SHE CONTINUES TO PURSUE SINGING, ACTING, DIRECTING, PRODUCING AND PHILANTHROPY.
"YOU HAVE GOT TO DISCOVER YOU, WHAT YOU DO, AND TRUST IT." -BARBRA STREISAND

LIZA MINNELLI

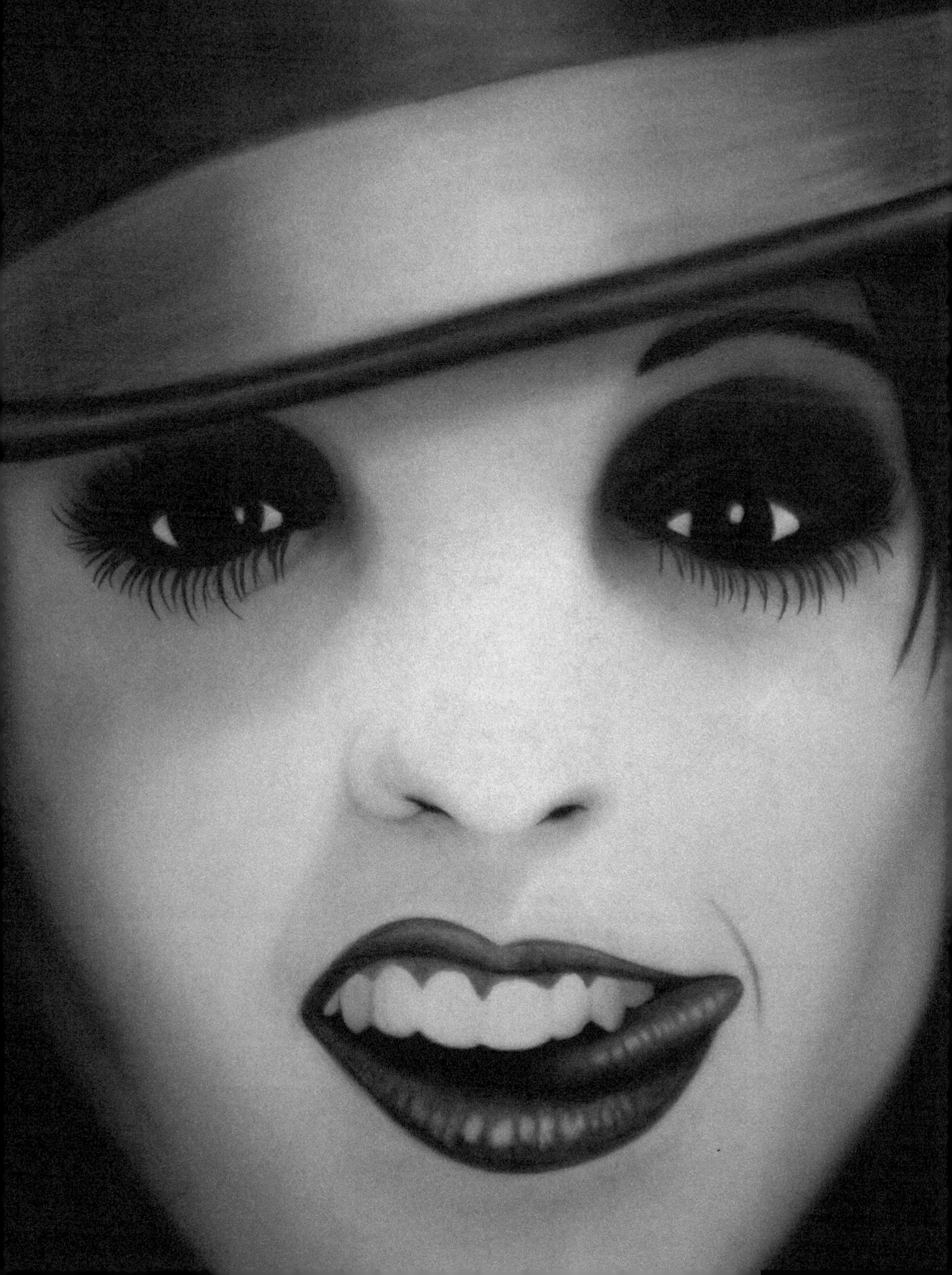

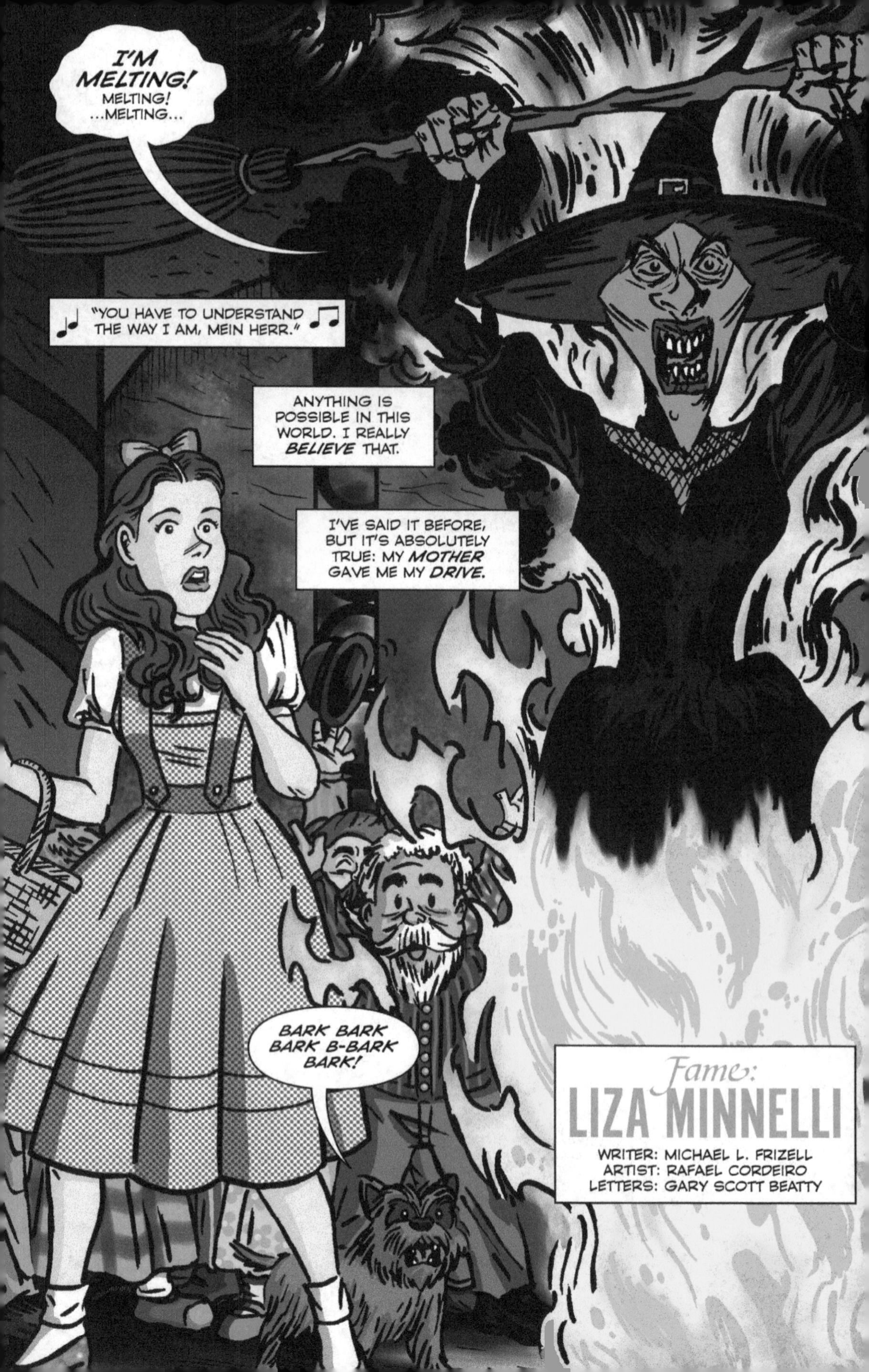
I'M MELTING! MELTING! ...MELTING...
"YOU HAVE TO UNDERSTAND THE WAY I AM, MEIN HERR."
ANYTHING IS POSSIBLE IN THIS WORLD. I REALLY BELIEVE THAT.
I'VE SAID IT BEFORE, BUT IT'S ABSOLUTELY TRUE: MY MOTHER GAVE ME MY DRIVE.
BARK BARK BARK B-BARK BARK!
Fame:
LIZA MINNELLI
WRITER: MICHAEL L. FRIZELL
ARTIST: RAFAEL CORDEIRO
LETTERS: GARY SCOTT BEATTY

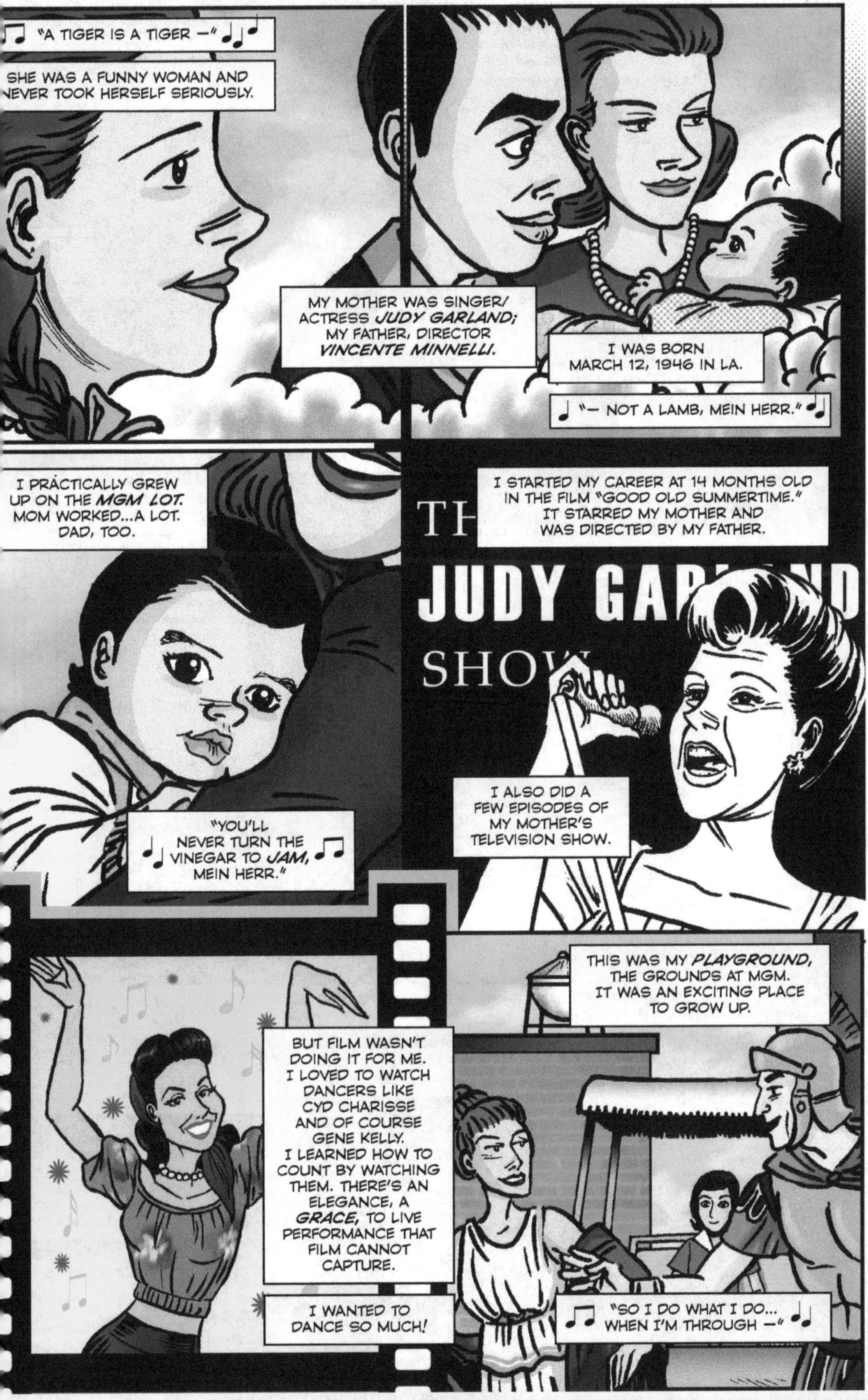
"A TIGER IS A TIGER —"
SHE WAS A FUNNY WOMAN AND NEVER TOOK HERSELF SERIOUSLY.
MY MOTHER WAS SINGER/ ACTRESS JUDY GARLAND; MY FATHER, DIRECTOR VINCENTE MINNELLI.
I WAS BORN MARCH 12, 1946 IN LA.
"— NOT A LAMB, MEIN HERR."
I PRACTICALLY GREW UP ON THE MGM LOT. MOM WORKED...A LOT. DAD, TOO.
"YOU'LL NEVER TURN THE VINEGAR TO JAM, MEIN HERR."
I STARTED MY CAREER AT 14 MONTHS OLD IN THE FILM "GOOD OLD SUMMERTIME." IT STARRED MY MOTHER AND WAS DIRECTED BY MY FATHER.
I ALSO DID A FEW EPISODES OF MY MOTHER'S TELEVISION SHOW.
BUT FILM WASN'T DOING IT FOR ME. I LOVED TO WATCH DANCERS LIKE CYD CHARISSE AND OF COURSE GENE KELLY. I LEARNED HOW TO COUNT BY WATCHING THEM. THERE'S AN ELEGANCE, A GRACE, TO LIVE PERFORMANCE THAT FILM CANNOT CAPTURE.
I WANTED TO DANCE SO MUCH!
THIS WAS MY PLAYGROUND, THE GROUNDS AT MGM. IT WAS AN EXCITING PLACE TO GROW UP.
"SO I DO WHAT I DO... WHEN I'M THROUGH —"

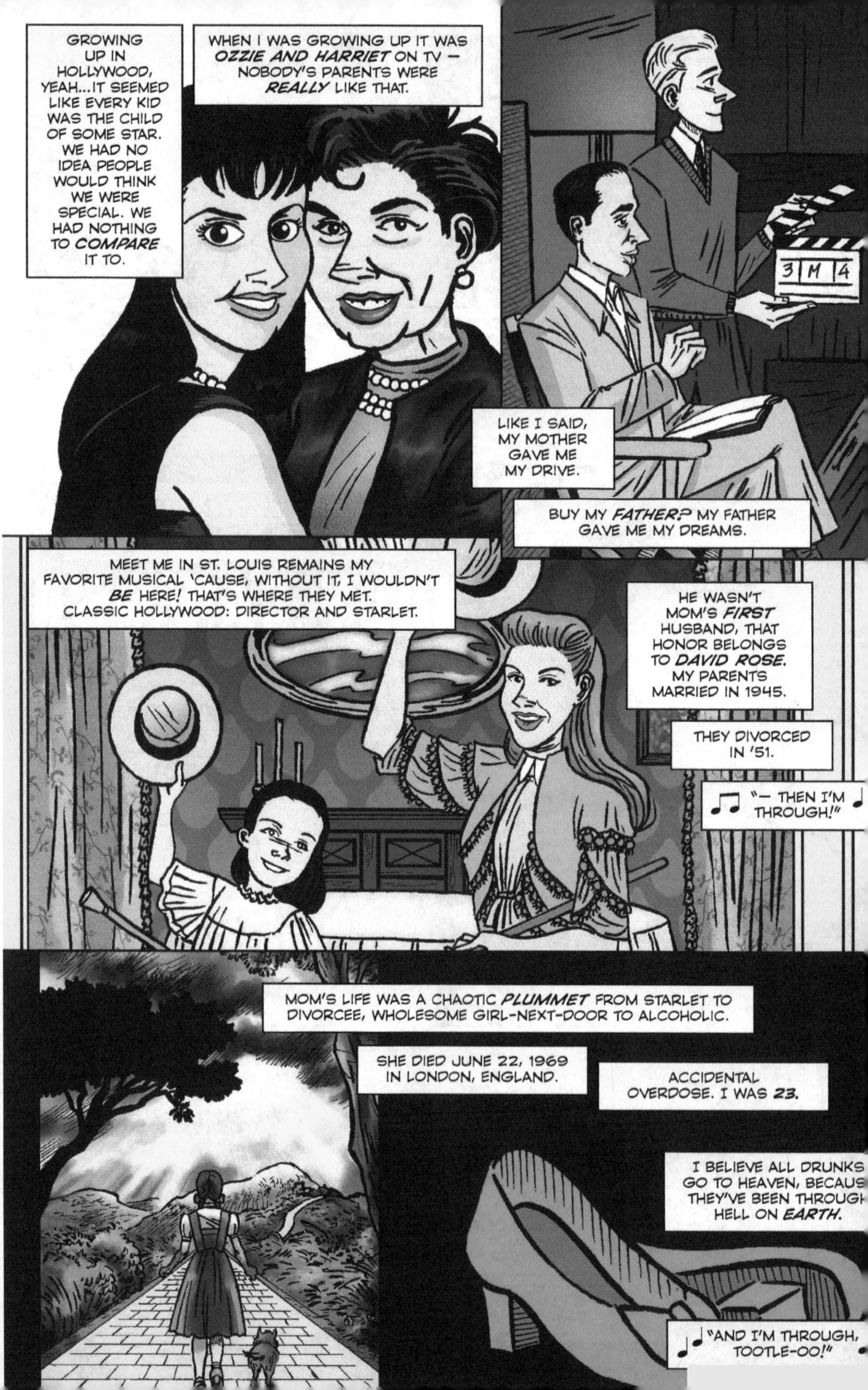

GROWING UP IN HOLLYWOOD, YEAH...IT SEEMED LIKE EVERY KID WAS THE CHILD OF SOME STAR. WE HAD NO IDEA PEOPLE WOULD THINK WE WERE SPECIAL. WE HAD NOTHING TO COMPARE IT TO.
WHEN I WAS GROWING UP IT WAS OZZIE AND HARRIET ON TV — NOBODY'S PARENTS WERE REALLY LIKE THAT.
3 M 4
LIKE I SAID, MY MOTHER GAVE ME MY DRIVE.
BUY MY FATHER? MY FATHER GAVE ME MY DREAMS.
MEET ME IN ST. LOUIS REMAINS MY FAVORITE MUSICAL 'CAUSE, WITHOUT IT, I WOULDN'T BE HERE! THAT'S WHERE THEY MET. CLASSIC HOLLYWOOD: DIRECTOR AND STARLET.
HE WASN'T MOM'S FIRST HUSBAND, THAT HONOR BELONGS TO DAVID ROSE. MY PARENTS MARRIED IN 1945.
THEY DIVORCED IN '51.
"— THEN I'M THROUGH!"
MOM'S LIFE WAS A CHAOTIC PLUMMET FROM STARLET TO DIVORCEE, WHOLESOME GIRL-NEXT-DOOR TO ALCOHOLIC.
SHE DIED JUNE 22, 1969 IN LONDON, ENGLAND.
ACCIDENTAL OVERDOSE. I WAS 23.
I BELIEVE ALL DRUNKS GO TO HEAVEN, BECAUS THEY'VE BEEN THROUGH HELL ON EARTH.
"AND I'M THROUGH, TOOTLE-OO!"

CABARET (1972)
I DECIDED TO GO IN A *DIFFERENT* DIRECTION.
"BYE BYE, MEIN LIEBER HERR"
"FAREWELL, MEIN LIEBER HERR"
"IT WAS A FINE AFFAIR, BUT NOW IT'S OVER"
"I USED TO CARE, I NEED THE OPEN AIR!"
"YOU'RE BETTER OFF WITHOUT ME, MEIN HERR!"
BOB FOSSE DIRECTED ME IN THIS. MY *BREAKTHROUGH* WAS PLAYING A FLOUNDERING NIGHTCLUB SINGER NAMED SALLY BOWLES.
STREISAND WAS OFFERED THE PART FIRST. SHE TURNED IT DOWN. MY LUCK.

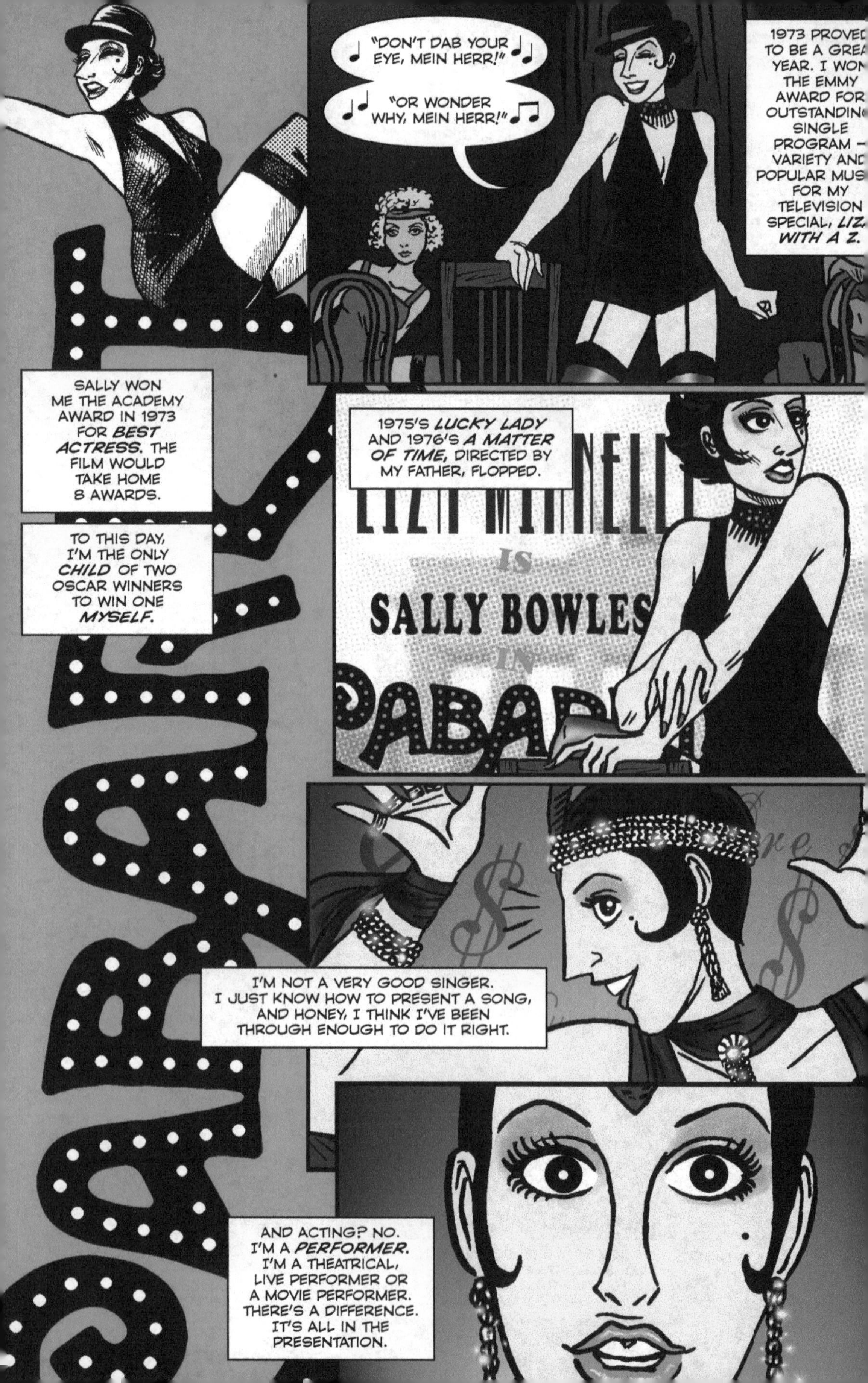
"DON'T DAB YOUR EYE, MEIN HERR!"
"OR WONDER WHY, MEIN HERR!"
1973 PROVED TO BE A GREAT YEAR. I WON THE EMMY AWARD FOR OUTSTANDING SINGLE PROGRAM – VARIETY AND POPULAR MUSIC FOR MY TELEVISION SPECIAL, *LIZA WITH A Z.*
SALLY WON ME THE ACADEMY AWARD IN 1973 FOR *BEST ACTRESS.* THE FILM WOULD TAKE HOME 8 AWARDS.
TO THIS DAY, I'M THE ONLY *CHILD* OF TWO OSCAR WINNERS TO WIN ONE *MYSELF.*
1975'S *LUCKY LADY* AND 1976'S *A MATTER OF TIME,* DIRECTED BY MY FATHER, FLOPPED.
IS
SALLY BOWLES
IN
I'M NOT A VERY GOOD SINGER. I JUST KNOW HOW TO PRESENT A SONG, AND HONEY, I THINK I'VE BEEN THROUGH ENOUGH TO DO IT RIGHT.
AND ACTING? NO. I'M A *PERFORMER.* I'M A THEATRICAL, LIVE PERFORMER OR A MOVIE PERFORMER. THERE'S A DIFFERENCE. IT'S ALL IN THE PRESENTATION.

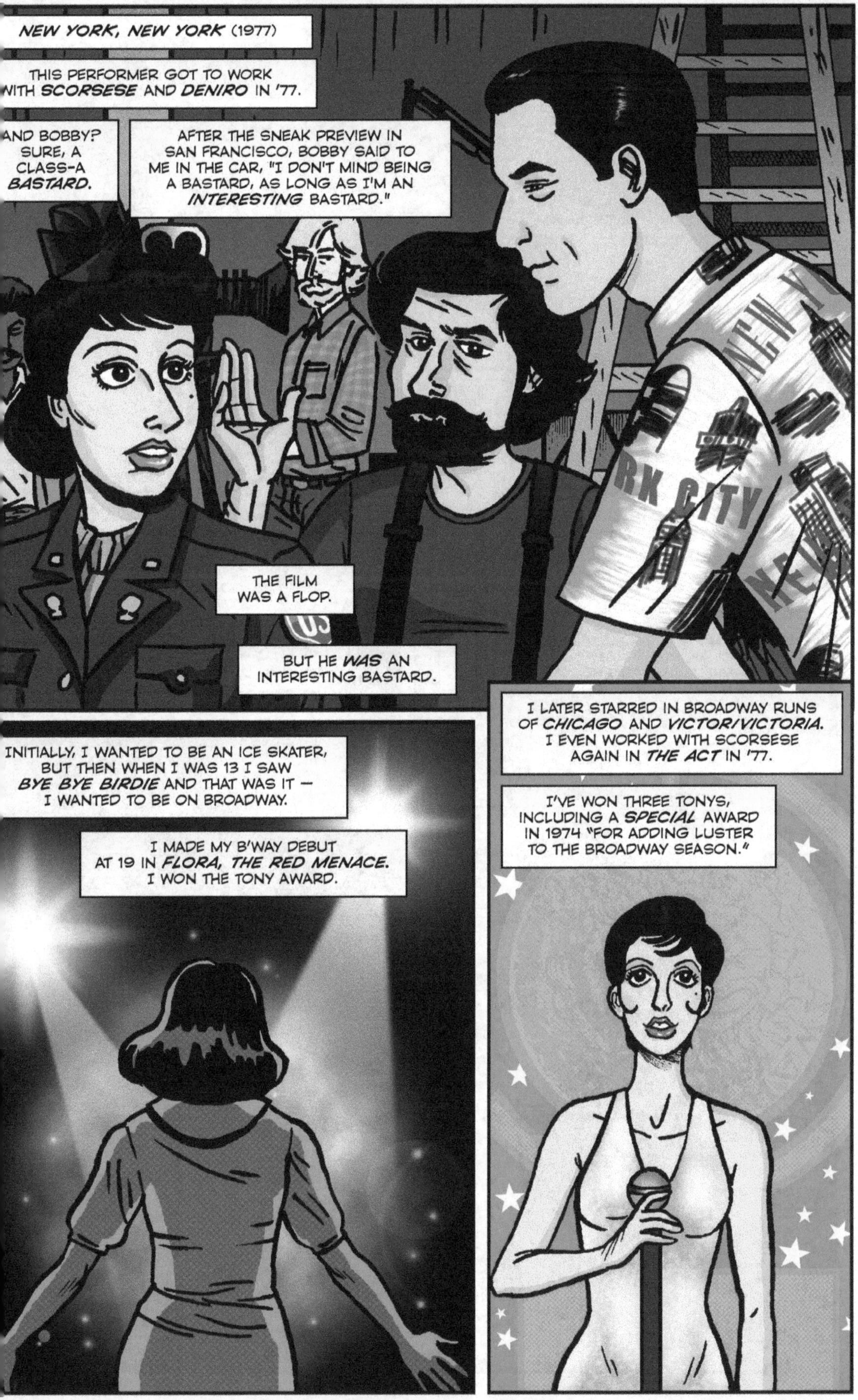
NEW YORK, NEW YORK (1977)
THIS PERFORMER GOT TO WORK WITH SCORSESE AND DENIRO IN '77.
AND BOBBY? SURE, A CLASS-A BASTARD.
AFTER THE SNEAK PREVIEW IN SAN FRANCISCO, BOBBY SAID TO ME IN THE CAR, "I DON'T MIND BEING A BASTARD, AS LONG AS I'M AN INTERESTING BASTARD."
THE FILM WAS A FLOP.
BUT HE WAS AN INTERESTING BASTARD.
INITIALLY, I WANTED TO BE AN ICE SKATER, BUT THEN WHEN I WAS 13 I SAW BYE BYE BIRDIE AND THAT WAS IT — I WANTED TO BE ON BROADWAY.
I MADE MY B'WAY DEBUT AT 19 IN FLORA, THE RED MENACE. I WON THE TONY AWARD.
I LATER STARRED IN BROADWAY RUNS OF CHICAGO AND VICTOR/VICTORIA. I EVEN WORKED WITH SCORSESE AGAIN IN THE ACT IN '77.
I'VE WON THREE TONYS, INCLUDING A SPECIAL AWARD IN 1974 "FOR ADDING LUSTER TO THE BROADWAY SEASON."

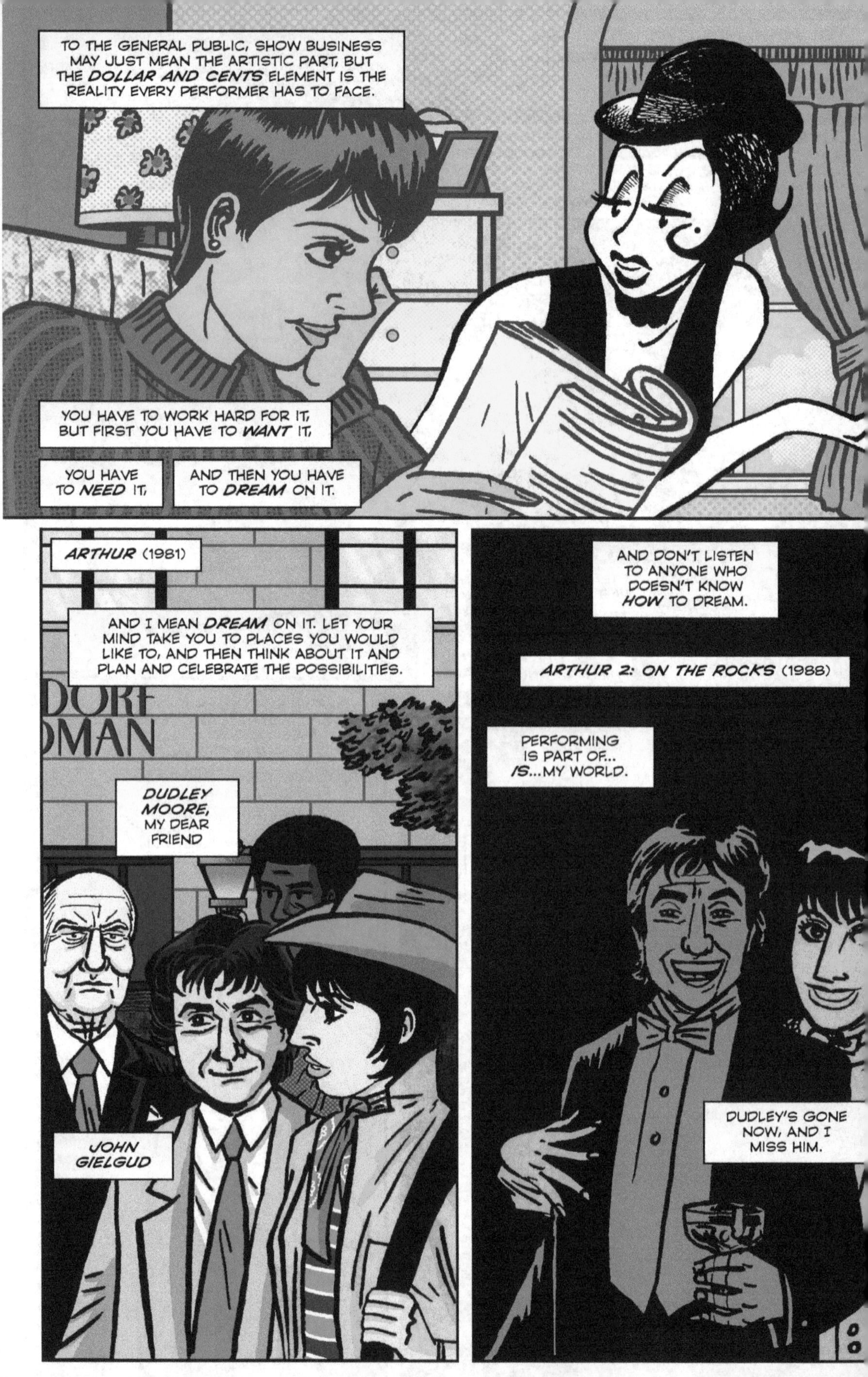

TO THE GENERAL PUBLIC, SHOW BUSINESS MAY JUST MEAN THE ARTISTIC PART, BUT THE DOLLAR AND CENTS ELEMENT IS THE REALITY EVERY PERFORMER HAS TO FACE.
YOU HAVE TO WORK HARD FOR IT, BUT FIRST YOU HAVE TO WANT IT,
YOU HAVE TO NEED IT,
AND THEN YOU HAVE TO DREAM ON IT.
ARTHUR (1981)
AND I MEAN DREAM ON IT. LET YOUR MIND TAKE YOU TO PLACES YOU WOULD LIKE TO, AND THEN THINK ABOUT IT AND PLAN AND CELEBRATE THE POSSIBILITIES.
DUDLEY MOORE, MY DEAR FRIEND
JOHN GIELGUD
AND DON'T LISTEN TO ANYONE WHO DOESN'T KNOW HOW TO DREAM.
ARTHUR 2: ON THE ROCKS (1988)
PERFORMING IS PART OF... IS...MY WORLD.
DUDLEY'S GONE NOW, AND I MISS HIM.

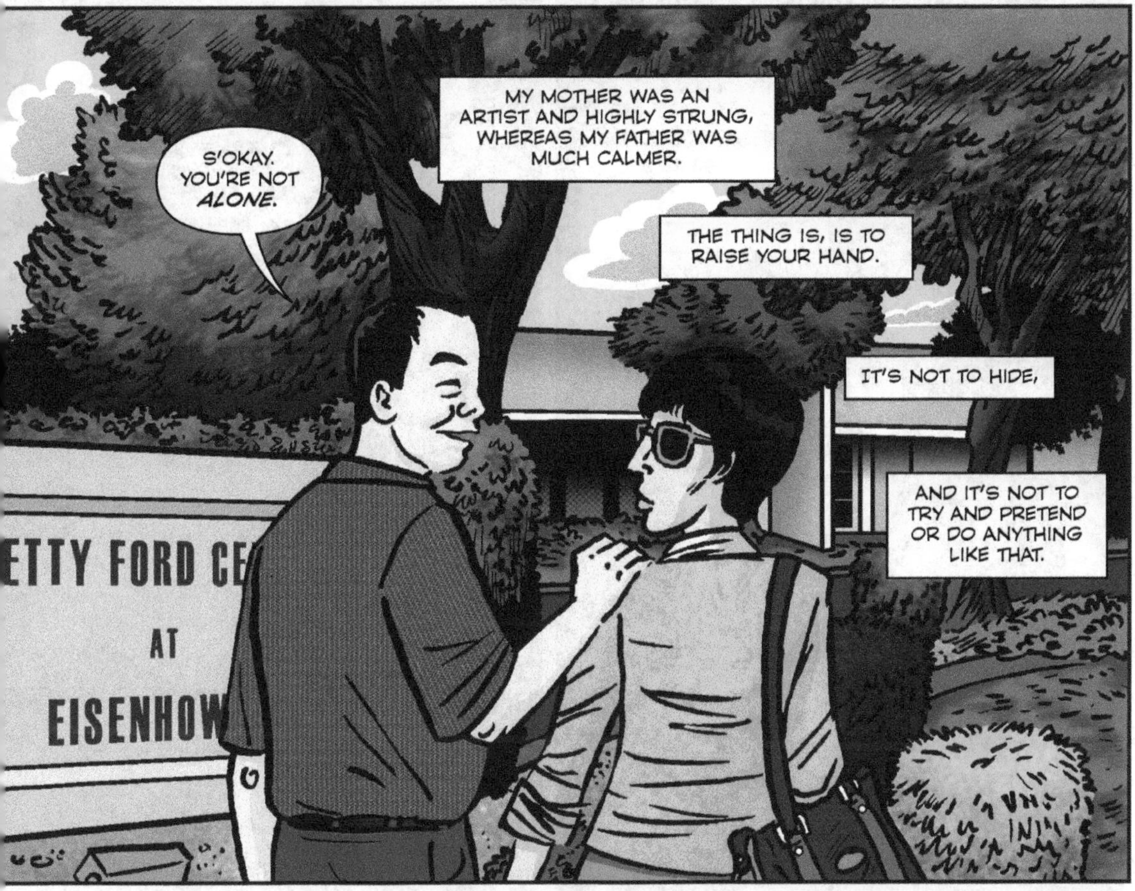
MY MOTHER WAS AN ARTIST AND HIGHLY STRUNG, WHEREAS MY FATHER WAS MUCH CALMER.
S'OKAY. YOU'RE NOT *ALONE.*
THE THING IS, IS TO RAISE YOUR HAND.
IT'S NOT TO HIDE,
AND IT'S NOT TO TRY AND PRETEND OR DO ANYTHING LIKE THAT.
ETTY FORD CE
AT
EISENHOW

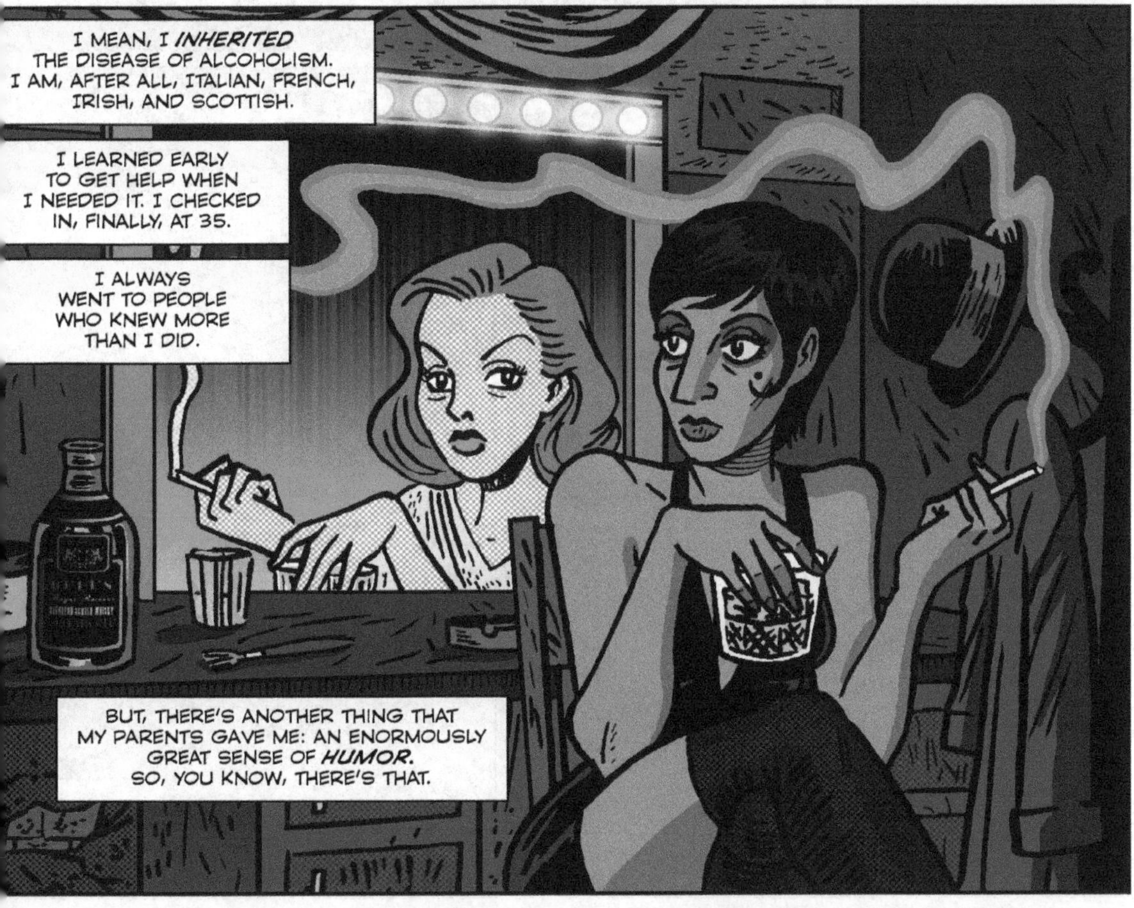
I MEAN, I *INHERITED* THE DISEASE OF ALCOHOLISM. I AM, AFTER ALL, ITALIAN, FRENCH, IRISH, AND SCOTTISH.
I LEARNED EARLY TO GET HELP WHEN I NEEDED IT. I CHECKED IN, FINALLY, AT 35.
I ALWAYS WENT TO PEOPLE WHO KNEW MORE THAN I DID.
BUT, THERE'S ANOTHER THING THAT MY PARENTS GAVE ME: AN ENORMOUSLY GREAT SENSE OF ***HUMOR.*** SO, YOU KNOW, THERE'S THAT.

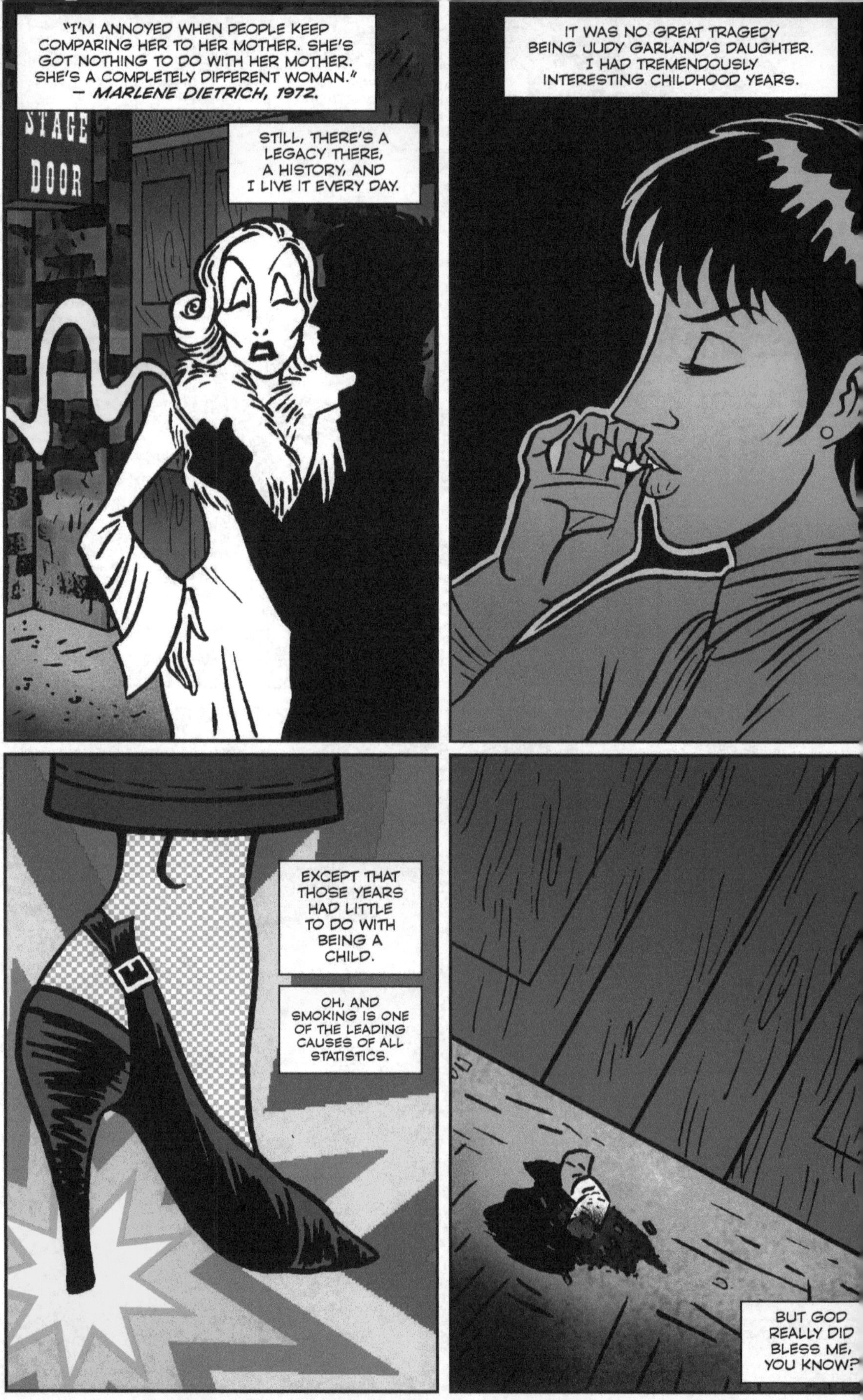
"I'M ANNOYED WHEN PEOPLE KEEP COMPARING HER TO HER MOTHER. SHE'S GOT NOTHING TO DO WITH HER MOTHER. SHE'S A COMPLETELY DIFFERENT WOMAN."
— MARLENE DIETRICH, 1972.
STAGE DOOR
STILL, THERE'S A LEGACY THERE, A HISTORY, AND I LIVE IT EVERY DAY.
IT WAS NO GREAT TRAGEDY BEING JUDY GARLAND'S DAUGHTER. I HAD TREMENDOUSLY INTERESTING CHILDHOOD YEARS.
EXCEPT THAT THOSE YEARS HAD LITTLE TO DO WITH BEING A CHILD.
OH, AND SMOKING IS ONE OF THE LEADING CAUSES OF ALL STATISTICS.
BUT GOD REALLY DID BLESS ME, YOU KNOW?

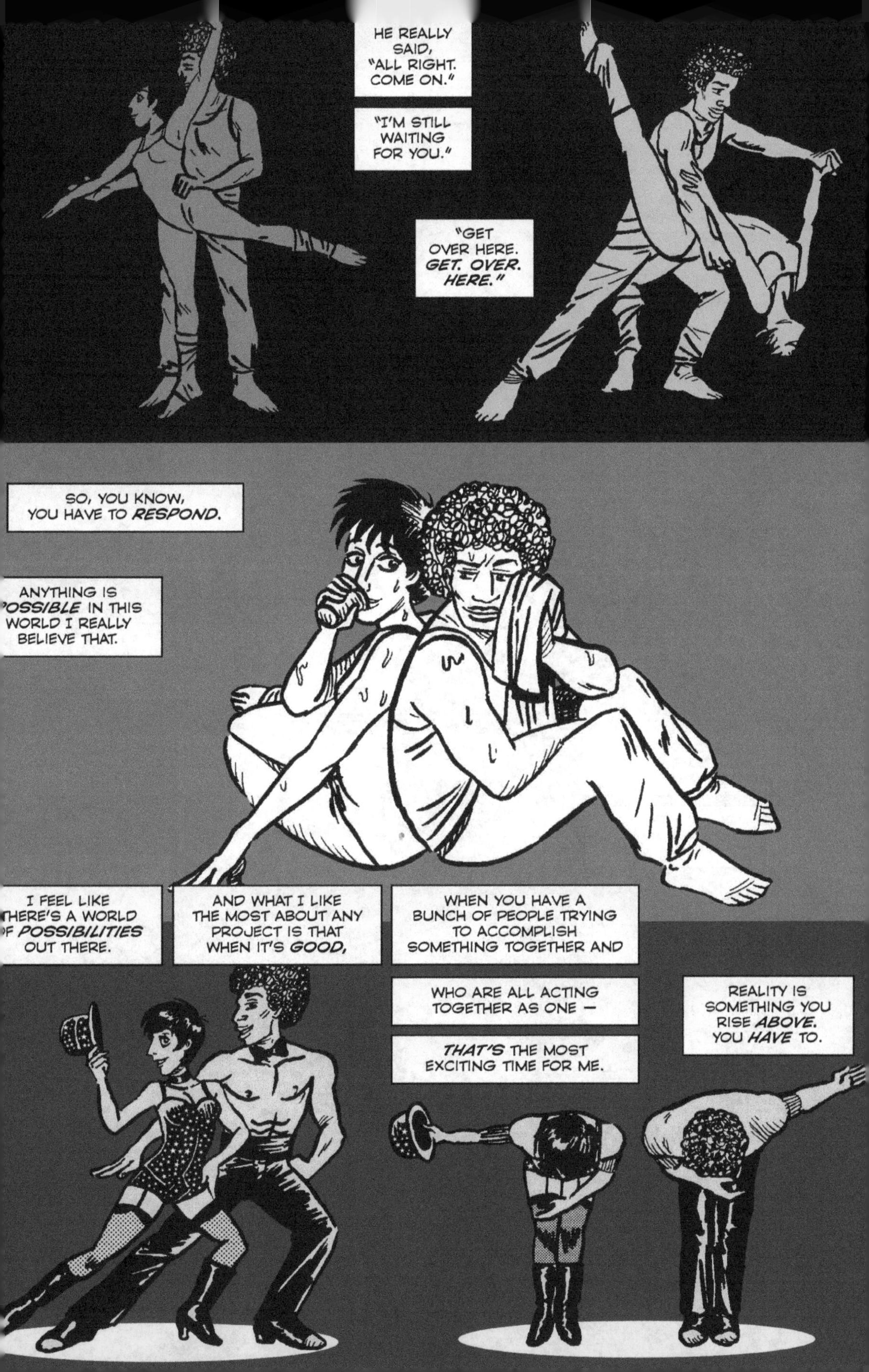
HE REALLY SAID, "ALL RIGHT. COME ON."
"I'M STILL WAITING FOR YOU."
"GET OVER HERE. *GET. OVER. HERE.*"
SO, YOU KNOW, YOU HAVE TO *RESPOND*.
ANYTHING IS *POSSIBLE* IN THIS WORLD I REALLY BELIEVE THAT.
I FEEL LIKE THERE'S A WORLD OF *POSSIBILITIES* OUT THERE.
AND WHAT I LIKE THE MOST ABOUT ANY PROJECT IS THAT WHEN IT'S *GOOD,*
WHEN YOU HAVE A BUNCH OF PEOPLE TRYING TO ACCOMPLISH SOMETHING TOGETHER AND
WHO ARE ALL ACTING TOGETHER AS ONE —
THAT'S THE MOST EXCITING TIME FOR ME.
REALITY IS SOMETHING YOU RISE *ABOVE*. YOU *HAVE* TO.

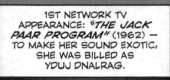

1ST NETWORK TV APPEARANCE: *"THE JACK PAAR PROGRAM"* (1962) — TO MAKE HER SOUND EXOTIC, SHE WAS BILLED AS YDUJ DNALRAG.

IT'S A WASTE OF TIME TO THINK ABOUT WHAT I *SHOULD* HAVE DONE AND *DIDN'T.*

VOICE OF DOROTHY IN *JOURNEY BACK TO OZ* (1974)

I REALLY *BELIEVE* THAT.

THE MUPPET SHOW (EPISODE 414, 1979)

THAT'S HOW I REACT TO THE *IF-ONLY'S* OF LIFE.

CAMEO IN *THE MUPPETS TAKE MANHATTAN* (1984)

TO MOAN AND GROAN ABOUT SOMETHING YOU SHOULDN'T HAVE DONE,

WITH BURT REYNOLDS IN *RENT-A-COP* (1987)

COULD HAVE DONE,

LIZA MINNELLI LIVE FROM RADIO CITY MUSIC HALL (1992)

MIGHT HAVE DONE... WHO KNOWS? IT IS WHAT IT IS.

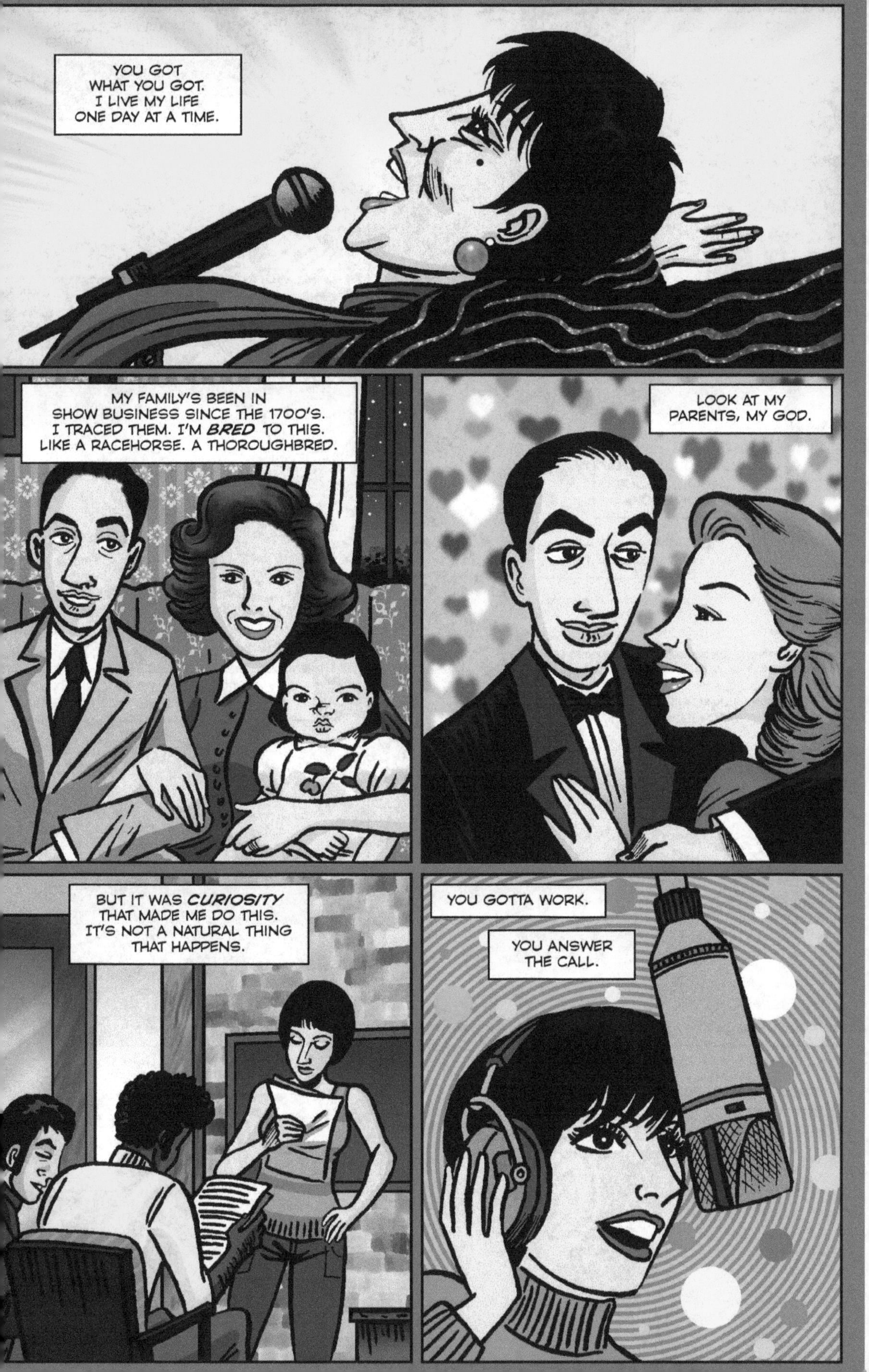
YOU GOT WHAT YOU GOT. I LIVE MY LIFE ONE DAY AT A TIME.
MY FAMILY'S BEEN IN SHOW BUSINESS SINCE THE 1700'S. I TRACED THEM. I'M *BRED* TO THIS. LIKE A RACEHORSE. A THOROUGHBRED.
LOOK AT MY PARENTS, MY GOD.
BUT IT WAS *CURIOSITY* THAT MADE ME DO THIS. IT'S NOT A NATURAL THING THAT HAPPENS.
YOU GOTTA WORK.
YOU ANSWER THE CALL.

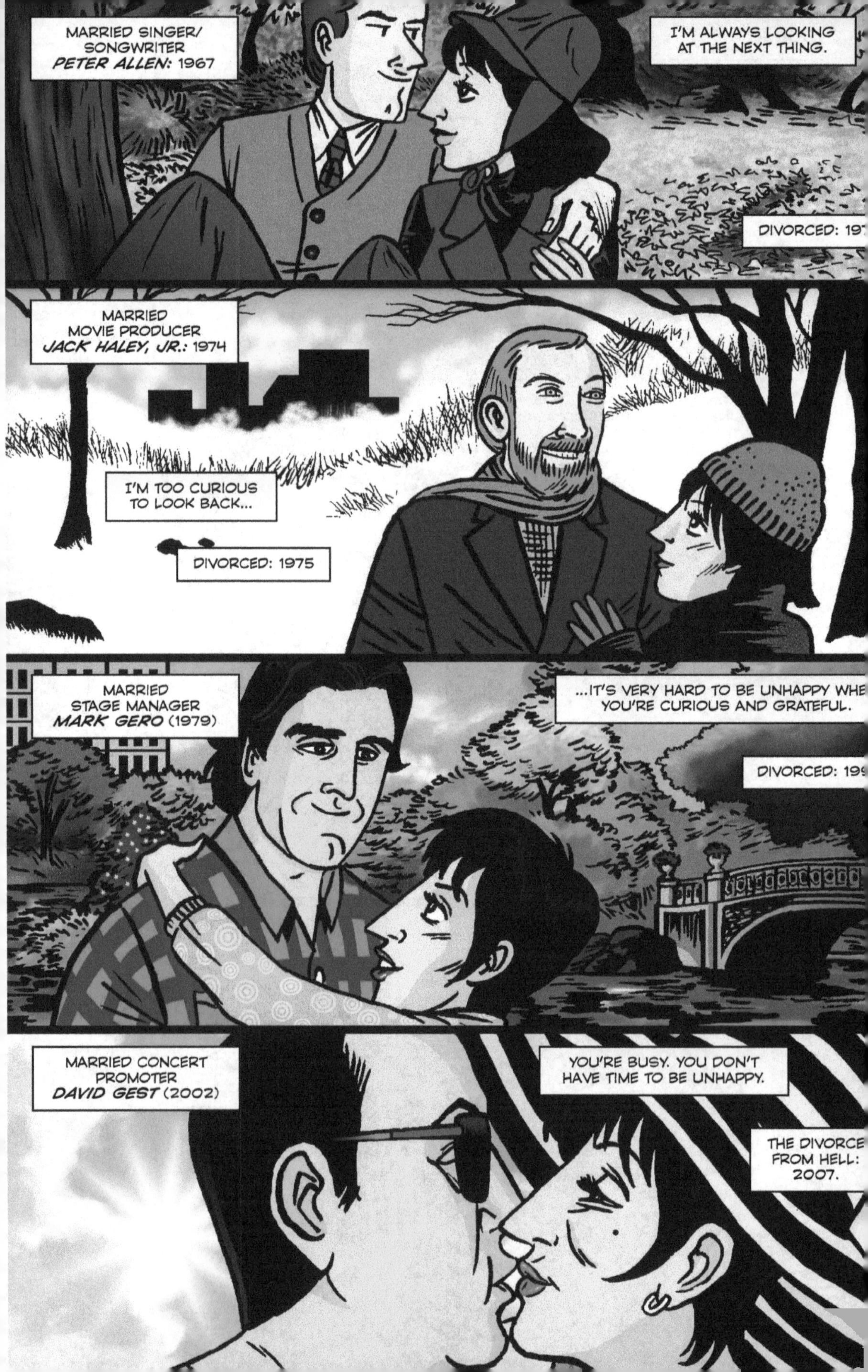
MARRIED SINGER/ SONGWRITER PETER ALLEN: 1967
I'M ALWAYS LOOKING AT THE NEXT THING.
DIVORCED: 19
MARRIED MOVIE PRODUCER JACK HALEY, JR.: 1974
I'M TOO CURIOUS TO LOOK BACK...
DIVORCED: 1975
MARRIED STAGE MANAGER MARK GERO (1979)
...IT'S VERY HARD TO BE UNHAPPY WHE YOU'RE CURIOUS AND GRATEFUL.
DIVORCED: 19
MARRIED CONCERT PROMOTER DAVID GEST (2002)
YOU'RE BUSY. YOU DON'T HAVE TIME TO BE UNHAPPY.
THE DIVORCE FROM HELL: 2007.

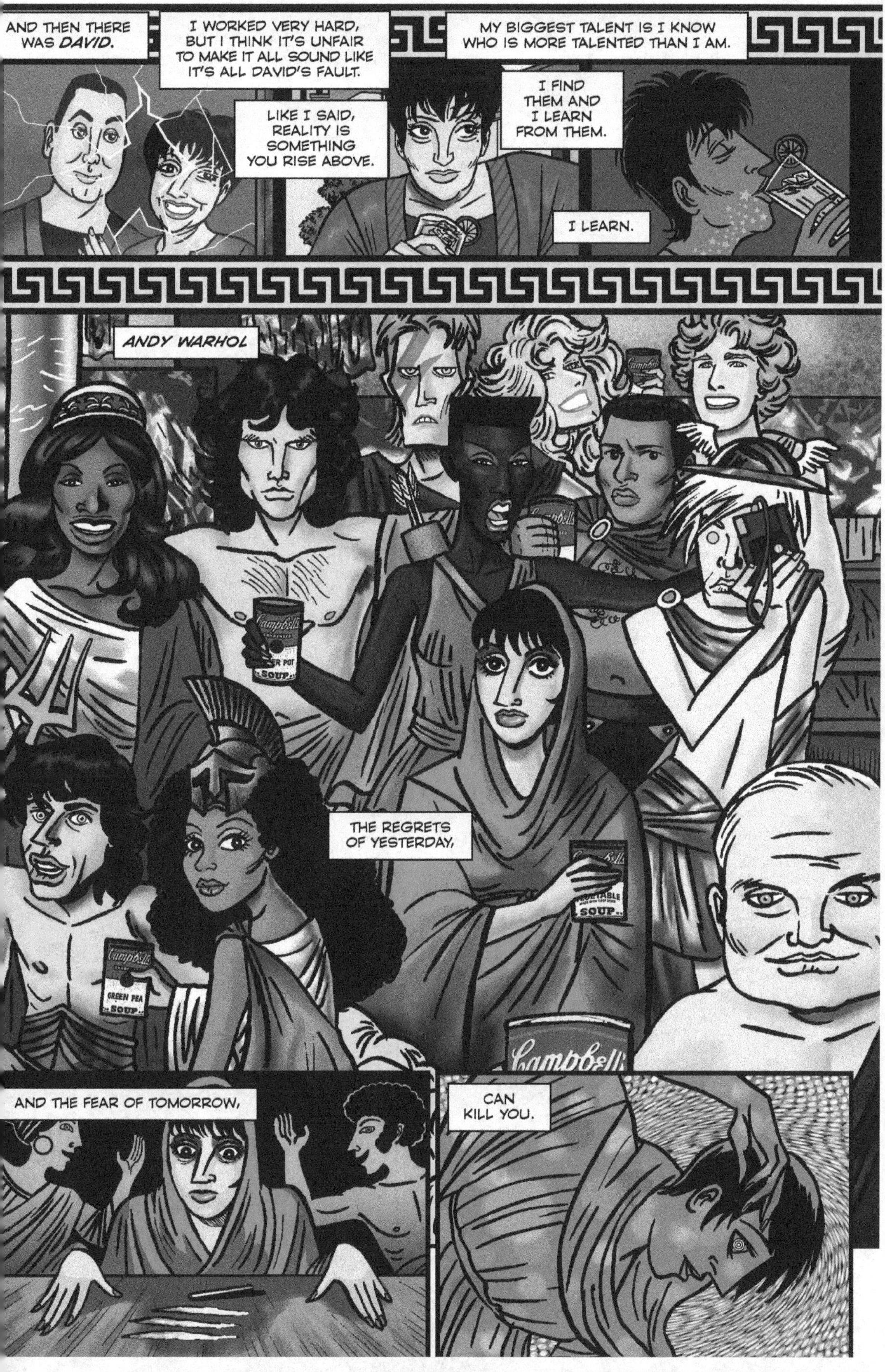
AND THEN THERE WAS DAVID.
I WORKED VERY HARD, BUT I THINK IT'S UNFAIR TO MAKE IT ALL SOUND LIKE IT'S ALL DAVID'S FAULT.
LIKE I SAID, REALITY IS SOMETHING YOU RISE ABOVE.
MY BIGGEST TALENT IS I KNOW WHO IS MORE TALENTED THAN I AM.
I FIND THEM AND I LEARN FROM THEM.
I LEARN.
ANDY WARHOL
Campbell's
SOUP
GREEN PEA SOUP
THE REGRETS OF YESTERDAY,
Campbell's
AND THE FEAR OF TOMORROW,
CAN KILL YOU.

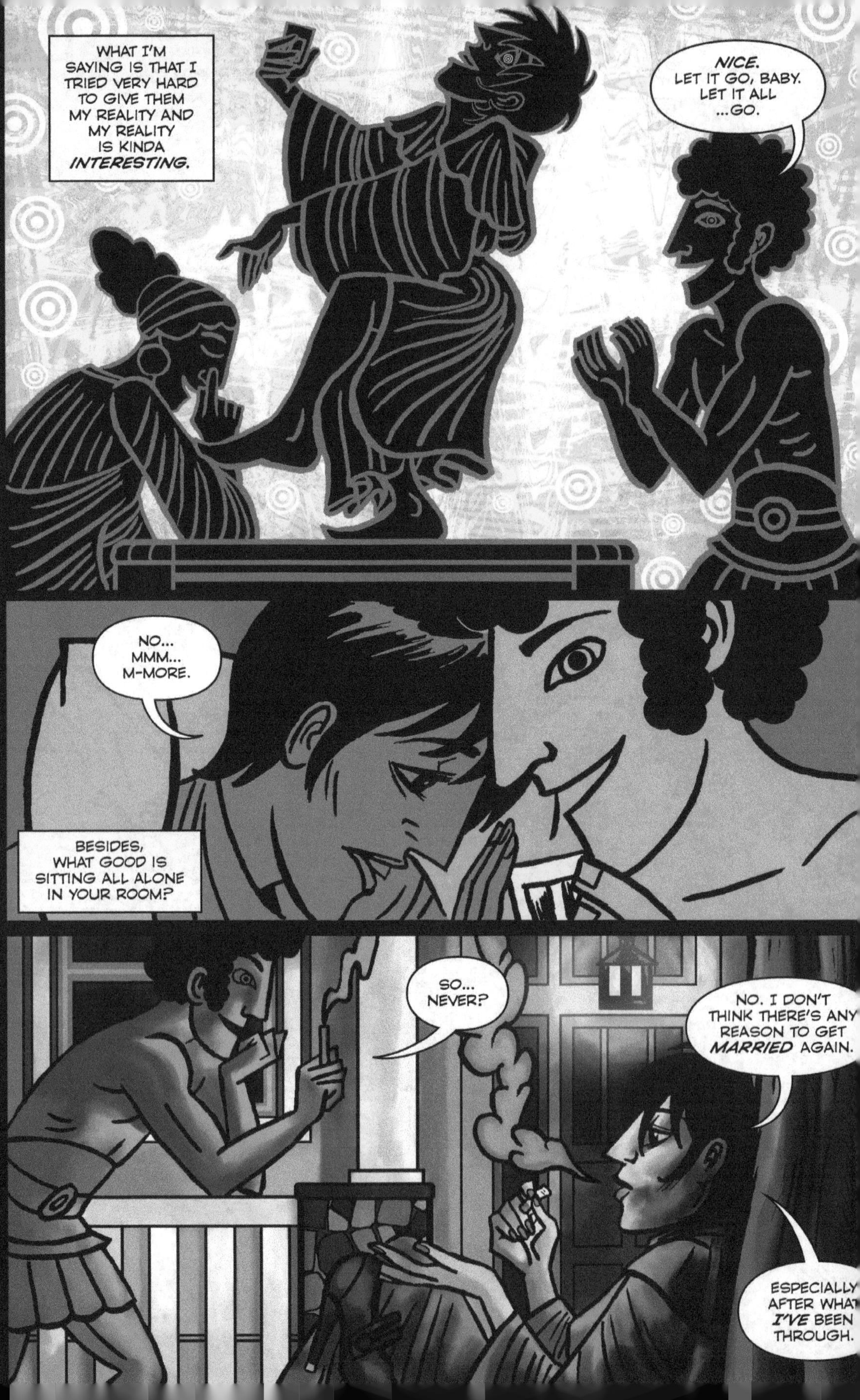
WHAT I'M SAYING IS THAT I TRIED VERY HARD TO GIVE THEM MY REALITY AND MY REALITY IS KINDA *INTERESTING*.
NICE. LET IT GO, BABY. LET IT ALL ...GO.
NO... MMM... M-MORE.
BESIDES, WHAT GOOD IS SITTING ALL ALONE IN YOUR ROOM?
SO... NEVER?
NO. I DON'T THINK THERE'S ANY REASON TO GET *MARRIED* AGAIN.
ESPECIALLY AFTER WHAT *I'VE* BEEN THROUGH.

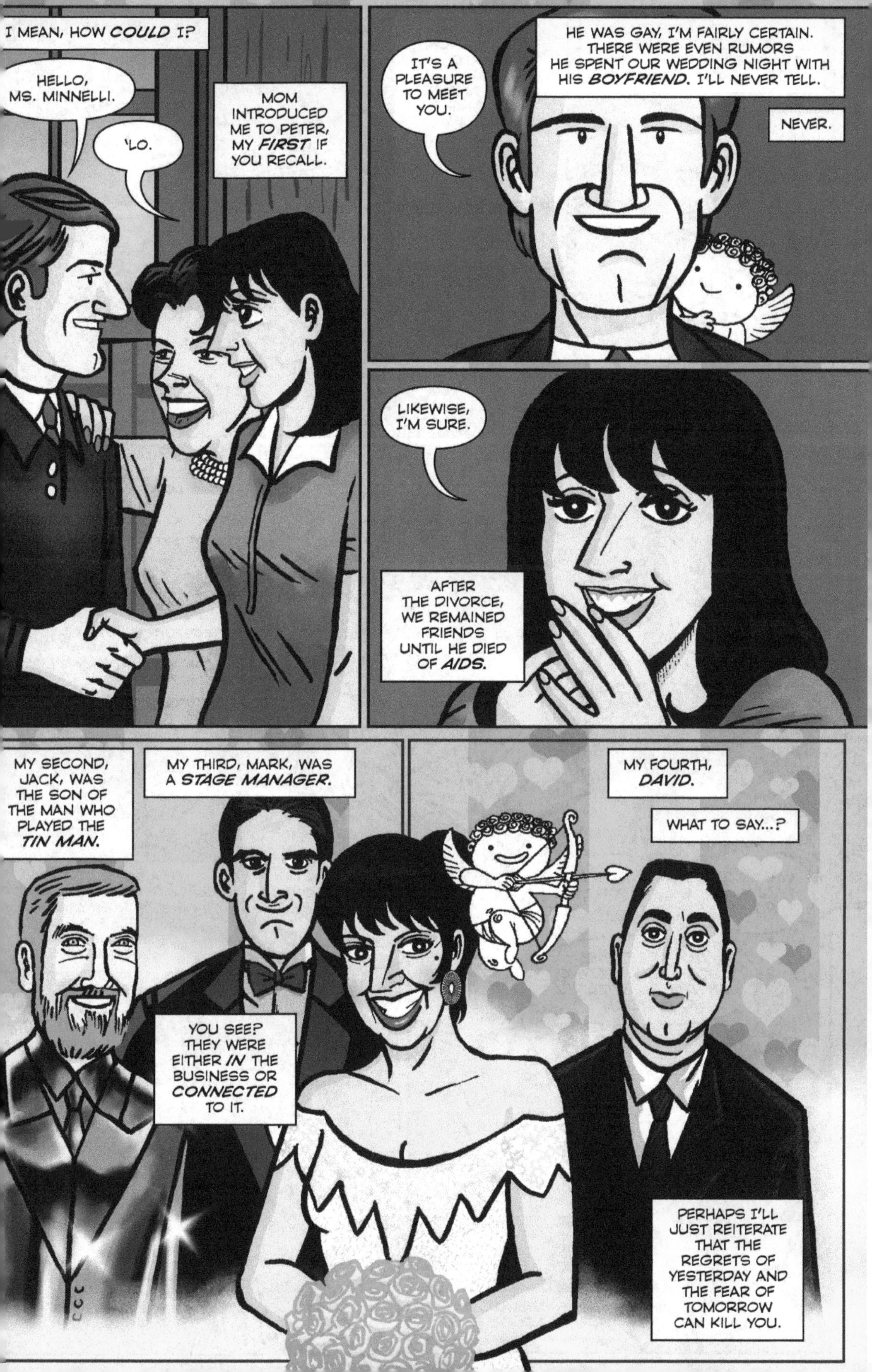

I MEAN, HOW *COULD* I?
HELLO, MS. MINNELLI.
'LO.
MOM INTRODUCED ME TO PETER, MY *FIRST* IF YOU RECALL.
IT'S A PLEASURE TO MEET YOU.
HE WAS GAY, I'M FAIRLY CERTAIN. THERE WERE EVEN RUMORS HE SPENT OUR WEDDING NIGHT WITH HIS *BOYFRIEND*. I'LL NEVER TELL.
NEVER.
LIKEWISE, I'M SURE.
AFTER THE DIVORCE, WE REMAINED FRIENDS UNTIL HE DIED OF *AIDS*.
MY SECOND, JACK, WAS THE SON OF THE MAN WHO PLAYED THE *TIN MAN*.
MY THIRD, MARK, WAS A *STAGE MANAGER*.
YOU SEE? THEY WERE EITHER *IN* THE BUSINESS OR *CONNECTED* TO IT.
MY FOURTH, *DAVID*.
WHAT TO SAY...?
PERHAPS I'LL JUST REITERATE THAT THE REGRETS OF YESTERDAY AND THE FEAR OF TOMORROW CAN KILL YOU.

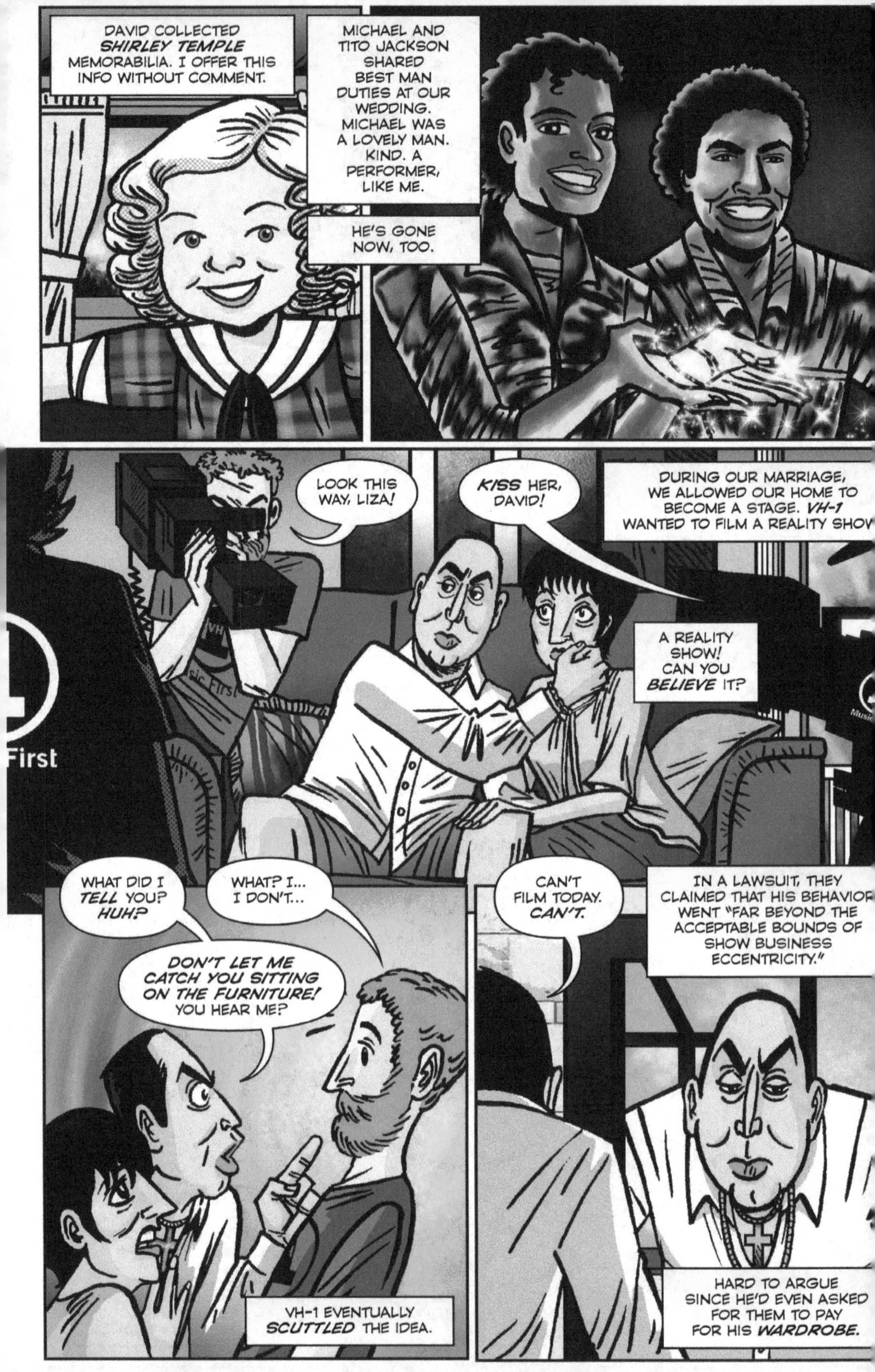

DAVID COLLECTED SHIRLEY TEMPLE MEMORABILIA. I OFFER THIS INFO WITHOUT COMMENT.
MICHAEL AND TITO JACKSON SHARED BEST MAN DUTIES AT OUR WEDDING. MICHAEL WAS A LOVELY MAN. KIND. A PERFORMER, LIKE ME.
HE'S GONE NOW, TOO.
LOOK THIS WAY, LIZA!
KISS HER, DAVID!
DURING OUR MARRIAGE, WE ALLOWED OUR HOME TO BECOME A STAGE. VH-1 WANTED TO FILM A REALITY SHOW
A REALITY SHOW! CAN YOU BELIEVE IT?
First
WHAT DID I TELL YOU? HUH?
WHAT? I... I DON'T...
DON'T LET ME CATCH YOU SITTING ON THE FURNITURE! YOU HEAR ME?
VH-1 EVENTUALLY SCUTTLED THE IDEA.
CAN'T FILM TODAY. CAN'T.
IN A LAWSUIT, THEY CLAIMED THAT HIS BEHAVIOR WENT "FAR BEYOND THE ACCEPTABLE BOUNDS OF SHOW BUSINESS ECCENTRICITY."
HARD TO ARGUE SINCE HE'D EVEN ASKED FOR THEM TO PAY FOR HIS WARDROBE.

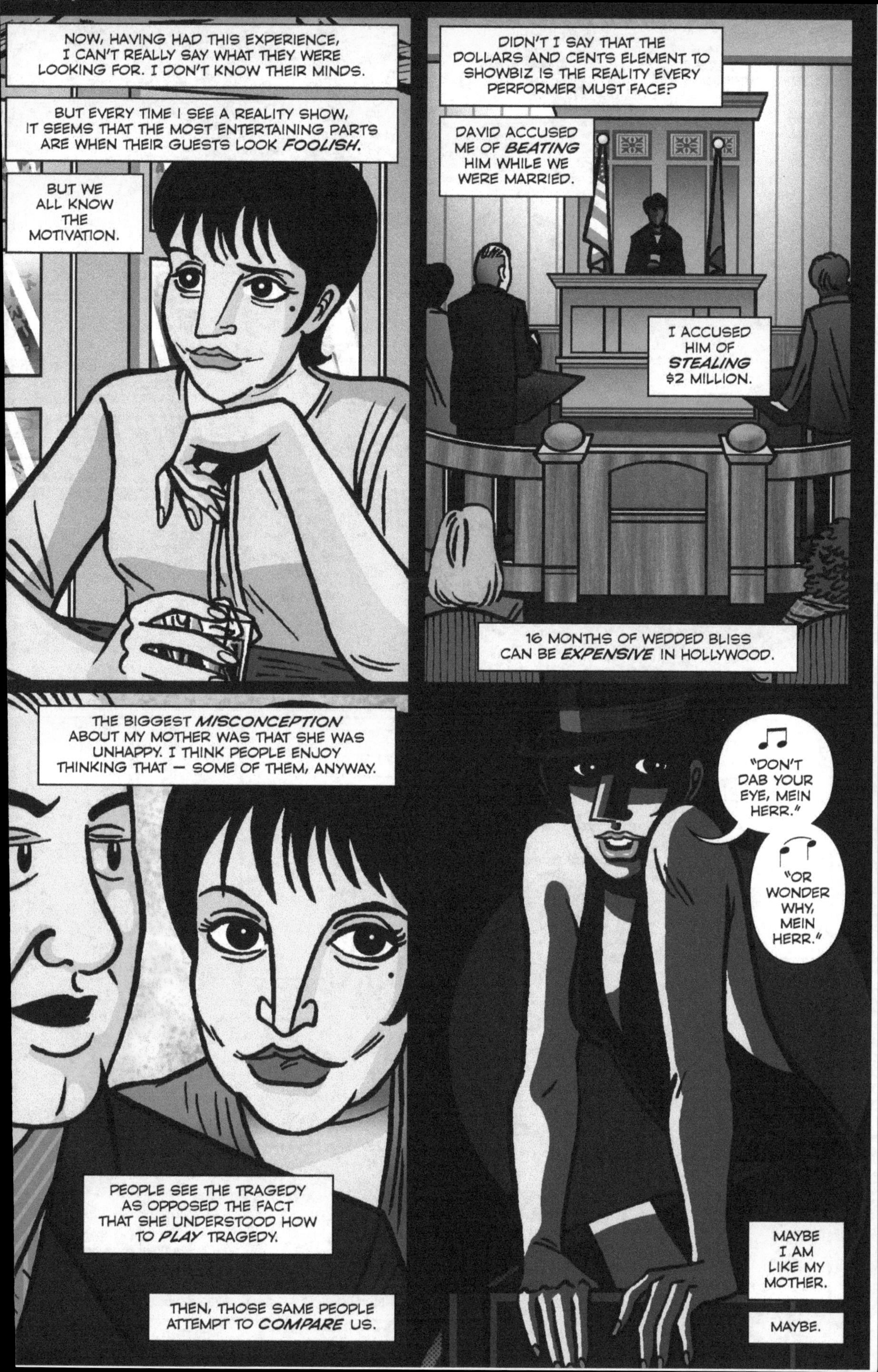
NOW, HAVING HAD THIS EXPERIENCE, I CAN'T REALLY SAY WHAT THEY WERE LOOKING FOR. I DON'T KNOW THEIR MINDS.
BUT EVERY TIME I SEE A REALITY SHOW, IT SEEMS THAT THE MOST ENTERTAINING PARTS ARE WHEN THEIR GUESTS LOOK *FOOLISH.*
BUT WE ALL KNOW THE MOTIVATION.
DIDN'T I SAY THAT THE DOLLARS AND CENTS ELEMENT TO SHOWBIZ IS THE REALITY EVERY PERFORMER MUST FACE?
DAVID ACCUSED ME OF *BEATING* HIM WHILE WE WERE MARRIED.
I ACCUSED HIM OF *STEALING* $2 MILLION.
16 MONTHS OF WEDDED BLISS CAN BE *EXPENSIVE* IN HOLLYWOOD.
THE BIGGEST *MISCONCEPTION* ABOUT MY MOTHER WAS THAT SHE WAS UNHAPPY. I THINK PEOPLE ENJOY THINKING THAT — SOME OF THEM, ANYWAY.
PEOPLE SEE THE TRAGEDY AS OPPOSED THE FACT THAT SHE UNDERSTOOD HOW TO *PLAY* TRAGEDY.
THEN, THOSE SAME PEOPLE ATTEMPT TO *COMPARE* US.
"DON'T DAB YOUR EYE, MEIN HERR."
"OR WONDER WHY, MEIN HERR."
MAYBE I AM LIKE MY MOTHER.
MAYBE.

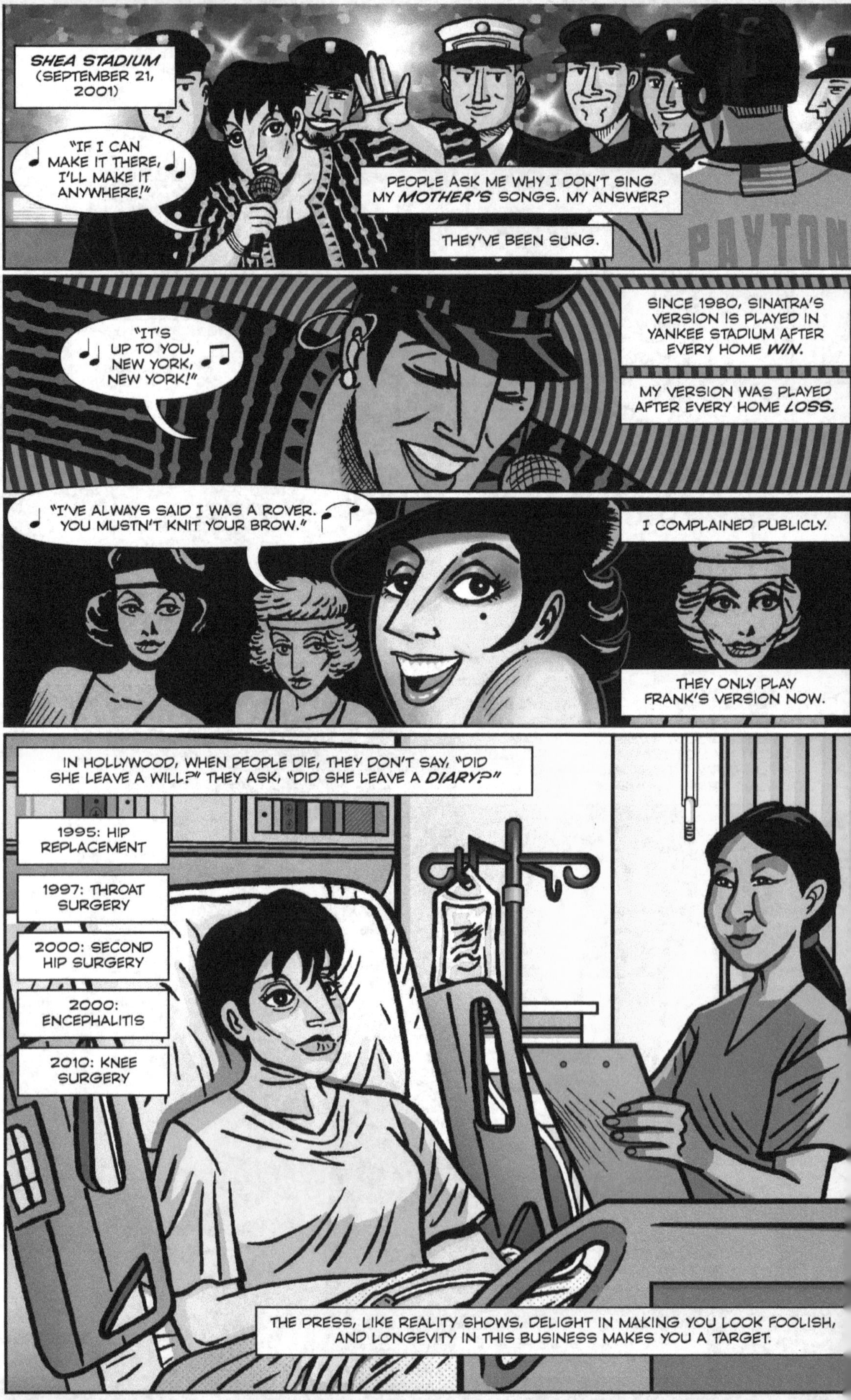
SHEA STADIUM (SEPTEMBER 21, 2001)
"IF I CAN MAKE IT THERE, I'LL MAKE IT ANYWHERE!"
PEOPLE ASK ME WHY I DON'T SING MY MOTHER'S SONGS. MY ANSWER?
THEY'VE BEEN SUNG.
PAYTON
"IT'S UP TO YOU, NEW YORK, NEW YORK!"
SINCE 1980, SINATRA'S VERSION IS PLAYED IN YANKEE STADIUM AFTER EVERY HOME WIN.
MY VERSION WAS PLAYED AFTER EVERY HOME LOSS.
"I'VE ALWAYS SAID I WAS A ROVER. YOU MUSTN'T KNIT YOUR BROW."
I COMPLAINED PUBLICLY.
THEY ONLY PLAY FRANK'S VERSION NOW.
IN HOLLYWOOD, WHEN PEOPLE DIE, THEY DON'T SAY, "DID SHE LEAVE A WILL?" THEY ASK, "DID SHE LEAVE A DIARY?"
1995: HIP REPLACEMENT
1997: THROAT SURGERY
2000: SECOND HIP SURGERY
2000: ENCEPHALITIS
2010: KNEE SURGERY
THE PRESS, LIKE REALITY SHOWS, DELIGHT IN MAKING YOU LOOK FOOLISH, AND LONGEVITY IN THIS BUSINESS MAKES YOU A TARGET.

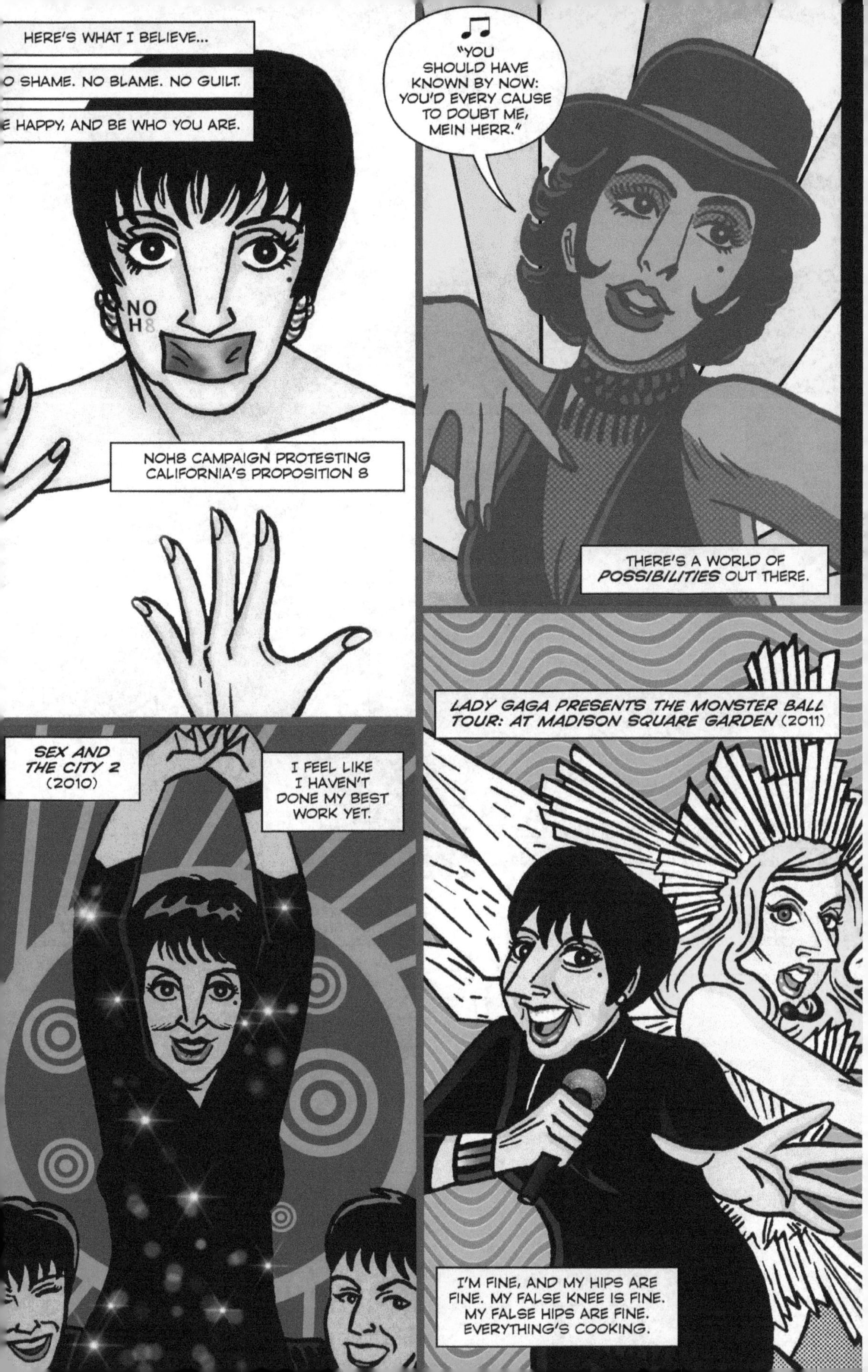

HERE'S WHAT I BELIEVE...
O SHAME. NO BLAME. NO GUILT.
E HAPPY, AND BE WHO YOU ARE.
NO H8
NOH8 CAMPAIGN PROTESTING CALIFORNIA'S PROPOSITION 8
"YOU SHOULD HAVE KNOWN BY NOW: YOU'D EVERY CAUSE TO DOUBT ME, MEIN HERR."
THERE'S A WORLD OF *POSSIBILITIES* OUT THERE.
SEX AND THE CITY 2 (2010)
I FEEL LIKE I HAVEN'T DONE MY BEST WORK YET.
LADY GAGA PRESENTS THE MONSTER BALL TOUR: AT MADISON SQUARE GARDEN (2011)
I'M FINE, AND MY HIPS ARE FINE. MY FALSE KNEE IS FINE. MY FALSE HIPS ARE FINE. EVERYTHING'S COOKING.

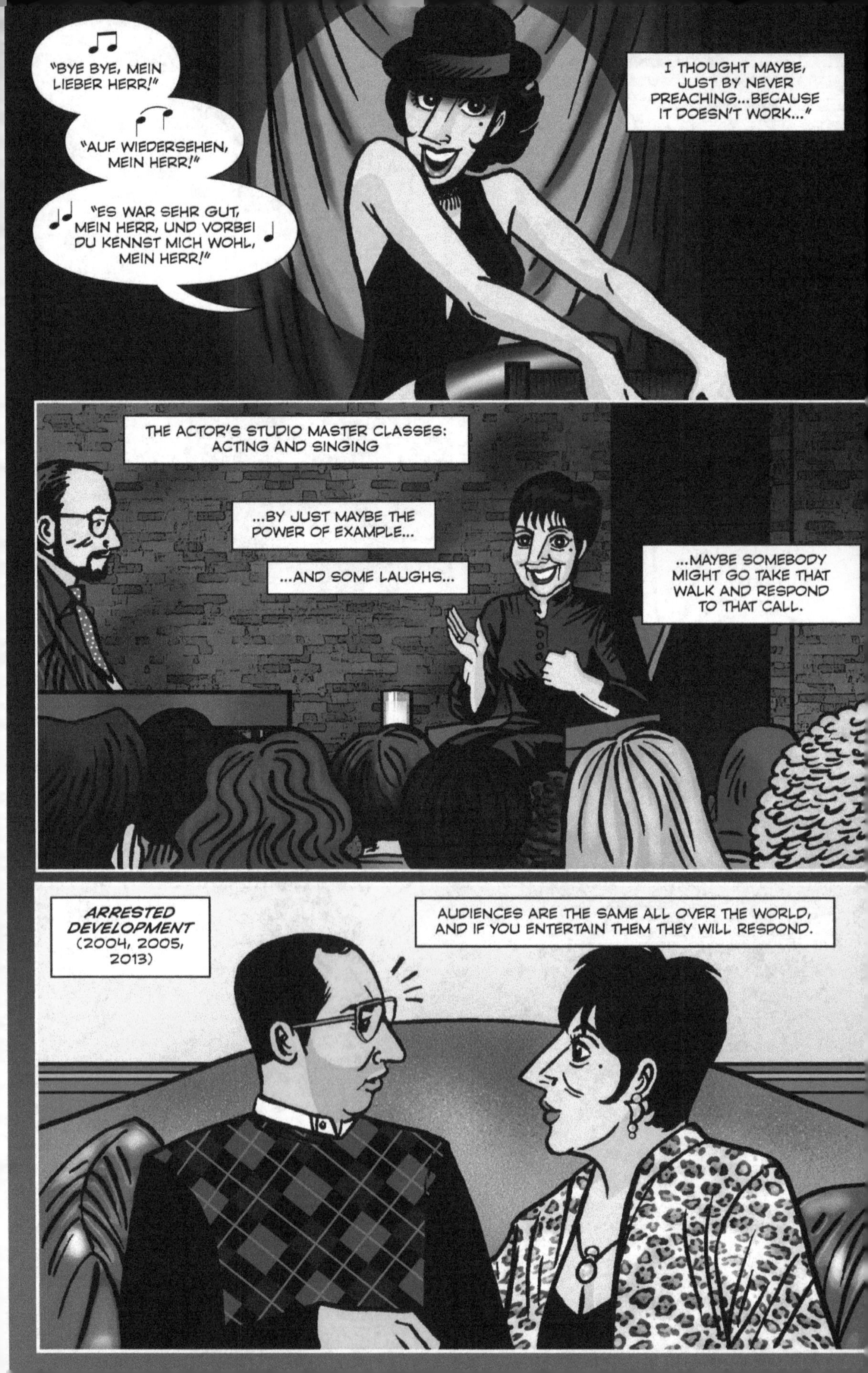
"BYE BYE, MEIN LIEBER HERR!"
"AUF WIEDERSEHEN, MEIN HERR!"
"ES WAR SEHR GUT, MEIN HERR, UND VORBEI DU KENNST MICH WOHL, MEIN HERR!"
I THOUGHT MAYBE, JUST BY NEVER PREACHING...BECAUSE IT DOESN'T WORK..."
THE ACTOR'S STUDIO MASTER CLASSES: ACTING AND SINGING
...BY JUST MAYBE THE POWER OF EXAMPLE...
...AND SOME LAUGHS...
...MAYBE SOMEBODY MIGHT GO TAKE THAT WALK AND RESPOND TO THAT CALL.
ARRESTED DEVELOPMENT (2004, 2005, 2013)
AUDIENCES ARE THE SAME ALL OVER THE WORLD, AND IF YOU ENTERTAIN THEM THEY WILL RESPOND.

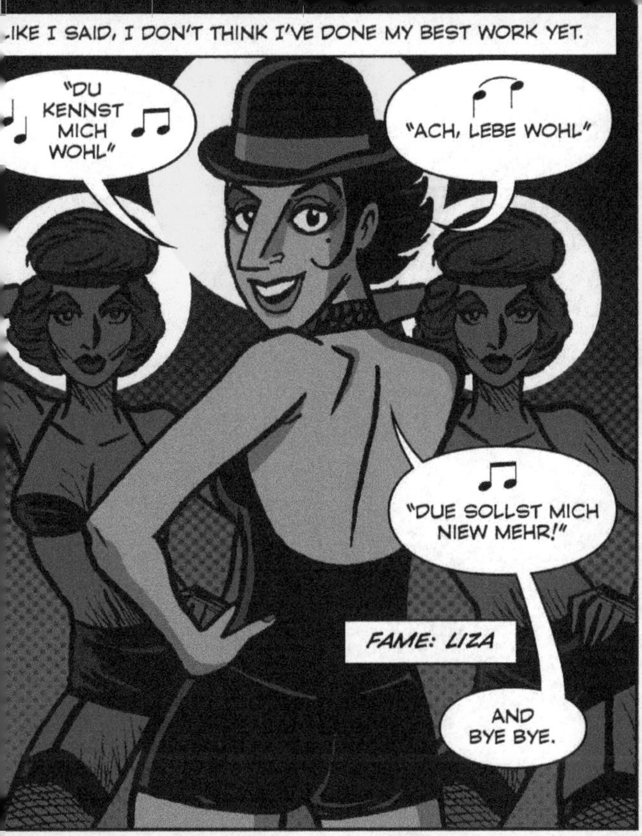
LIKE I SAID, I DON'T THINK I'VE DONE MY BEST WORK YET.
"DU KENNST MICH WOHL"
"ACH, LEBE WOHL"
"DUE SOLLST MICH NIEW MEHR!"
FAME: LIZA
AND BYE BYE.

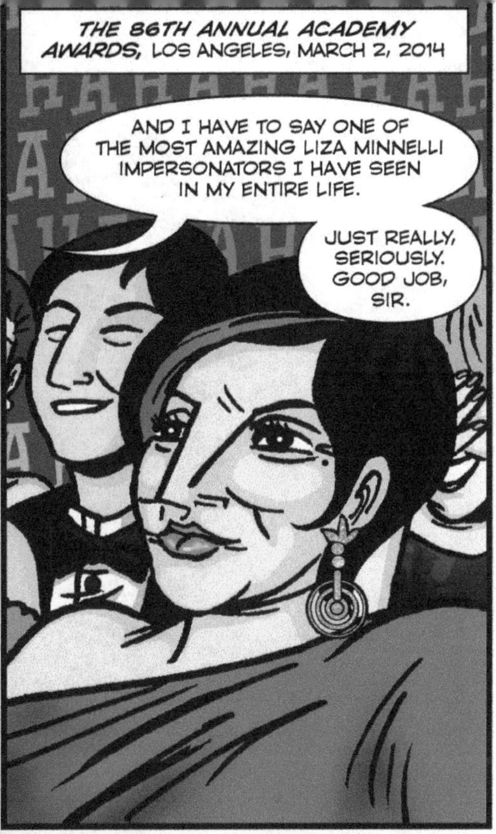
THE 86TH ANNUAL ACADEMY AWARDS, LOS ANGELES, MARCH 2, 2014
AND I HAVE TO SAY ONE OF THE MOST AMAZING LIZA MINNELLI IMPERSONATORS I HAVE SEEN IN MY ENTIRE LIFE.
JUST REALLY, SERIOUSLY. GOOD JOB, SIR.

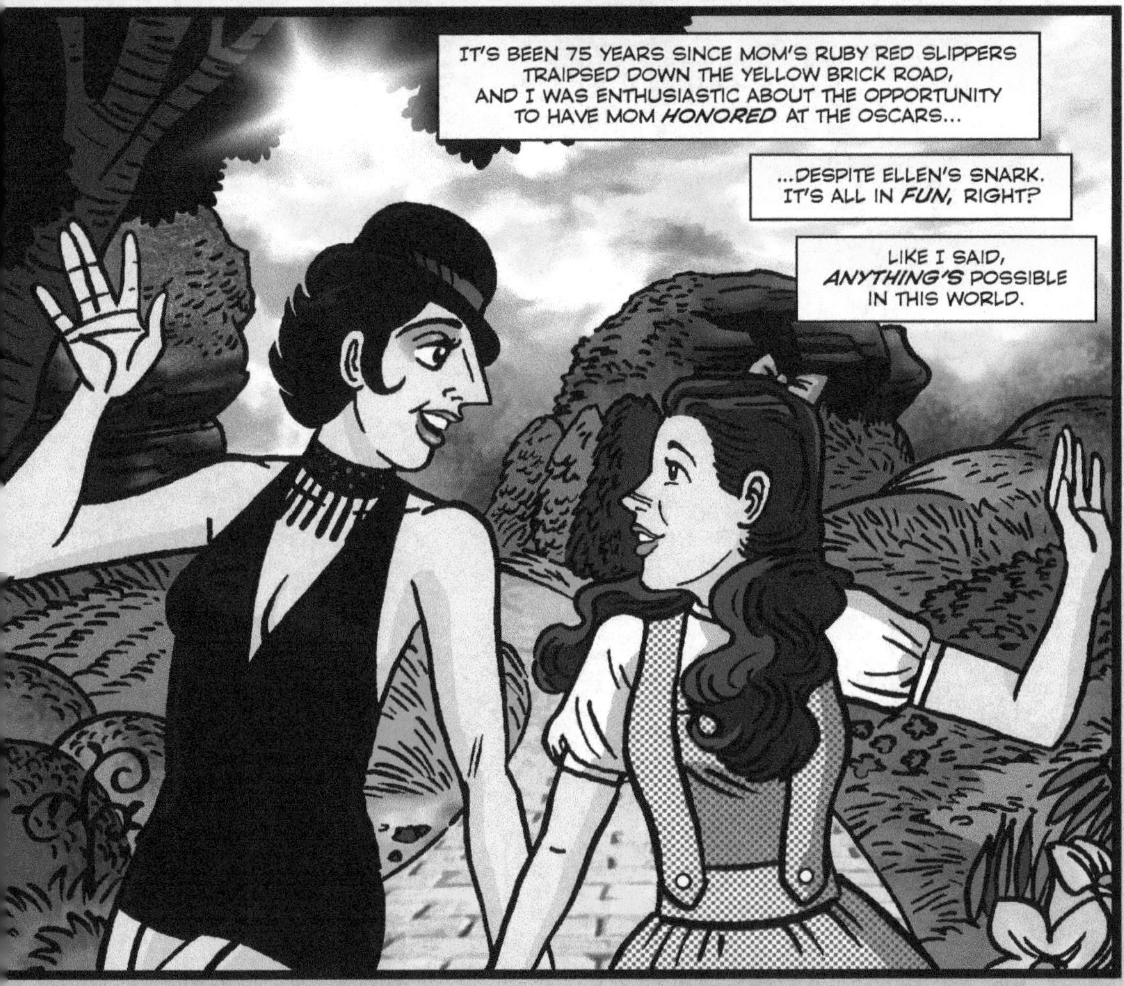
IT'S BEEN 75 YEARS SINCE MOM'S RUBY RED SLIPPERS TRAIPSED DOWN THE YELLOW BRICK ROAD, AND I WAS ENTHUSIASTIC ABOUT THE OPPORTUNITY TO HAVE MOM HONORED AT THE OSCARS...
...DESPITE ELLEN'S SNARK. IT'S ALL IN FUN, RIGHT?
LIKE I SAID, ANYTHING'S POSSIBLE IN THIS WORLD.

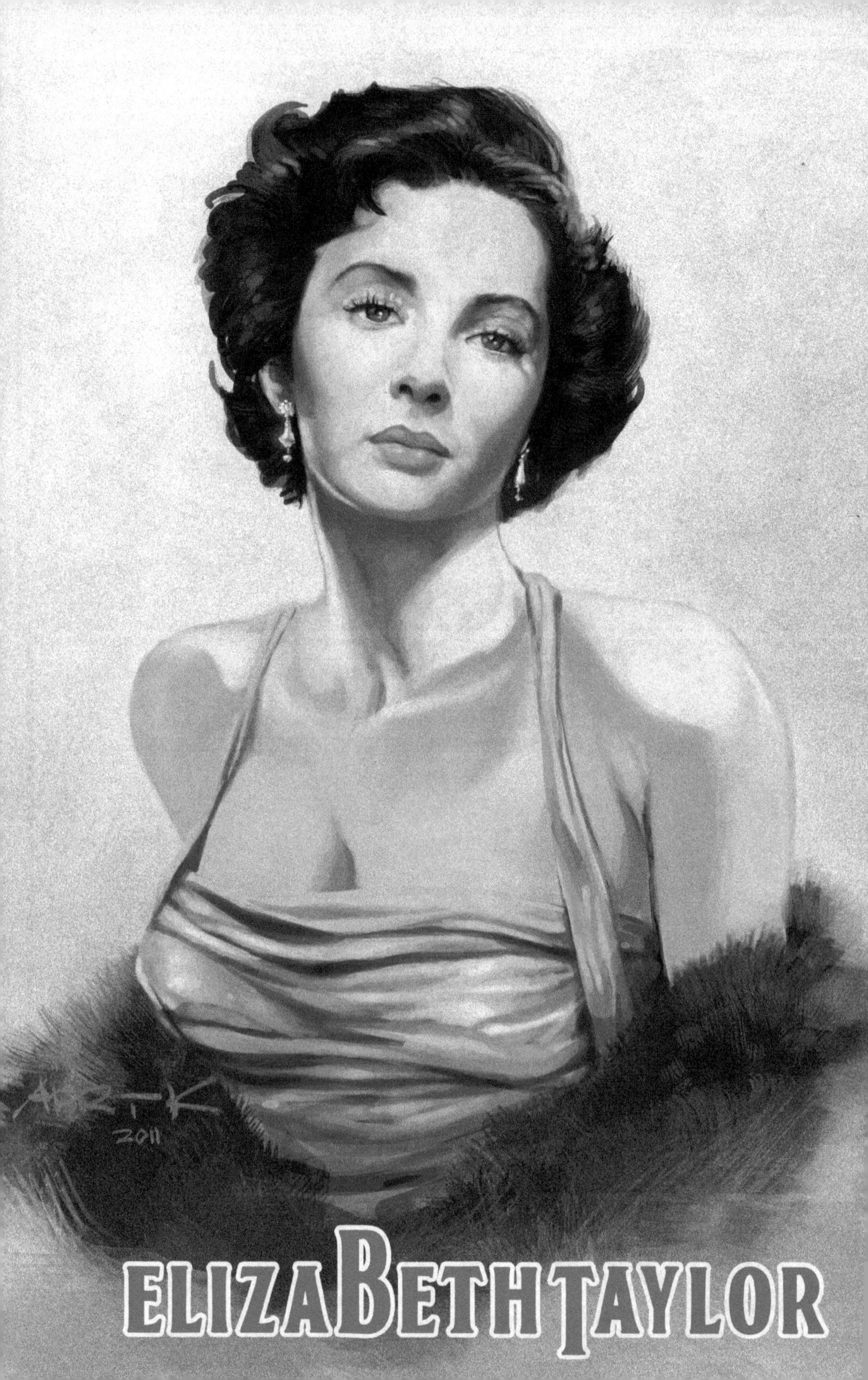
2011
ELIZABETH TAYLOR

ELIZABETH TAYLOR
Let's get one thing straight.
Elizabeth Taylor wasn't a fan of being called "Liz."
Not even "Dame Liz" will do, people.
She was a great lady.
FEMALE FORCE

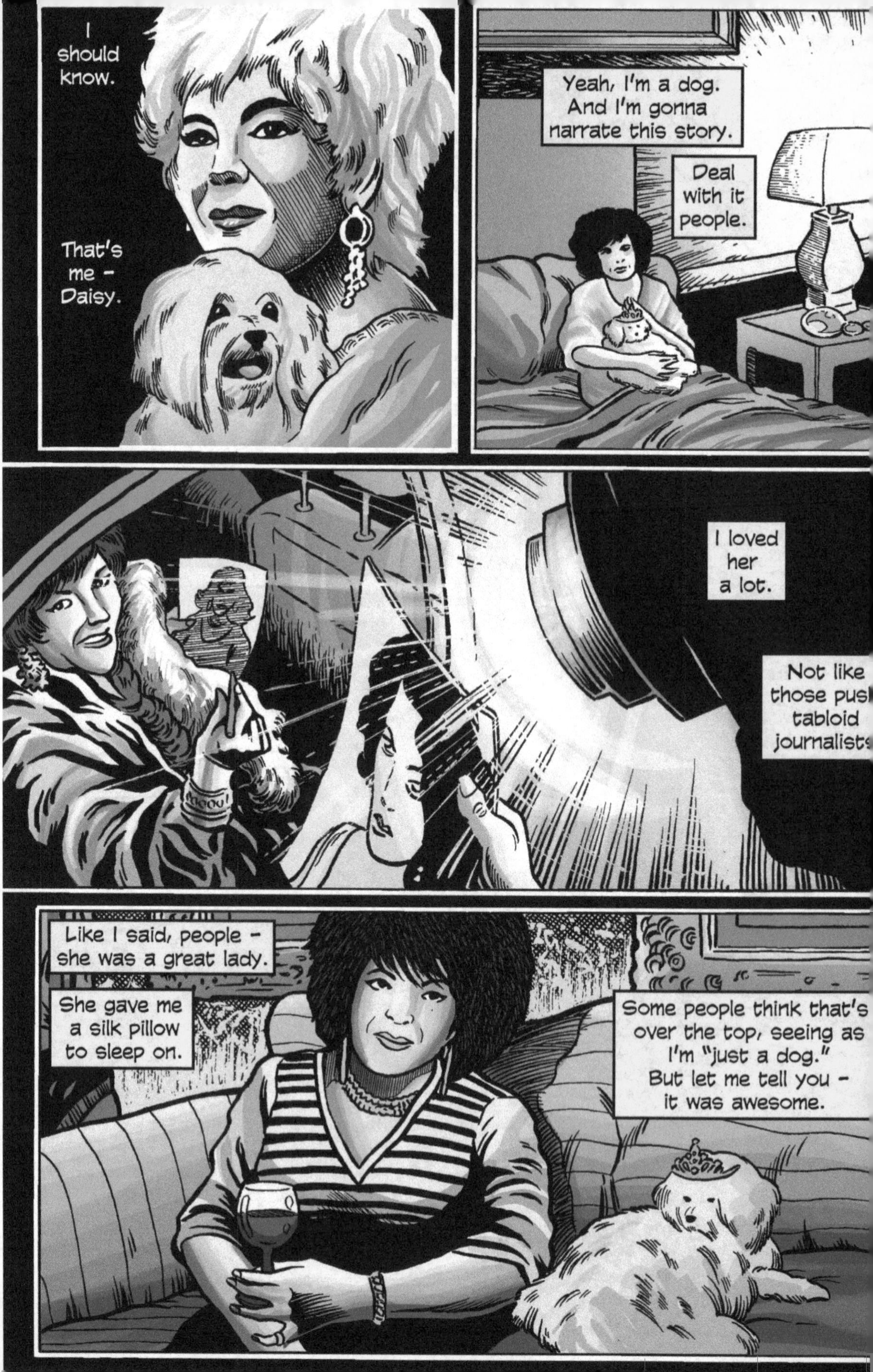
I should know.
That's me - Daisy.
Yeah, I'm a dog. And I'm gonna narrate this story.
Deal with it people.
I loved her a lot.
Not like those pus tabloid journalist
Like I said, people - she was a great lady.
She gave me a silk pillow to sleep on.
Some people think that's over the top, seeing as I'm "just a dog." But let me tell you - it was awesome.

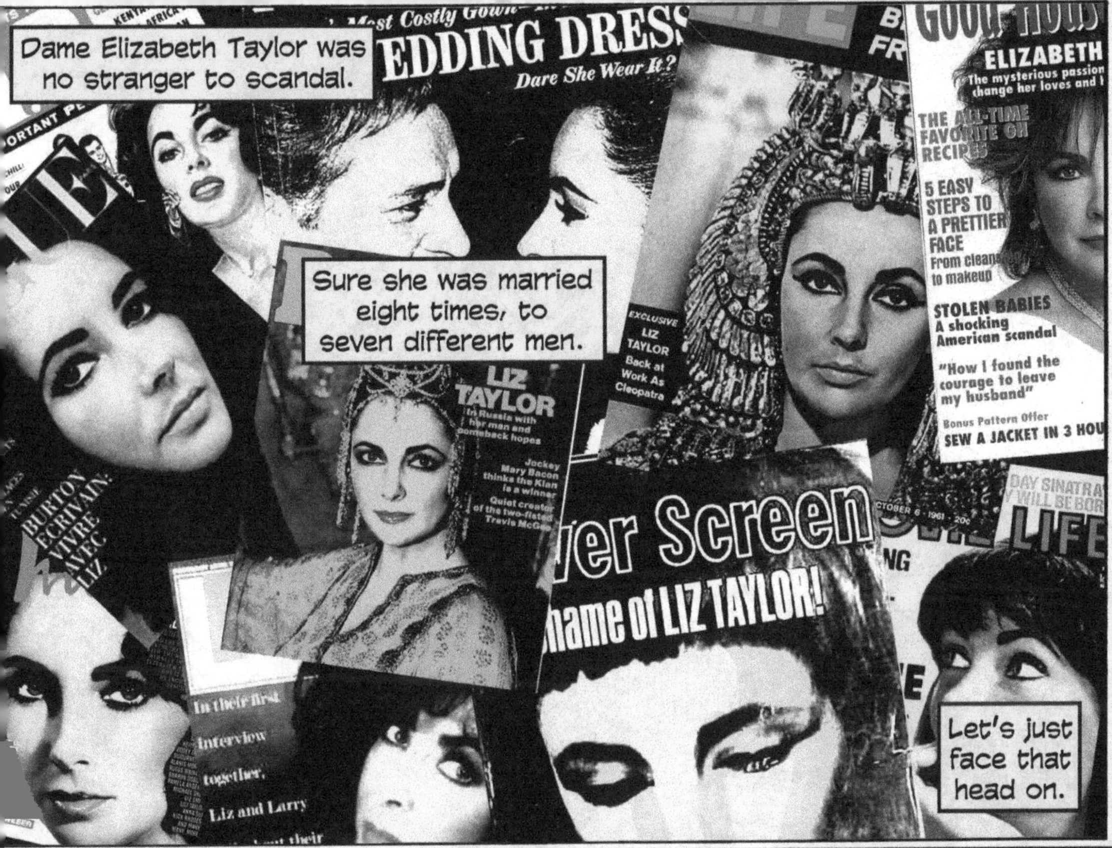
Dame Elizabeth Taylor was no stranger to scandal.
Sure she was married eight times, to seven different men.
Let's just face that head on.

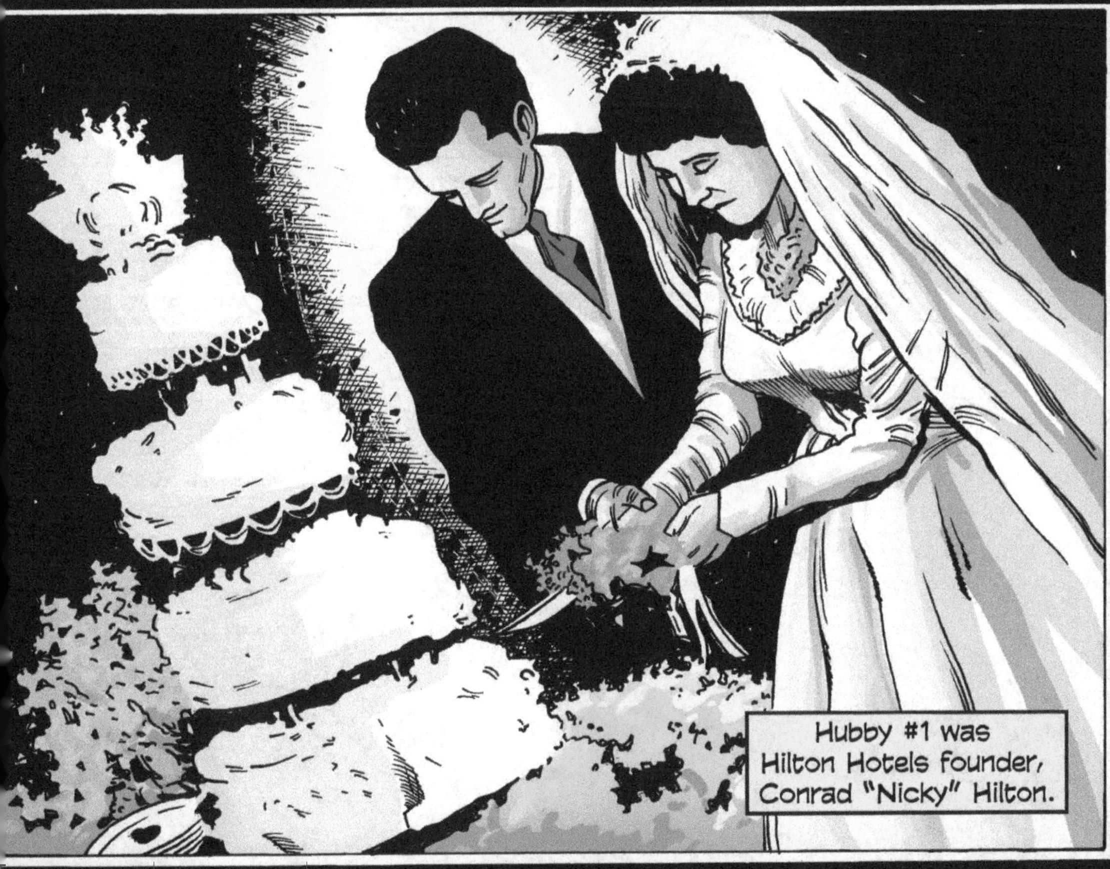
Hubby #1 was Hilton Hotels founder, Conrad "Nicky" Hilton.

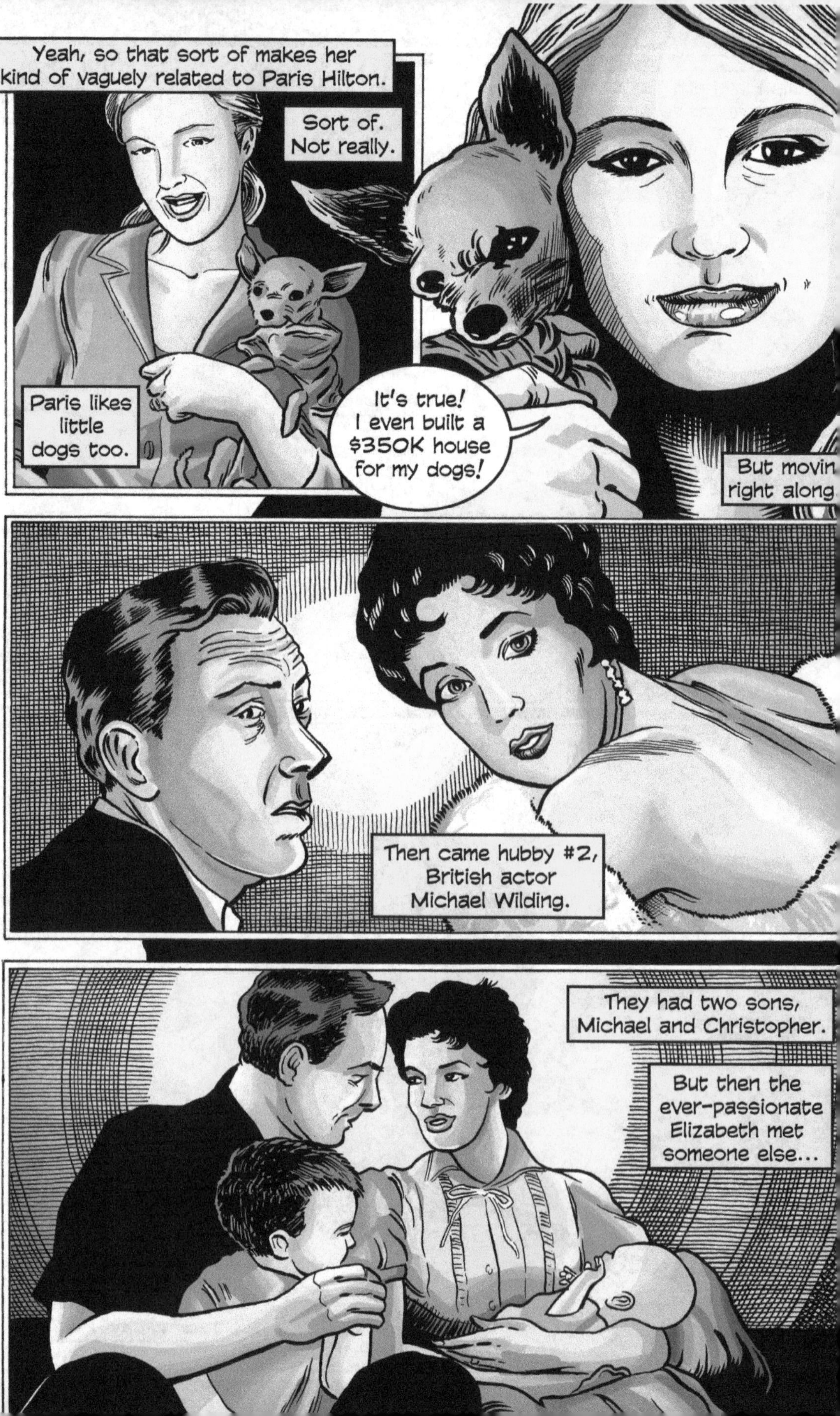
Yeah, so that sort of makes her kind of vaguely related to Paris Hilton.
Sort of. Not really.
Paris likes little dogs too.
It's true! I even built a $350K house for my dogs!
But movin right along
Then came hubby #2, British actor Michael Wilding.
They had two sons, Michael and Christopher.
But then the ever-passionate Elizabeth met someone else...

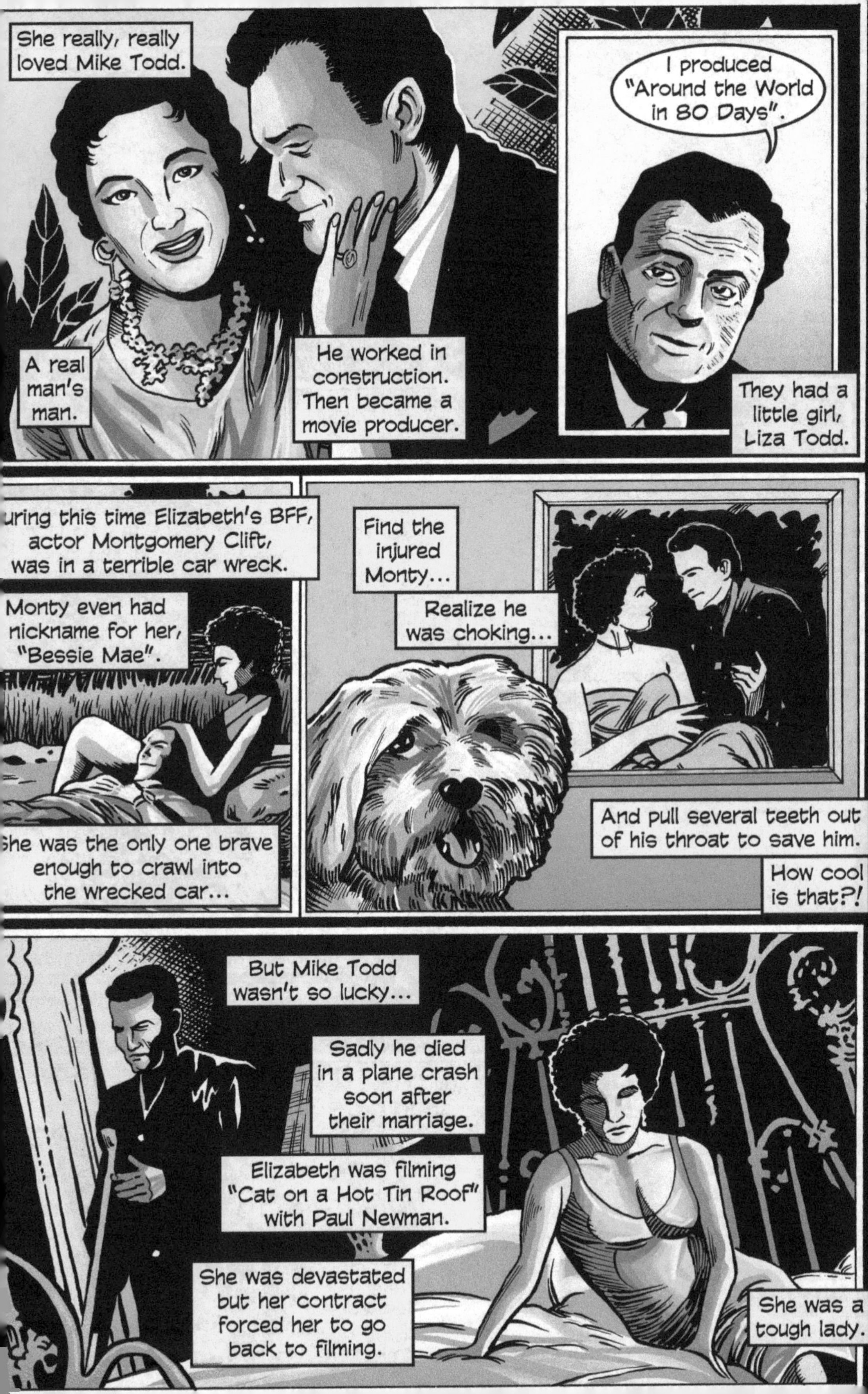
She really, really loved Mike Todd.
A real man's man.
He worked in construction. Then became a movie producer.
I produced "Around the World in 80 Days".
They had a little girl, Liza Todd.
uring this time Elizabeth's BFF, actor Montgomery Clift, was in a terrible car wreck.
Monty even had nickname for her, "Bessie Mae".
he was the only one brave enough to crawl into the wrecked car...
Find the injured Monty...
Realize he was choking...
And pull several teeth out of his throat to save him.
How cool is that?!
But Mike Todd wasn't so lucky...
Sadly he died in a plane crash soon after their marriage.
Elizabeth was filming "Cat on a Hot Tin Roof" with Paul Newman.
She was devastated but her contract forced her to go back to filming.
She was a tough lady.

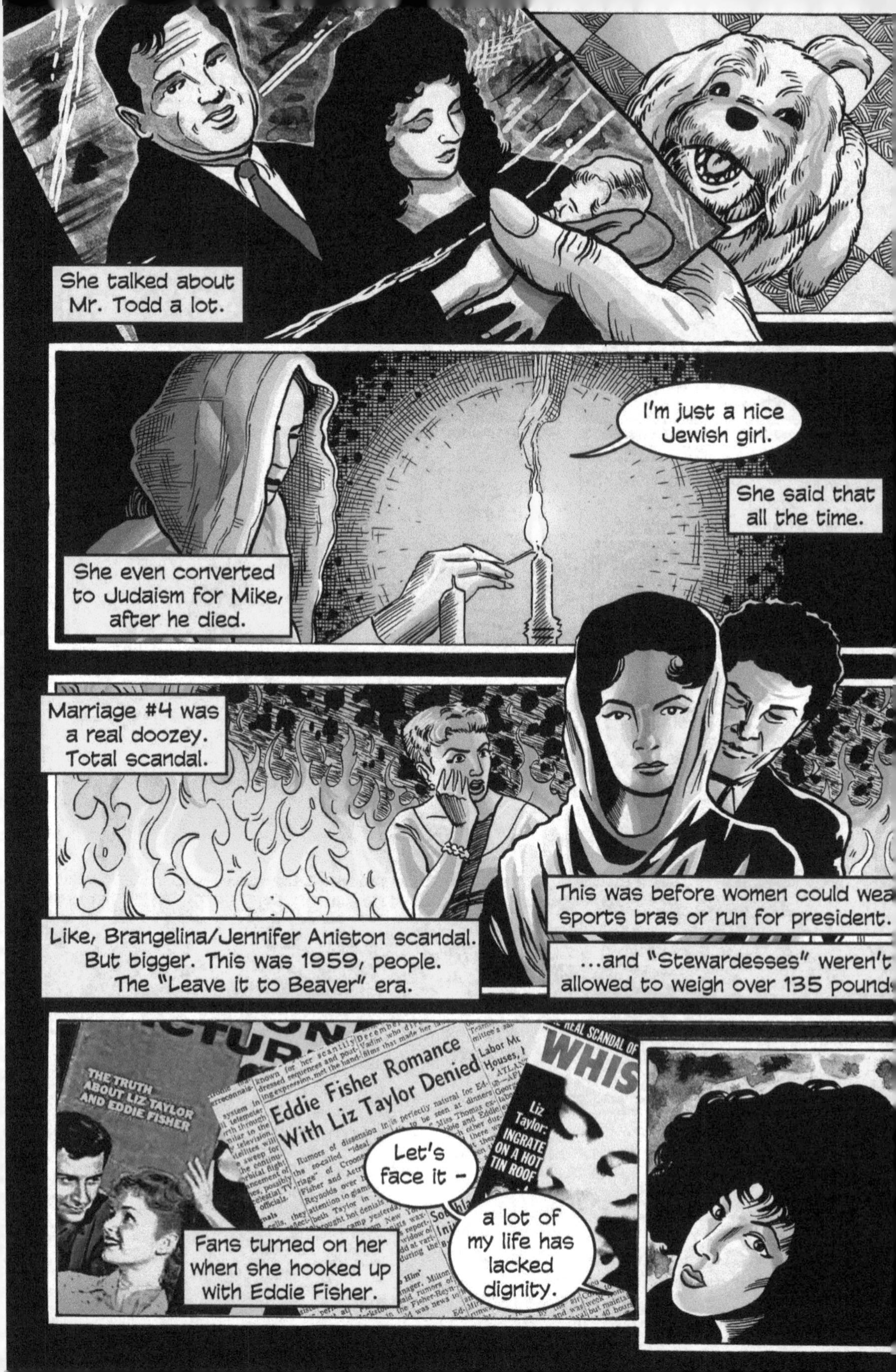
She talked about Mr. Todd a lot.
She even converted to Judaism for Mike, after he died.
I'm just a nice Jewish girl.
She said that all the time.
Marriage #4 was a real doozey. Total scandal.
Like, Brangelina/Jennifer Aniston scandal. But bigger. This was 1959, people. The "Leave it to Beaver" era.
This was before women could wea
sports bras or run for president.
...and "Stewardesses" weren't
allowed to weigh over 135 pound
THE TRUTH ABOUT LIZ TAYLOR AND EDDIE FISHER
Eddie Fisher Romance With Liz Taylor Denied
THE REAL SCANDAL OF
WHIS
Liz Taylor: INGRATE ON A HOT TIN ROOF
Fans turned on her when she hooked up with Eddie Fisher.
Let's face it –
a lot of my life has lacked dignity.

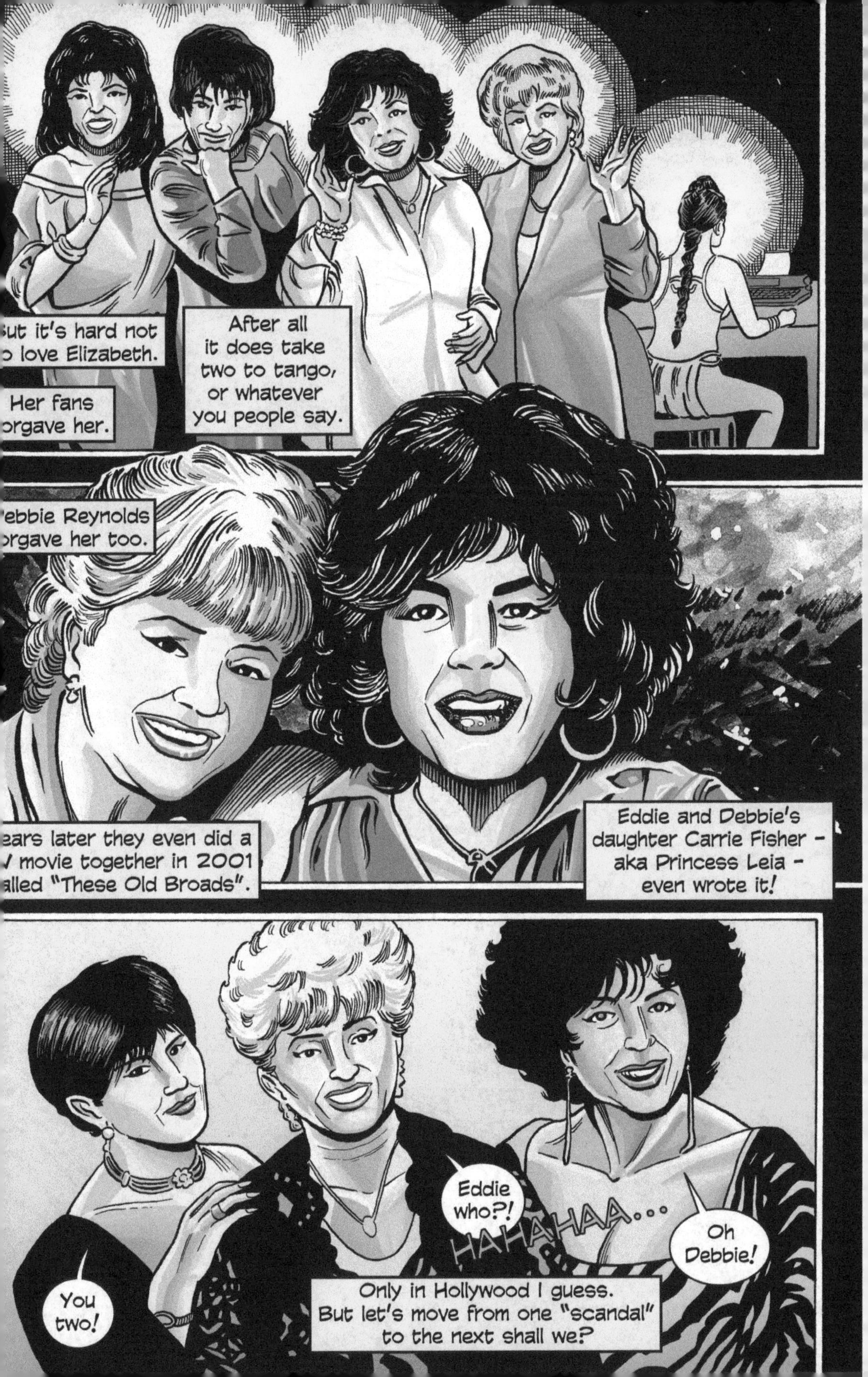
ut it's hard not
o love Elizabeth.
After all
it does take
two to tango,
or whatever
you people say.
Her fans
orgave her.
ebbie Reynolds
orgave her too.
ears later they even did a
V movie together in 2001
alled "These Old Broads".
Eddie and Debbie's
daughter Carrie Fisher -
aka Princess Leia -
even wrote it!
You
two!
Eddie
who?!
HAHAHAA...
Oh
Debbie!
Only in Hollywood I guess.
But let's move from one "scandal"
to the next shall we?

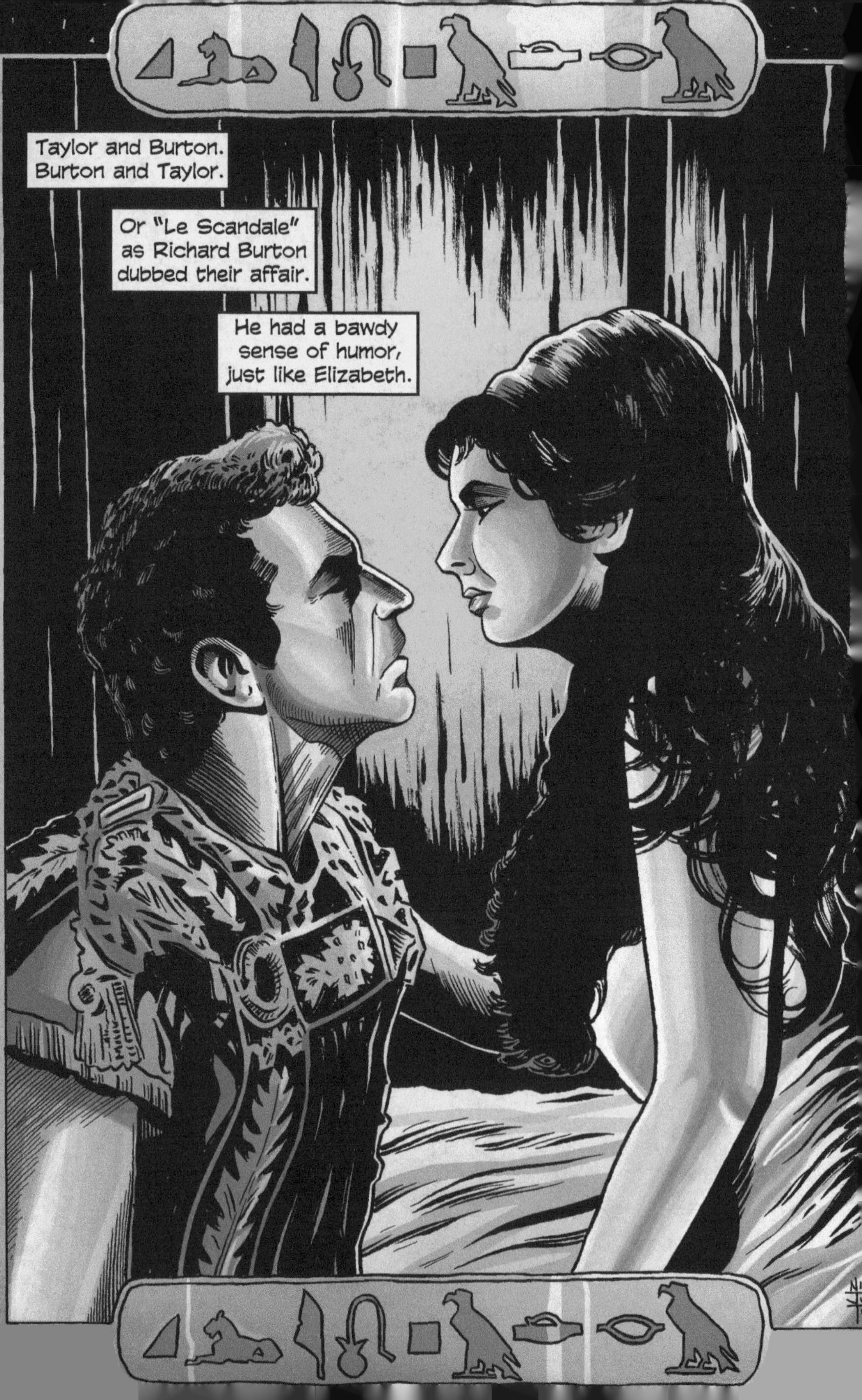

Taylor and Burton. Burton and Taylor.
Or "Le Scandale" as Richard Burton dubbed their affair.
He had a bawdy sense of humor, just like Elizabeth.

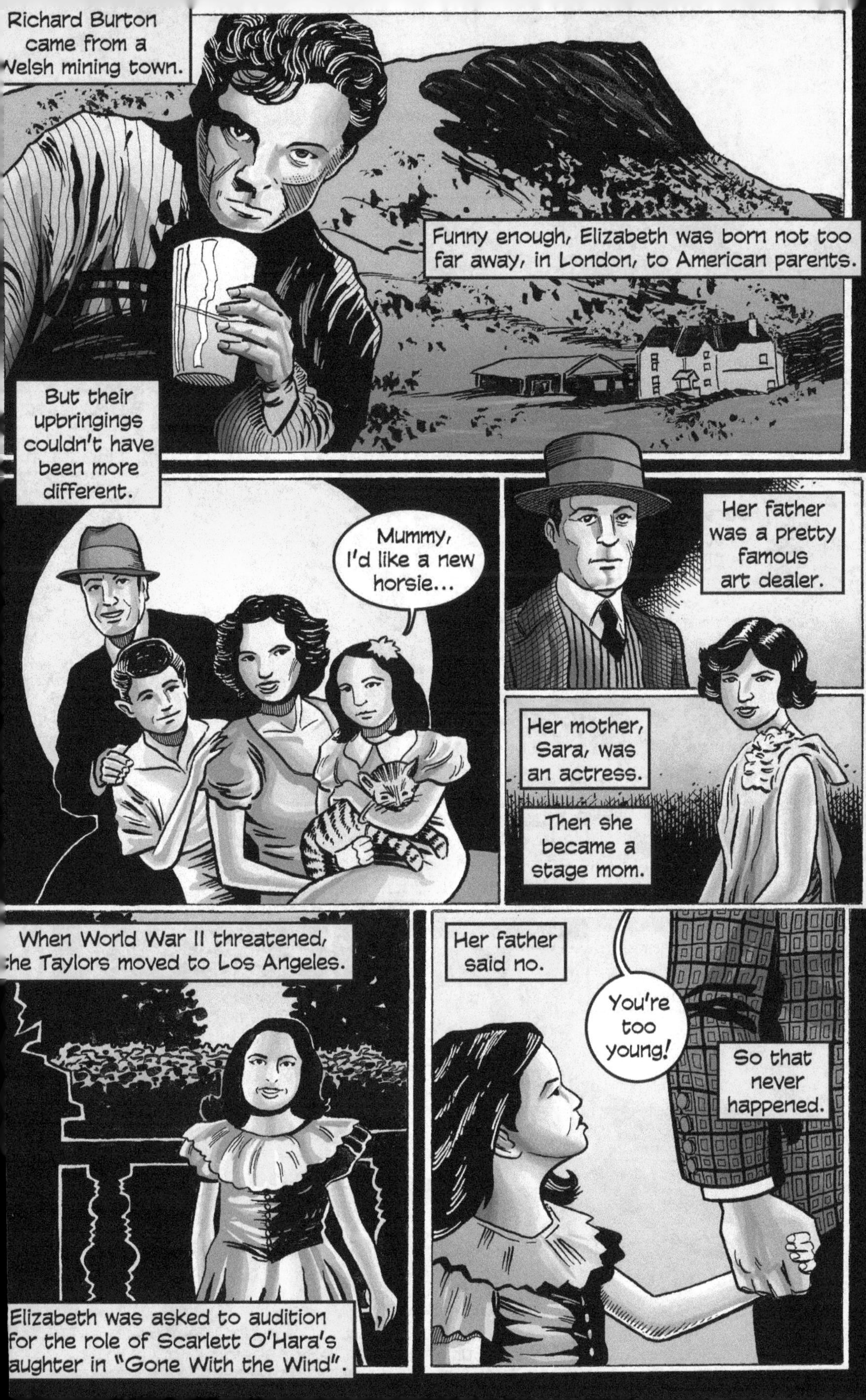

Richard Burton came from a Welsh mining town.
Funny enough, Elizabeth was born not too far away, in London, to American parents.
But their upbringings couldn't have been more different.
Mummy, I'd like a new horsie...
Her father was a pretty famous art dealer.
Her mother, Sara, was an actress.
Then she became a stage mom.
When World War II threatened, the Taylors moved to Los Angeles.
Elizabeth was asked to audition for the role of Scarlett O'Hara's daughter in "Gone With the Wind".
Her father said no.
You're too young!
So that never happened.

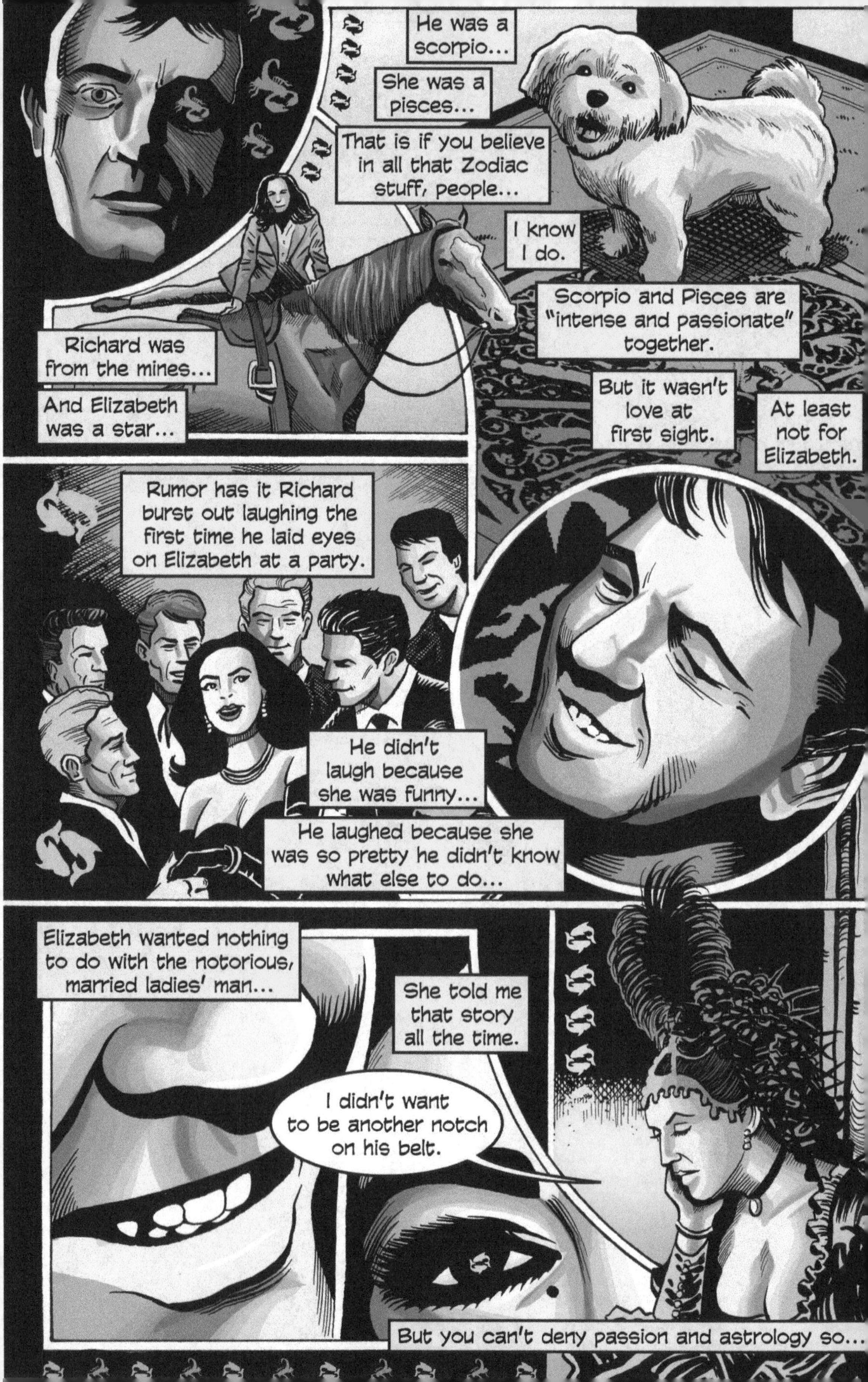
He was a scorpio...
She was a pisces...
That is if you believe in all that Zodiac stuff, people...
I know I do.
Richard was from the mines...
And Elizabeth was a star...
Scorpio and Pisces are "intense and passionate" together.
But it wasn't love at first sight.
At least not for Elizabeth.
Rumor has it Richard burst out laughing the first time he laid eyes on Elizabeth at a party.
He didn't laugh because she was funny...
He laughed because she was so pretty he didn't know what else to do...
Elizabeth wanted nothing to do with the notorious, married ladies' man...
She told me that story all the time.
I didn't want to be another notch on his belt.
But you can't deny passion and astrology so...

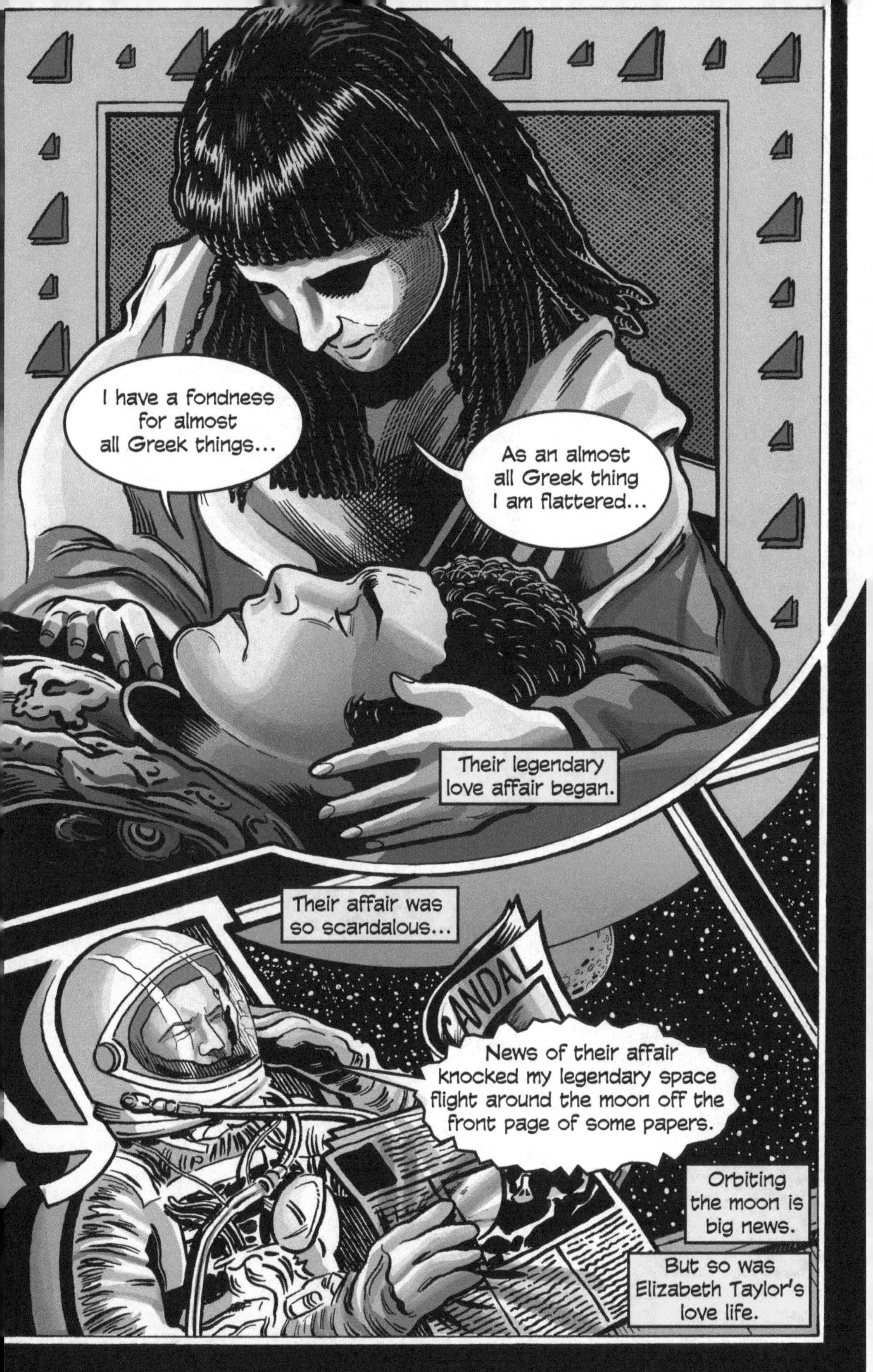
I have a fondness for almost all Greek things...
As an almost all Greek thing I am flattered...
Their legendary love affair began.
Their affair was so scandalous...
CANDAL
News of their affair knocked my legendary space flight around the moon off the front page of some papers.
Orbiting the moon is big news.
But so was Elizabeth Taylor's love life.

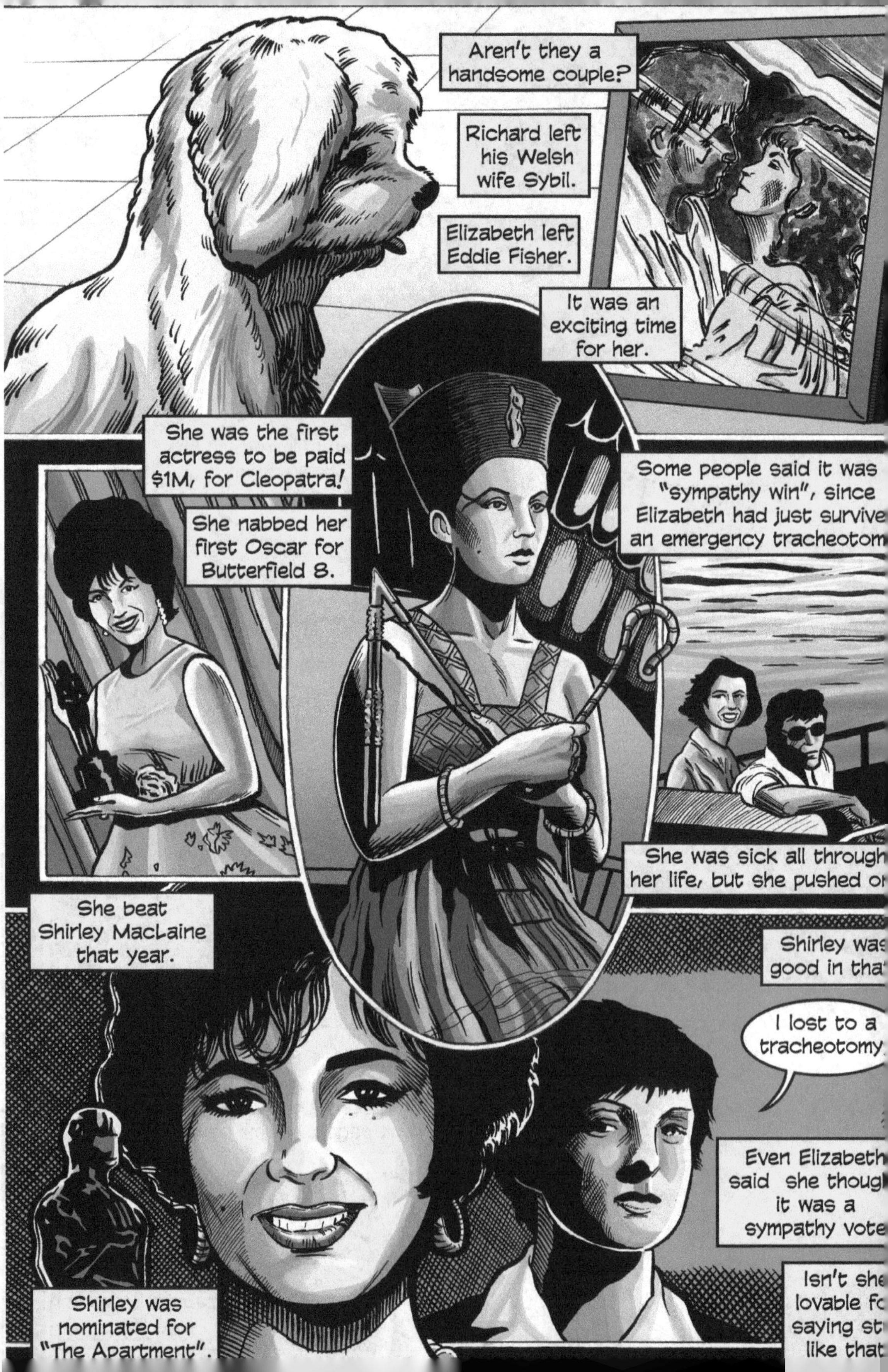
Aren't they a handsome couple?
Richard left his Welsh wife Sybil.
Elizabeth left Eddie Fisher.
It was an exciting time for her.
She was the first actress to be paid $1M, for Cleopatra!
She nabbed her first Oscar for Butterfield 8.
Some people said it was "sympathy win", since Elizabeth had just survive an emergency tracheotom
She was sick all through her life, but she pushed o
She beat Shirley MacLaine that year.
Shirley was good in tha
I lost to a tracheotomy.
Even Elizabeth said she thoug it was a sympathy vote
Isn't she lovable f saying s like that
Shirley was nominated for "The Apartment".

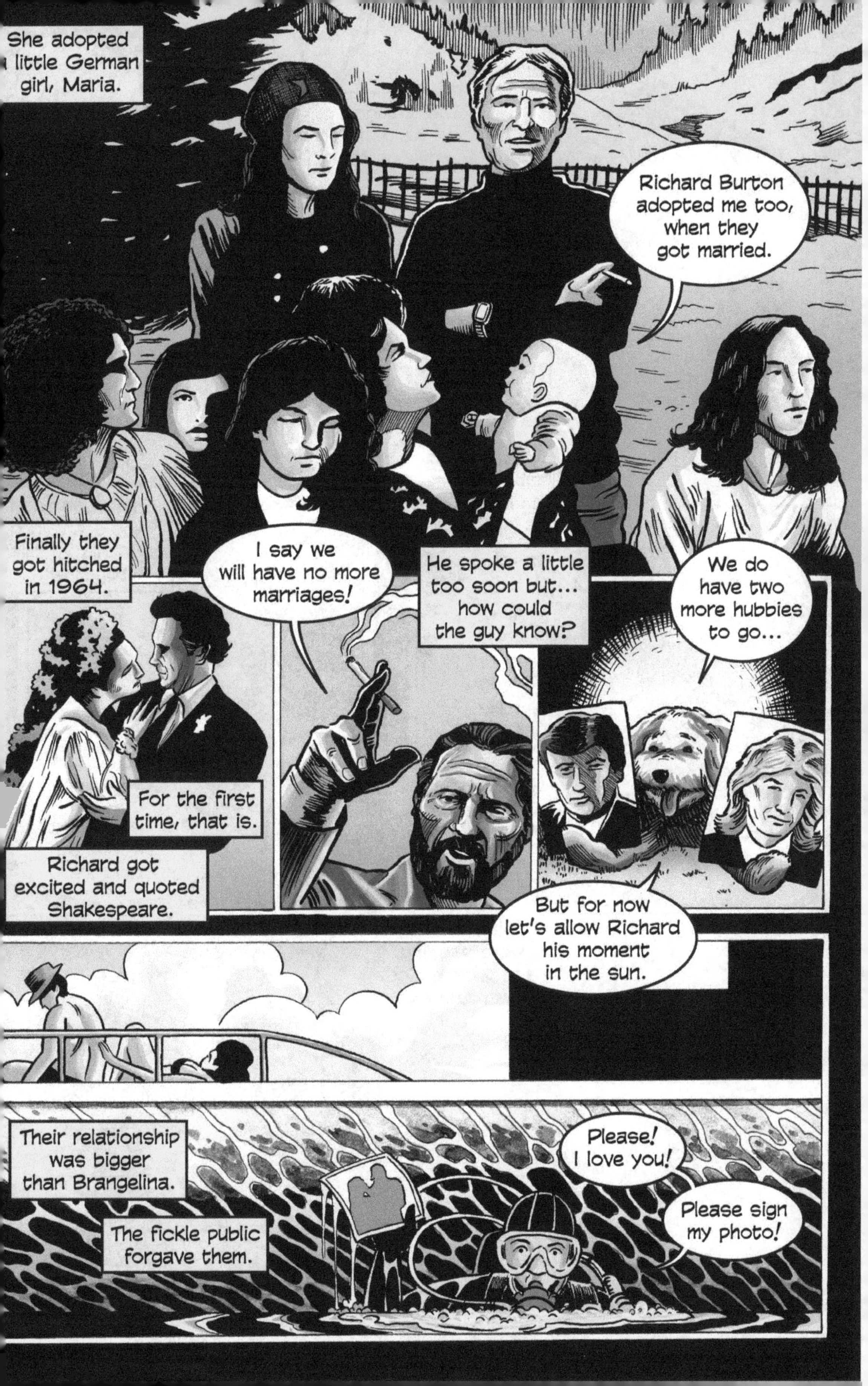
She adopted little German girl, Maria.
Richard Burton adopted me too, when they got married.
Finally they got hitched in 1964.
I say we will have no more marriages!
He spoke a little too soon but... how could the guy know?
We do have two more hubbies to go...
For the first time, that is.
Richard got excited and quoted Shakespeare.
But for now let's allow Richard his moment in the sun.
Their relationship was bigger than Brangelina.
The fickle public forgave them.
Please! I love you!
Please sign my photo!

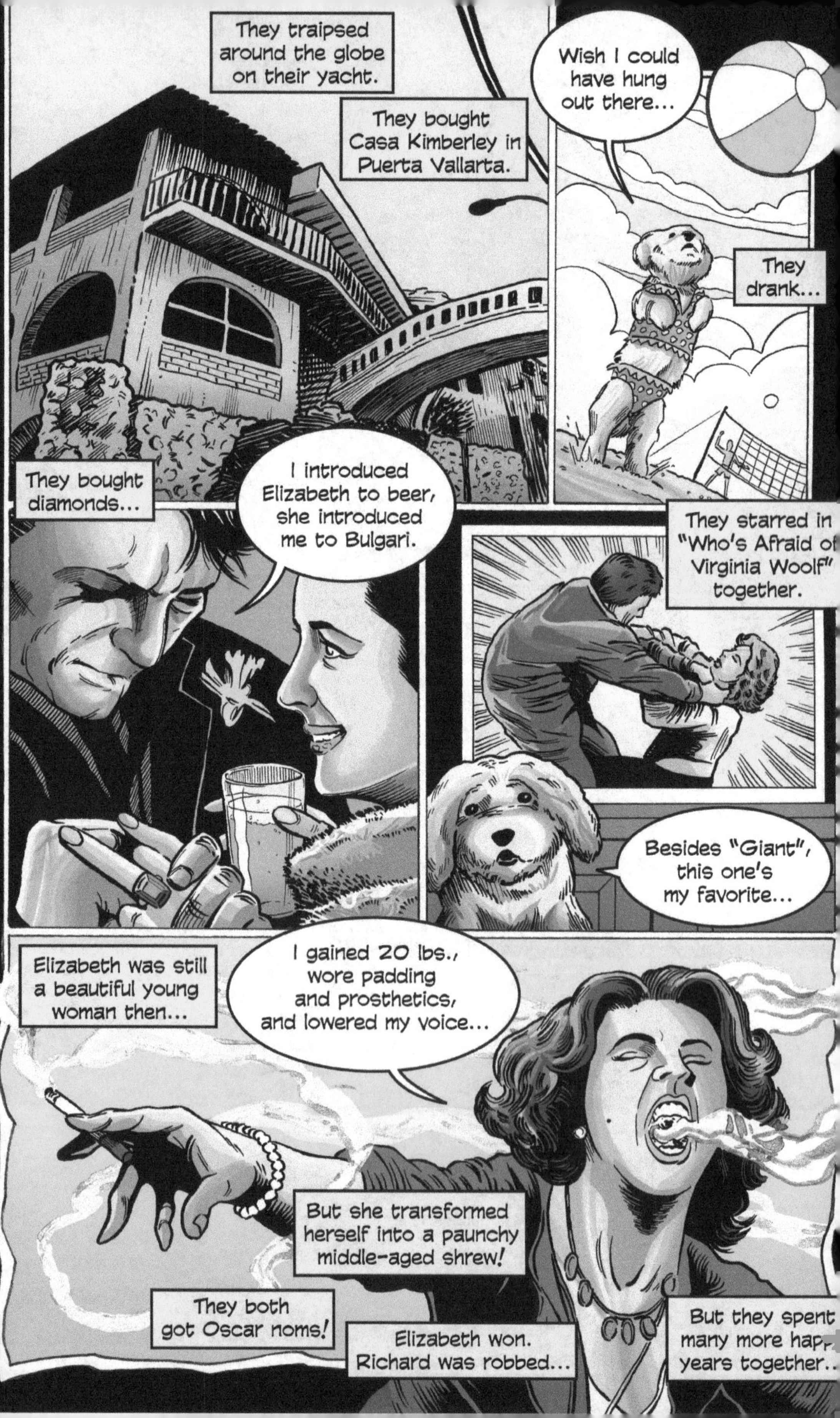
They traipsed around the globe on their yacht.
They bought Casa Kimberley in Puerta Vallarta.
Wish I could have hung out there...
They drank...
They bought diamonds...
I introduced Elizabeth to beer, she introduced me to Bulgari.
They starred in "Who's Afraid of Virginia Woolf" together.
Besides "Giant", this one's my favorite...
Elizabeth was still a beautiful young woman then...
I gained 20 lbs., wore padding and prosthetics, and lowered my voice...
But she transformed herself into a paunchy middle-aged shrew!
They both got Oscar noms!
Elizabeth won. Richard was robbed...
But they spent many more hap years together...

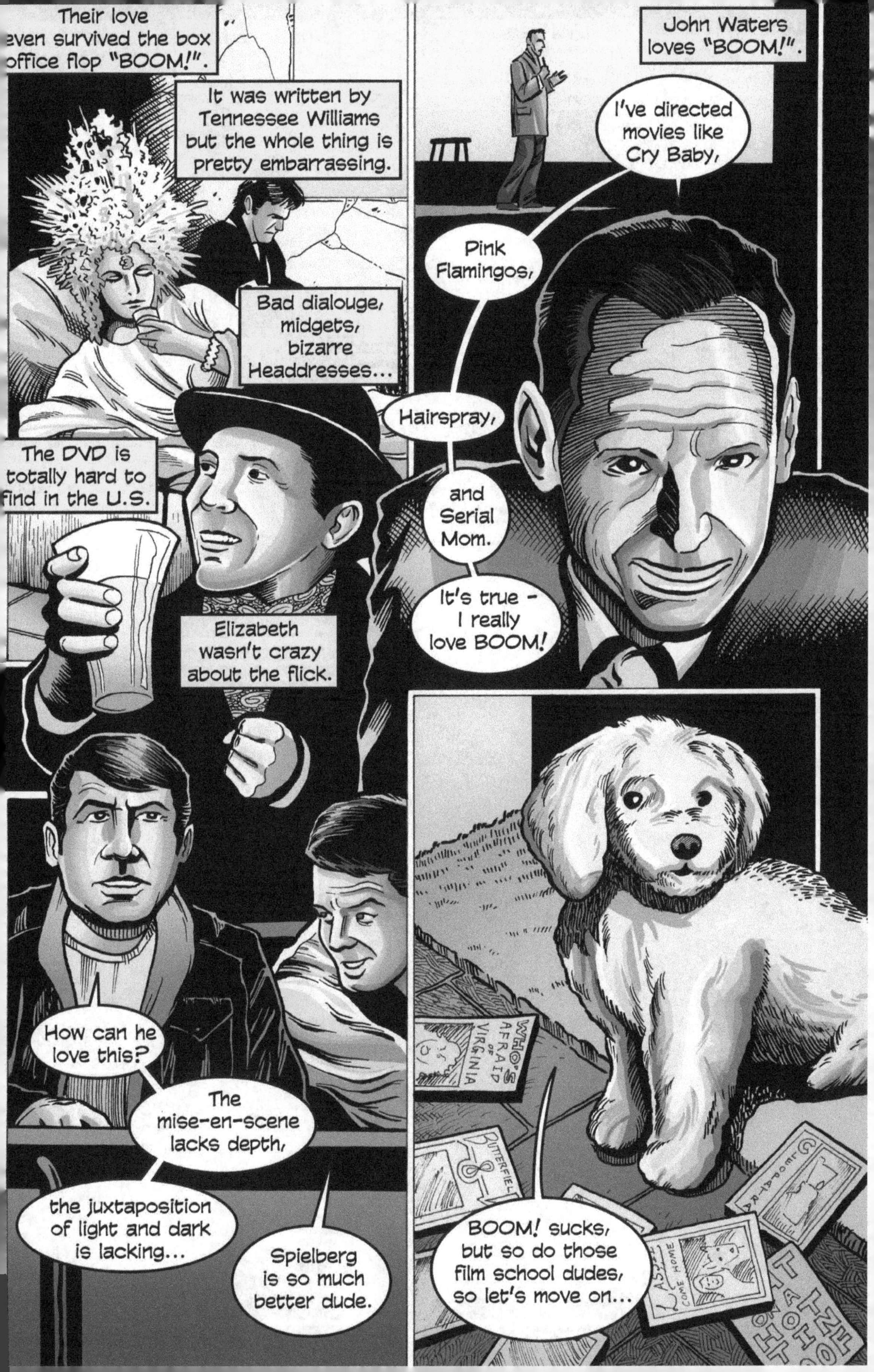
Their love even survived the box office flop "BOOM!".
It was written by Tennessee Williams but the whole thing is pretty embarrassing.
Bad dialouge, midgets, bizarre Headdresses...
The DVD is totally hard to find in the U.S.
Elizabeth wasn't crazy about the flick.
John Waters loves "BOOM!".
I've directed movies like Cry Baby,
Pink Flamingos,
Hairspray,
and Serial Mom.
It's true - I really love BOOM!
How can he love this?
The mise-en-scene lacks depth,
the juxtaposition of light and dark is lacking...
Spielberg is so much better dude.
BOOM! sucks, but so do those film school dudes, so let's move on...
WHO'S AFRAID OF VIRGINIA
BUTTERFIELD 8
LASSIE COME HOME

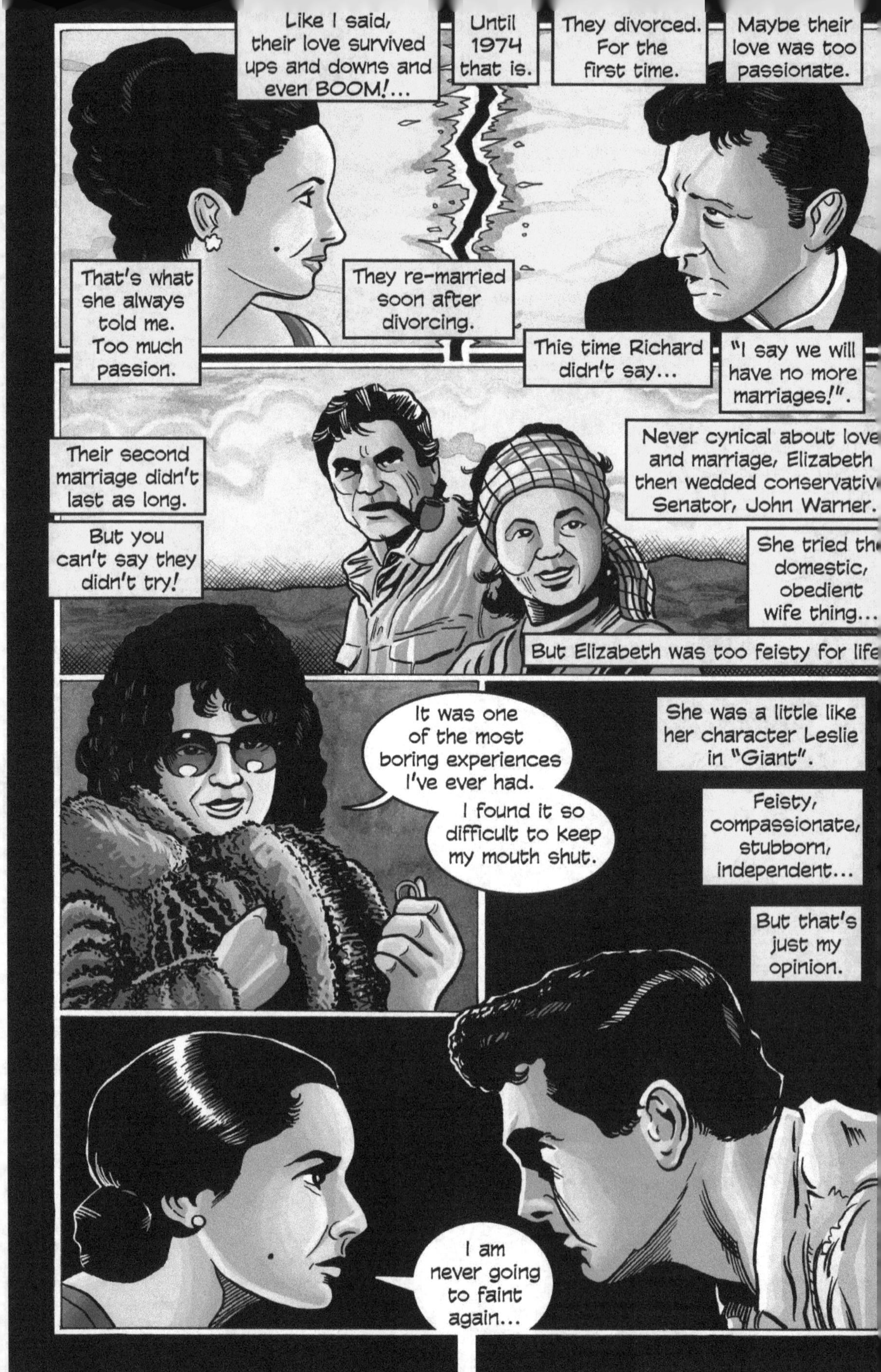
Like I said, their love survived ups and downs and even BOOM!...
Until 1974 that is.
They divorced. For the first time.
Maybe their love was too passionate.
That's what she always told me. Too much passion.
They re-married soon after divorcing.
This time Richard didn't say...
"I say we will have no more marriages!".
Their second marriage didn't last as long.
But you can't say they didn't try!
Never cynical about love and marriage, Elizabeth then wedded conservative Senator, John Warner.
She tried the domestic, obedient wife thing...
But Elizabeth was too feisty for life
It was one of the most boring experiences I've ever had.
I found it so difficult to keep my mouth shut.
She was a little like her character Leslie in "Giant".
Feisty, compassionate, stubborn, independent...
But that's just my opinion.
I am never going to faint again...

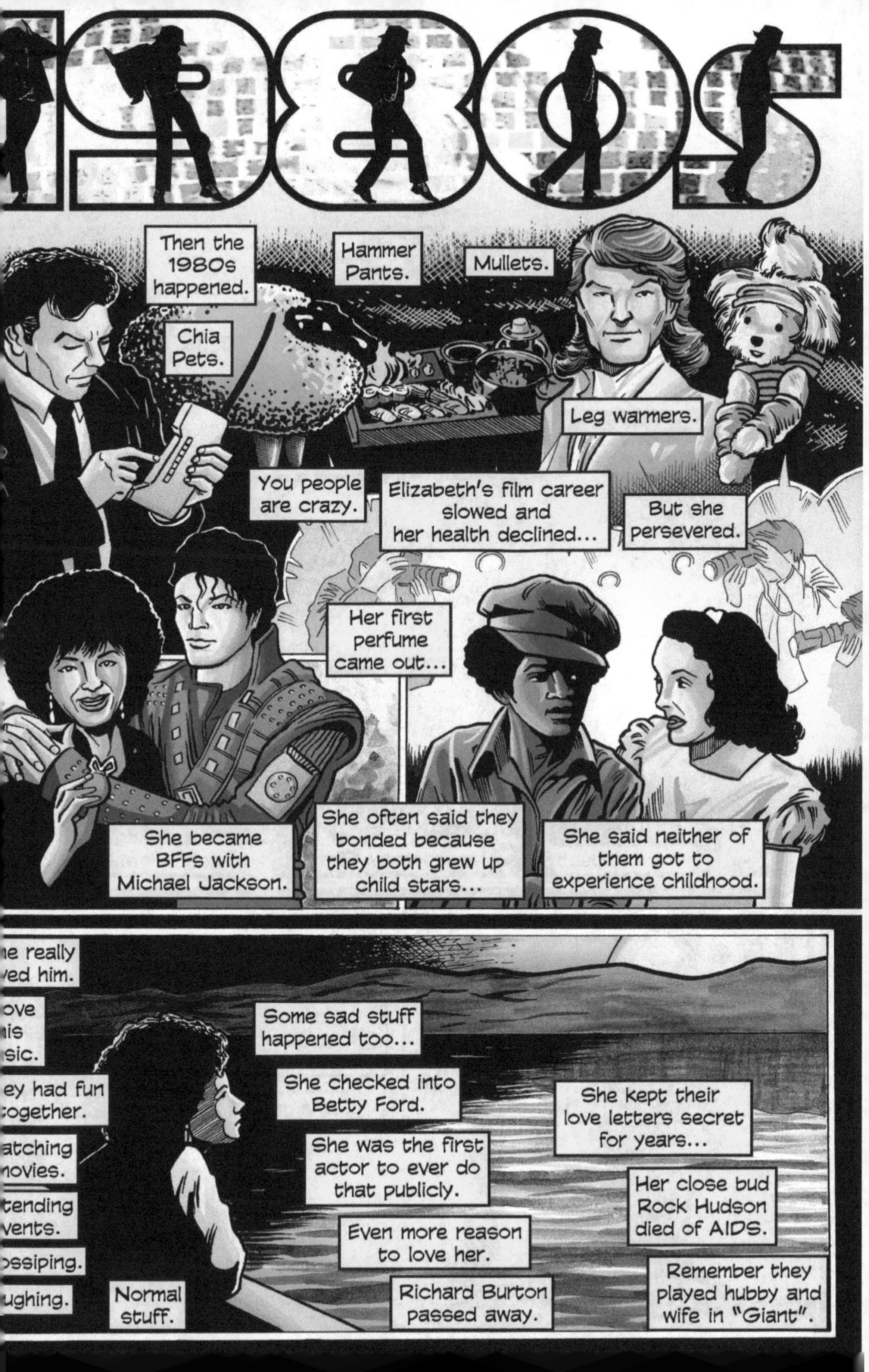
1980s
Then the 1980s happened.
Chia Pets.
Hammer Pants.
Mullets.
Leg warmers.
You people are crazy.
Elizabeth's film career slowed and her health declined...
But she persevered.
Her first perfume came out...
She became BFFs with Michael Jackson.
She often said they bonded because they both grew up child stars...
She said neither of them got to experience childhood.
ne really
ved him.
ove
nis
sic.
ey had fun
together.
atching
movies.
tending
vents.
ossiping.
ughing.
Normal stuff.
Some sad stuff happened too...
She checked into Betty Ford.
She was the first actor to ever do that publicly.
Even more reason to love her.
Richard Burton passed away.
She kept their love letters secret for years...
Her close bud Rock Hudson died of AIDS.
Remember they played hubby and wife in "Giant".

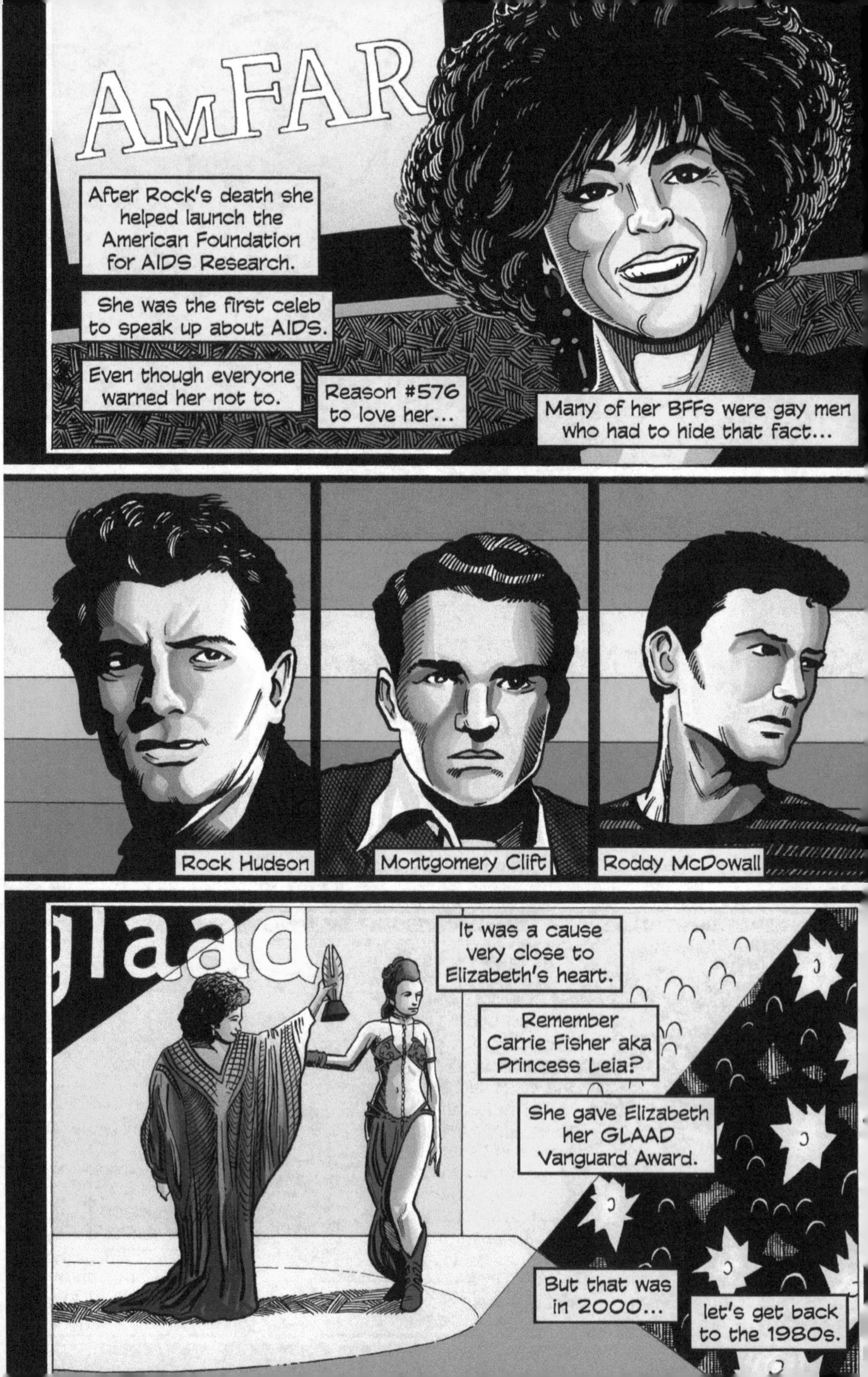
AmFAR
After Rock's death she helped launch the American Foundation for AIDS Research.
She was the first celeb to speak up about AIDS.
Even though everyone warned her not to.
Reason #576 to love her...
Many of her BFFs were gay men who had to hide that fact...
Rock Hudson
Montgomery Clift
Roddy McDowall
glaad
It was a cause very close to Elizabeth's heart.
Remember Carrie Fisher aka Princess Leia?
She gave Elizabeth her GLAAD Vanguard Award.
But that was in 2000...
let's get back to the 1980s.

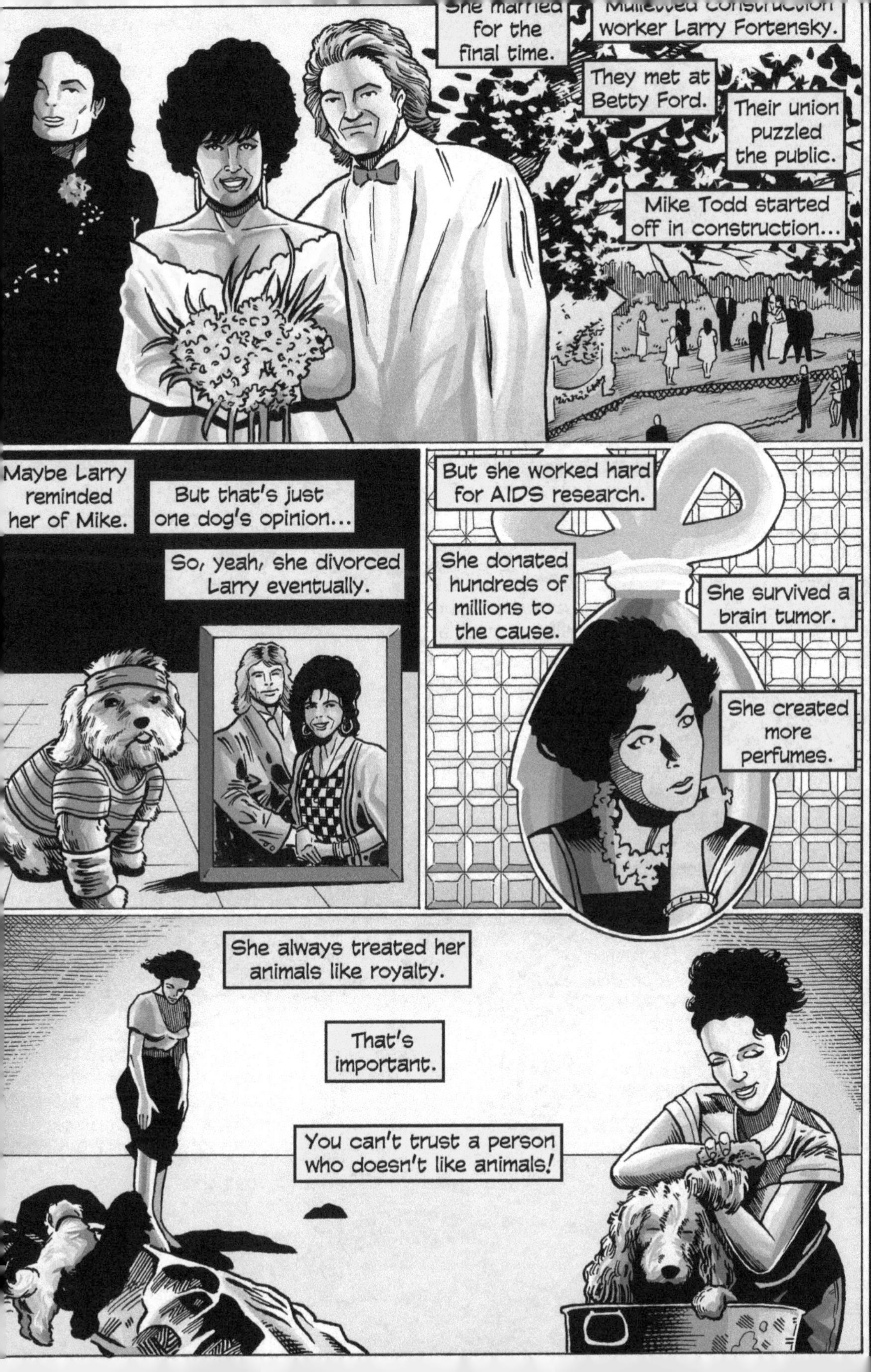
She married for the final time.
Mulletted construction worker Larry Fortensky.
They met at Betty Ford.
Their union puzzled the public.
Mike Todd started off in construction...
Maybe Larry reminded her of Mike.
But that's just one dog's opinion...
So, yeah, she divorced Larry eventually.
But she worked hard for AIDS research.
She donated hundreds of millions to the cause.
She survived a brain tumor.
She created more perfumes.
She always treated her animals like royalty.
That's important.
You can't trust a person who doesn't like animals!

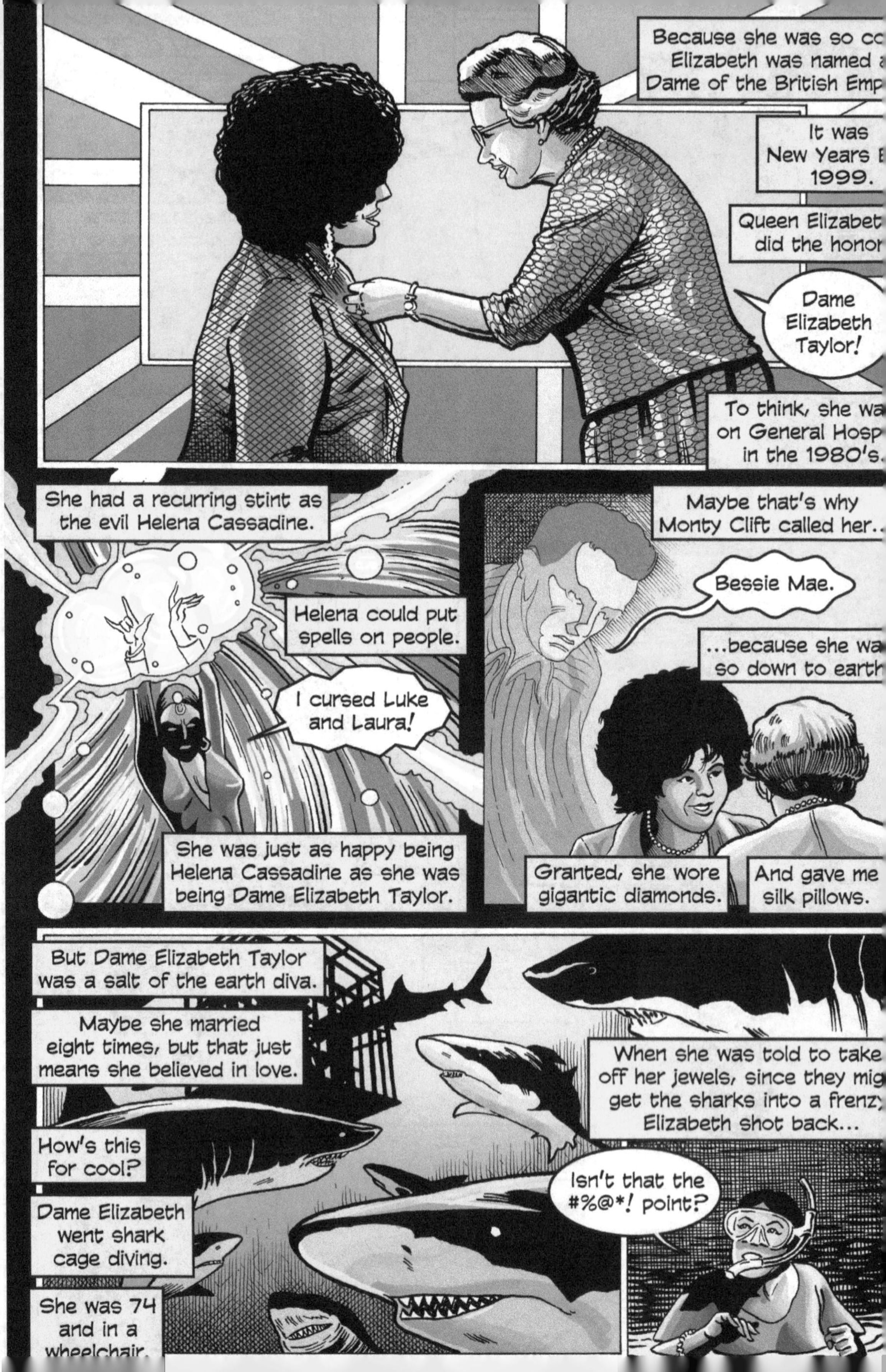

Because she was so co
Elizabeth was named a
Dame of the British Emp
It was
New Years E
1999.
Queen Elizabet
did the honor
Dame
Elizabeth
Taylor!
To think, she wa
on General Hosp
in the 1980's.
She had a recurring stint as
the evil Helena Cassadine.
Helena could put
spells on people.
I cursed Luke
and Laura!
She was just as happy being
Helena Cassadine as she was
being Dame Elizabeth Taylor.
Maybe that's why
Monty Clift called her...
Bessie Mae.
...because she wa
so down to earth
Granted, she wore
gigantic diamonds.
And gave me
silk pillows.
But Dame Elizabeth Taylor
was a salt of the earth diva.
Maybe she married
eight times, but that just
means she believed in love.
How's this
for cool?
Dame Elizabeth
went shark
cage diving.
She was 74
and in a
wheelchair.
When she was told to take
off her jewels, since they mig
get the sharks into a frenzy
Elizabeth shot back...
Isn't that the
#%@*! point?

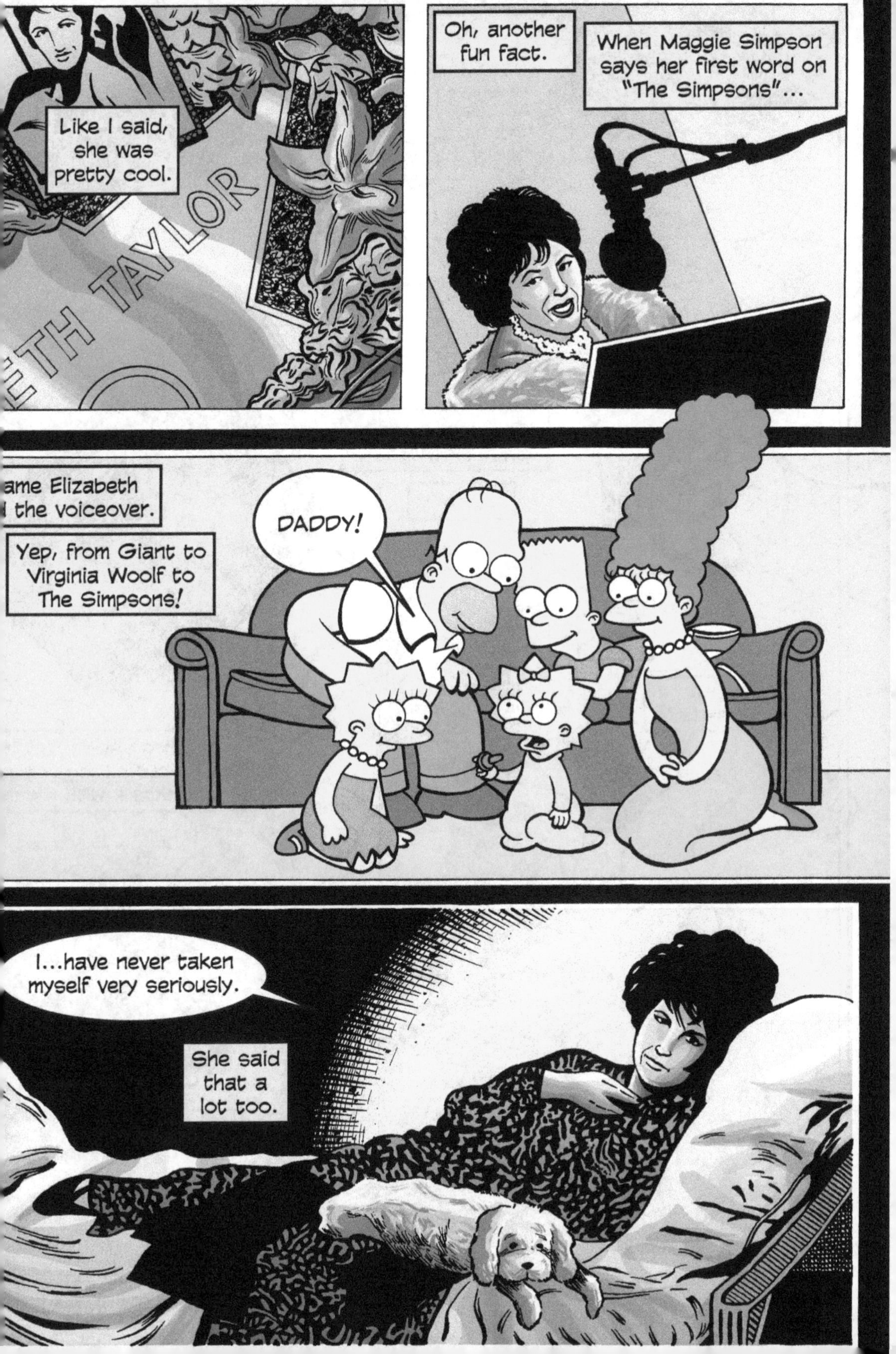
Like I said, she was pretty cool.
ETH TAYLOR
Oh, another fun fact.
When Maggie Simpson says her first word on "The Simpsons"...
ame Elizabeth
the voiceover.
Yep, from Giant to Virginia Woolf to The Simpsons!
DADDY!
I...have never taken myself very seriously.
She said that a lot too.

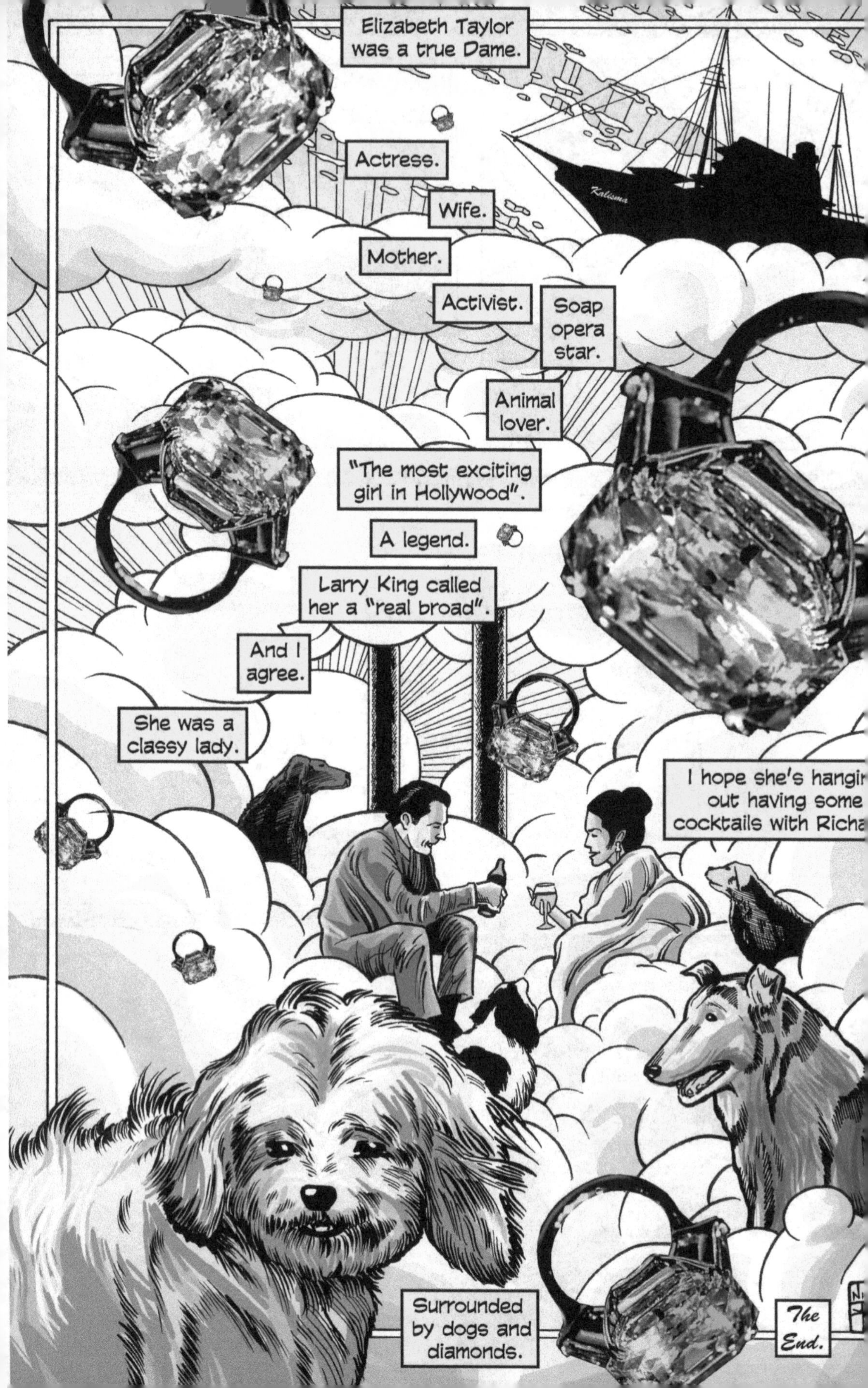
Elizabeth Taylor was a true Dame.
Kalisma
Actress.
Wife.
Mother.
Activist.
Soap opera star.
Animal lover.
"The most exciting girl in Hollywood".
A legend.
Larry King called her a "real broad".
And I agree.
She was a classy lady.
I hope she's hangir out having some cocktails with Richa
Surrounded by dogs and diamonds.
The End.

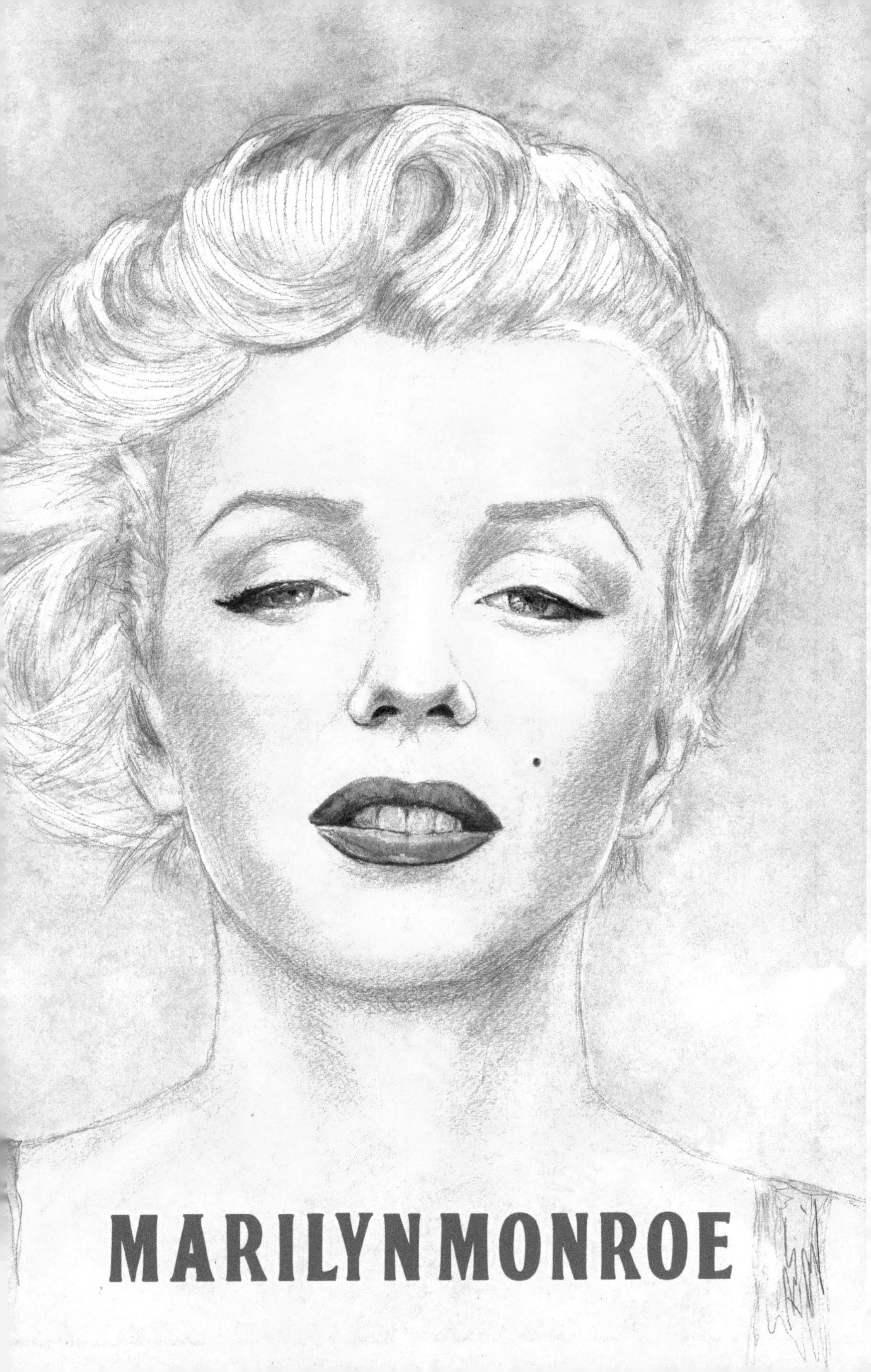
MARILYNMONROE

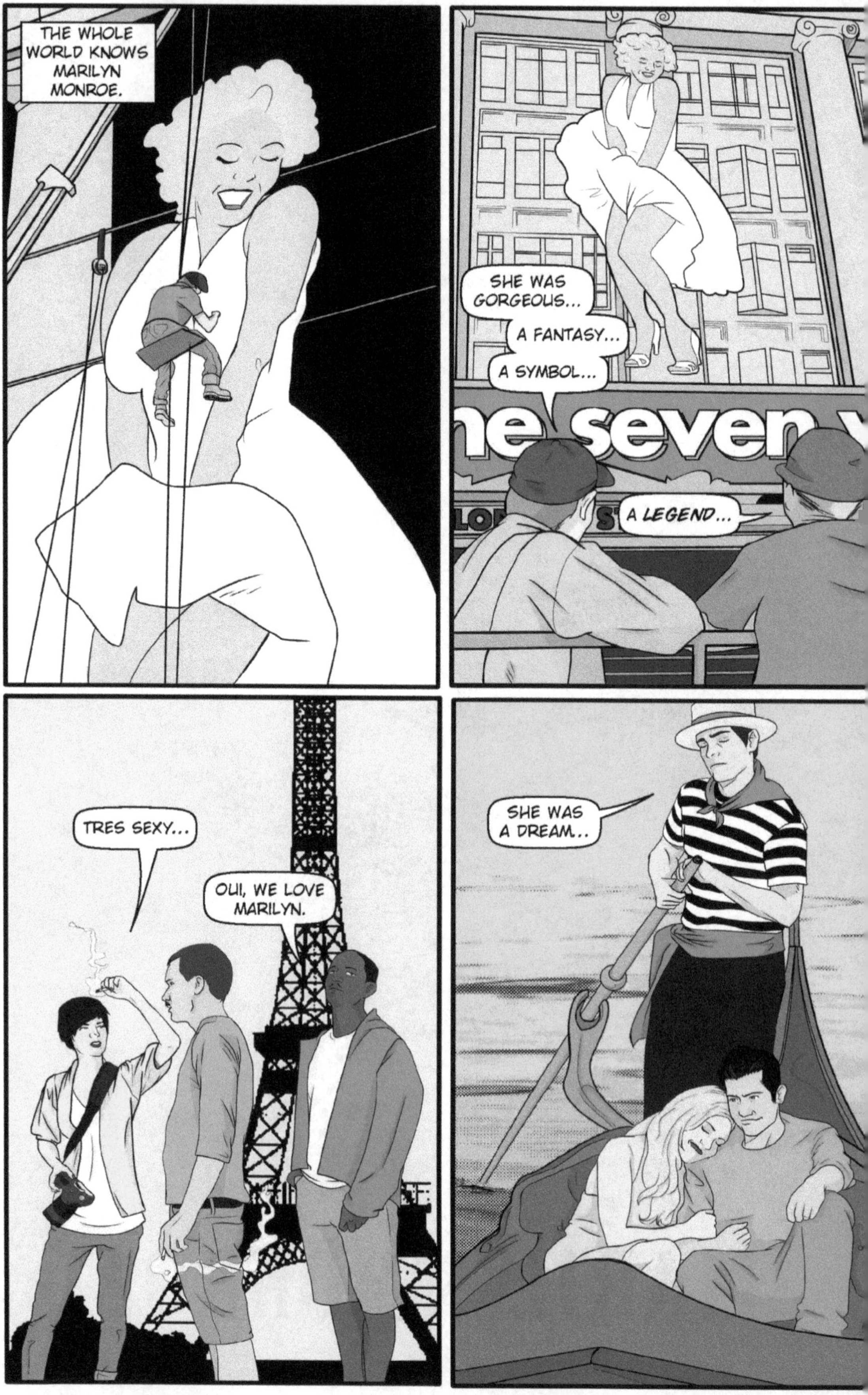
THE WHOLE WORLD KNOWS MARILYN MONROE.
SHE WAS GORGEOUS...
A FANTASY...
A SYMBOL...
A LEGEND...
TRES SEXY...
OUI, WE LOVE MARILYN.
SHE WAS A DREAM...

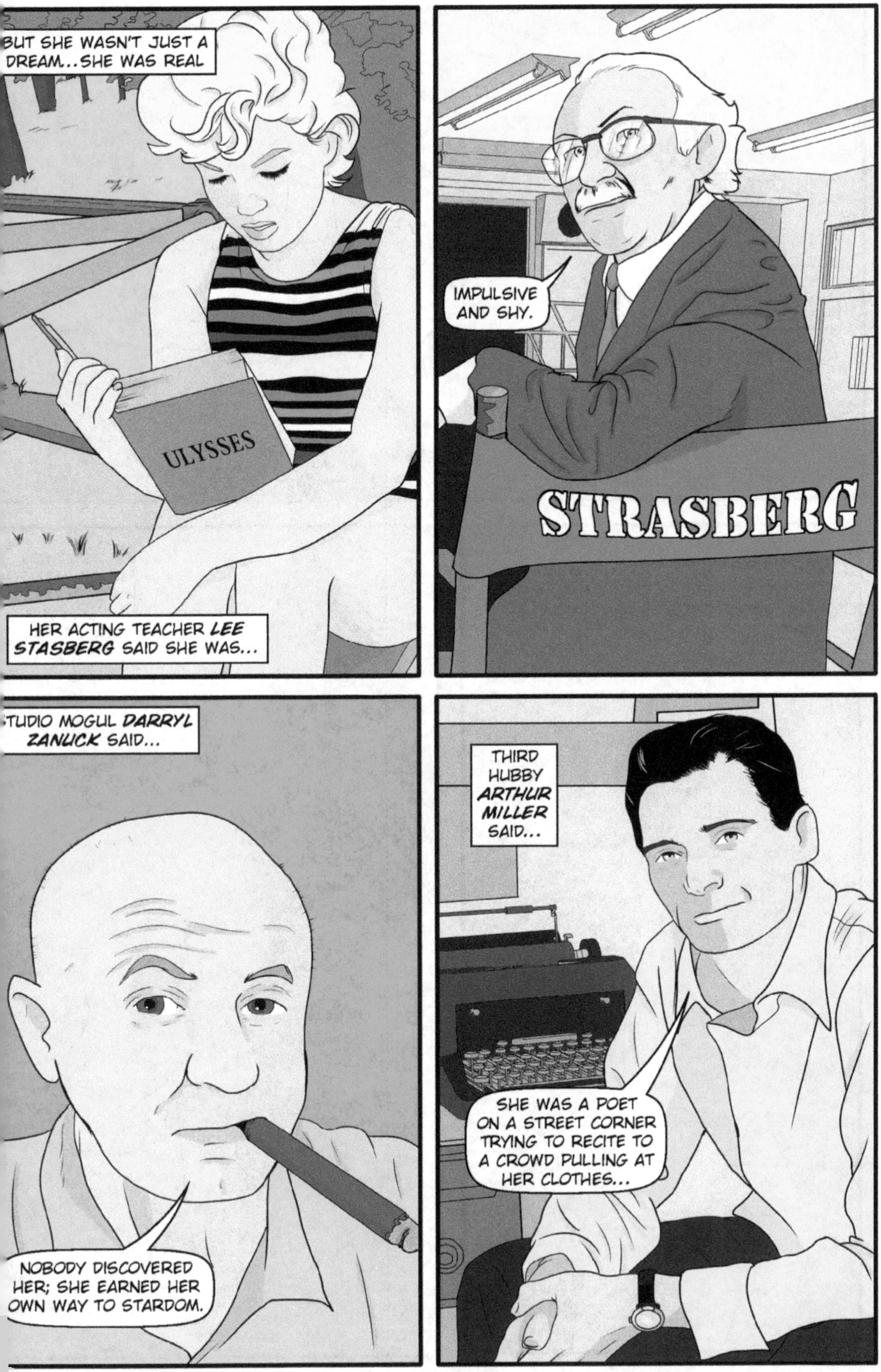
BUT SHE WASN'T JUST A DREAM...SHE WAS REAL
ULYSSES
HER ACTING TEACHER LEE STASBERG SAID SHE WAS...
IMPULSIVE AND SHY.
STRASBERG
STUDIO MOGUL DARRYL ZANUCK SAID...
NOBODY DISCOVERED HER; SHE EARNED HER OWN WAY TO STARDOM.
THIRD HUBBY ARTHUR MILLER SAID...
SHE WAS A POET ON A STREET CORNER TRYING TO RECITE TO A CROWD PULLING AT HER CLOTHES...

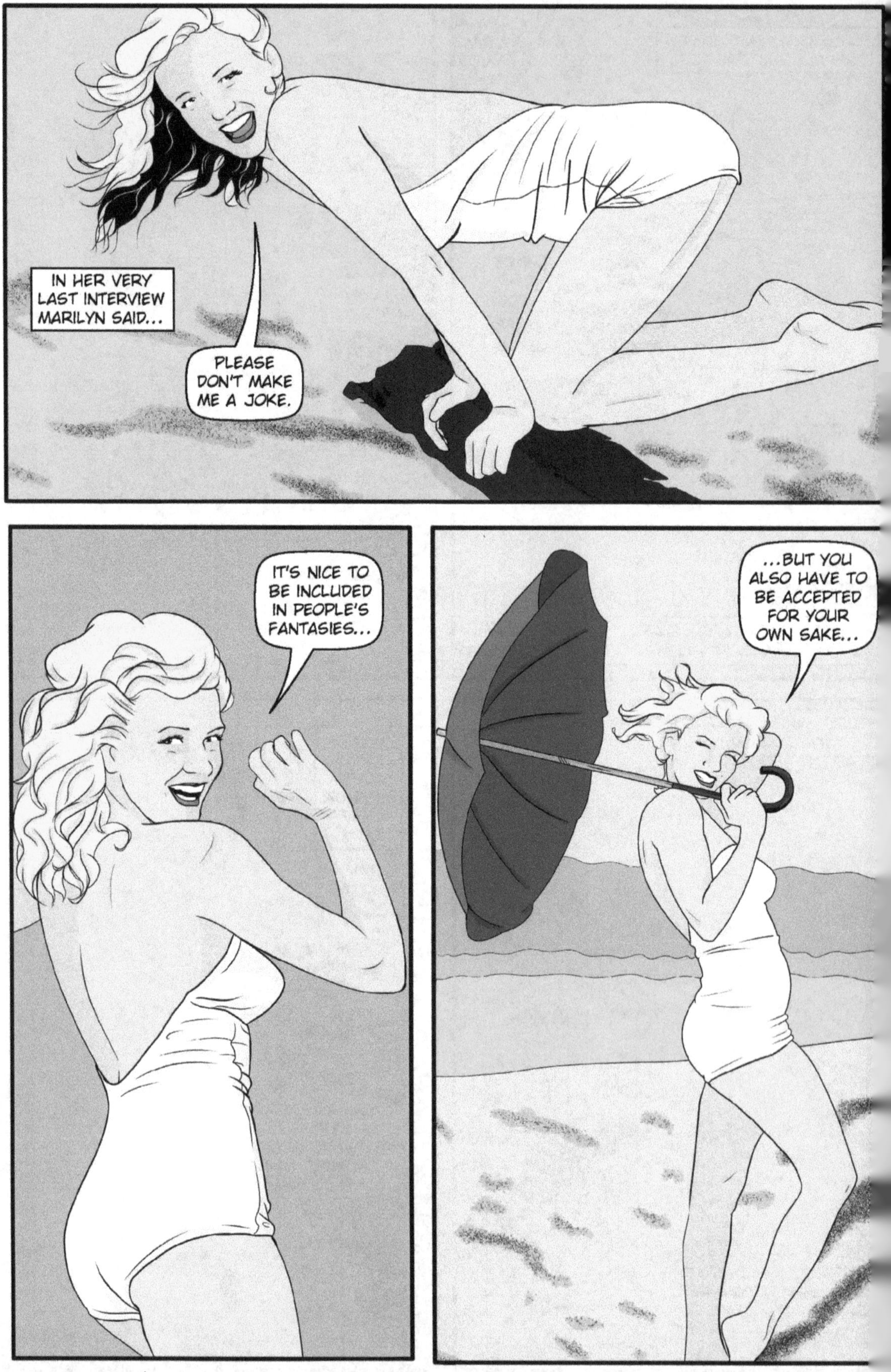
IN HER VERY LAST INTERVIEW MARILYN SAID...
PLEASE DON'T MAKE ME A JOKE.
IT'S NICE TO BE INCLUDED IN PEOPLE'S FANTASIES...
...BUT YOU ALSO HAVE TO BE ACCEPTED FOR YOUR OWN SAKE...

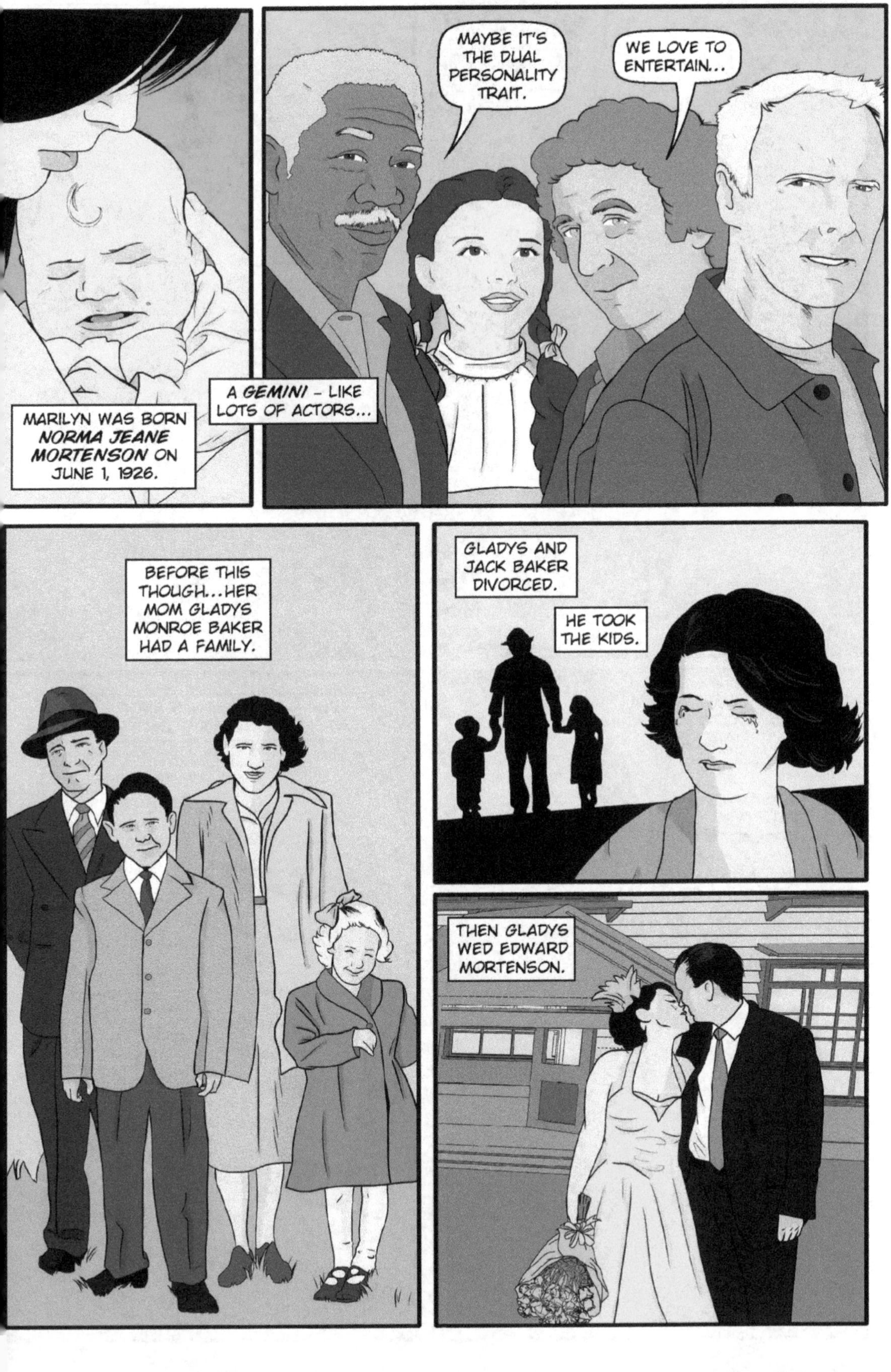

MARILYN WAS BORN ***NORMA JEANE MORTENSON*** ON JUNE 1, 1926.
A ***GEMINI*** – LIKE LOTS OF ACTORS...
MAYBE IT'S THE DUAL PERSONALITY TRAIT.
WE LOVE TO ENTERTAIN...
BEFORE THIS THOUGH...HER MOM GLADYS MONROE BAKER HAD A FAMILY.
GLADYS AND JACK BAKER DIVORCED.
HE TOOK THE KIDS.
THEN GLADYS WED EDWARD MORTENSON.

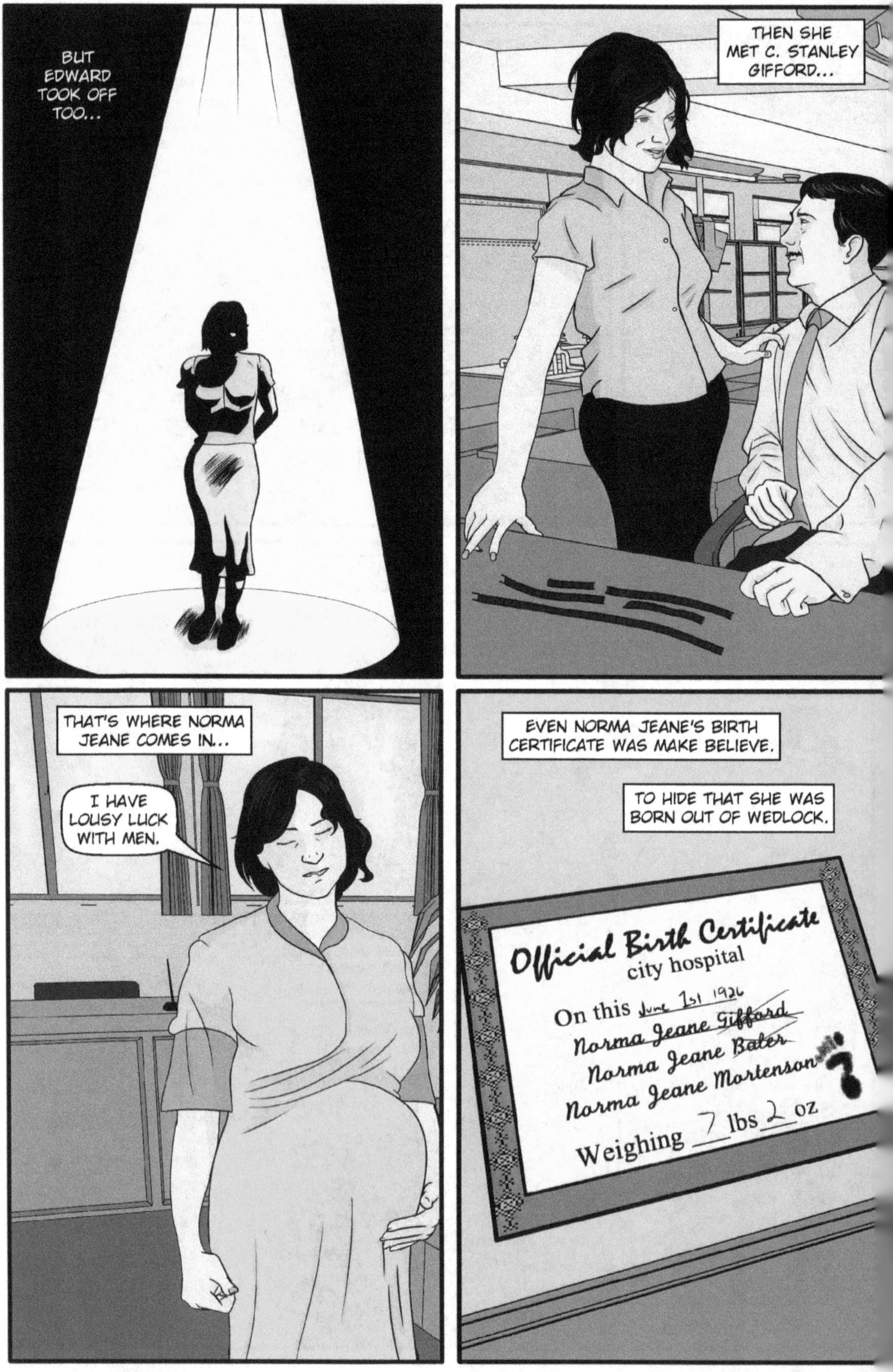
BUT EDWARD TOOK OFF TOO...
THEN SHE MET C. STANLEY GIFFORD...
THAT'S WHERE NORMA JEANE COMES IN...
I HAVE LOUSY LUCK WITH MEN.
EVEN NORMA JEANE'S BIRTH CERTIFICATE WAS MAKE BELIEVE.
TO HIDE THAT SHE WAS BORN OUT OF WEDLOCK.
Official Birth Certificate
city hospital
On this June 1st 1926
Norma Jeane Gifford
Norma Jeane Baker
Norma Jeane Mortenson
?
Weighing 7 lbs 2 oz

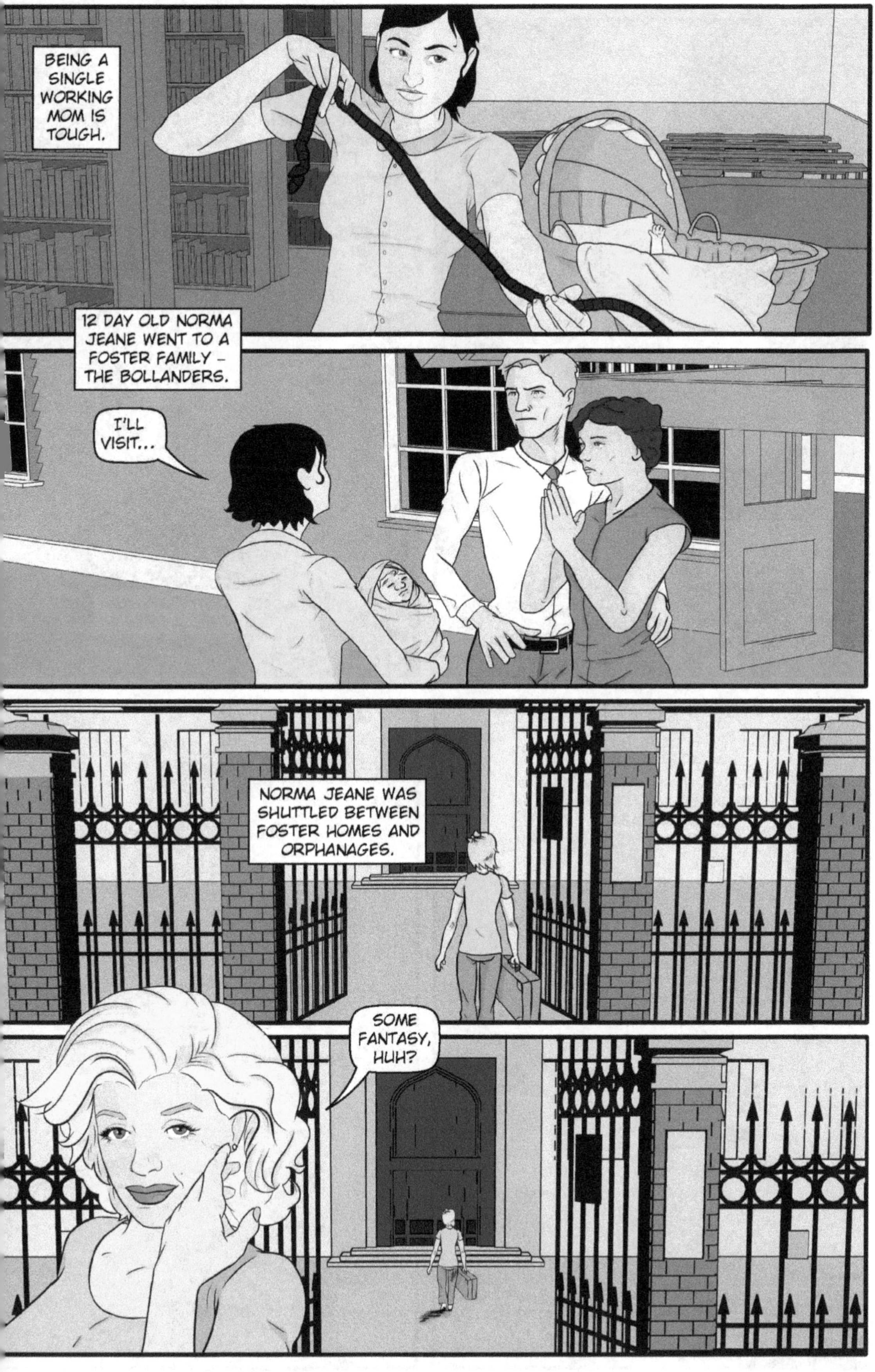
BEING A SINGLE WORKING MOM IS TOUGH.
12 DAY OLD NORMA JEANE WENT TO A FOSTER FAMILY – THE BOLLANDERS.
I'LL VISIT...
NORMA JEANE WAS SHUTTLED BETWEEN FOSTER HOMES AND ORPHANAGES.
SOME FANTASY, HUH?

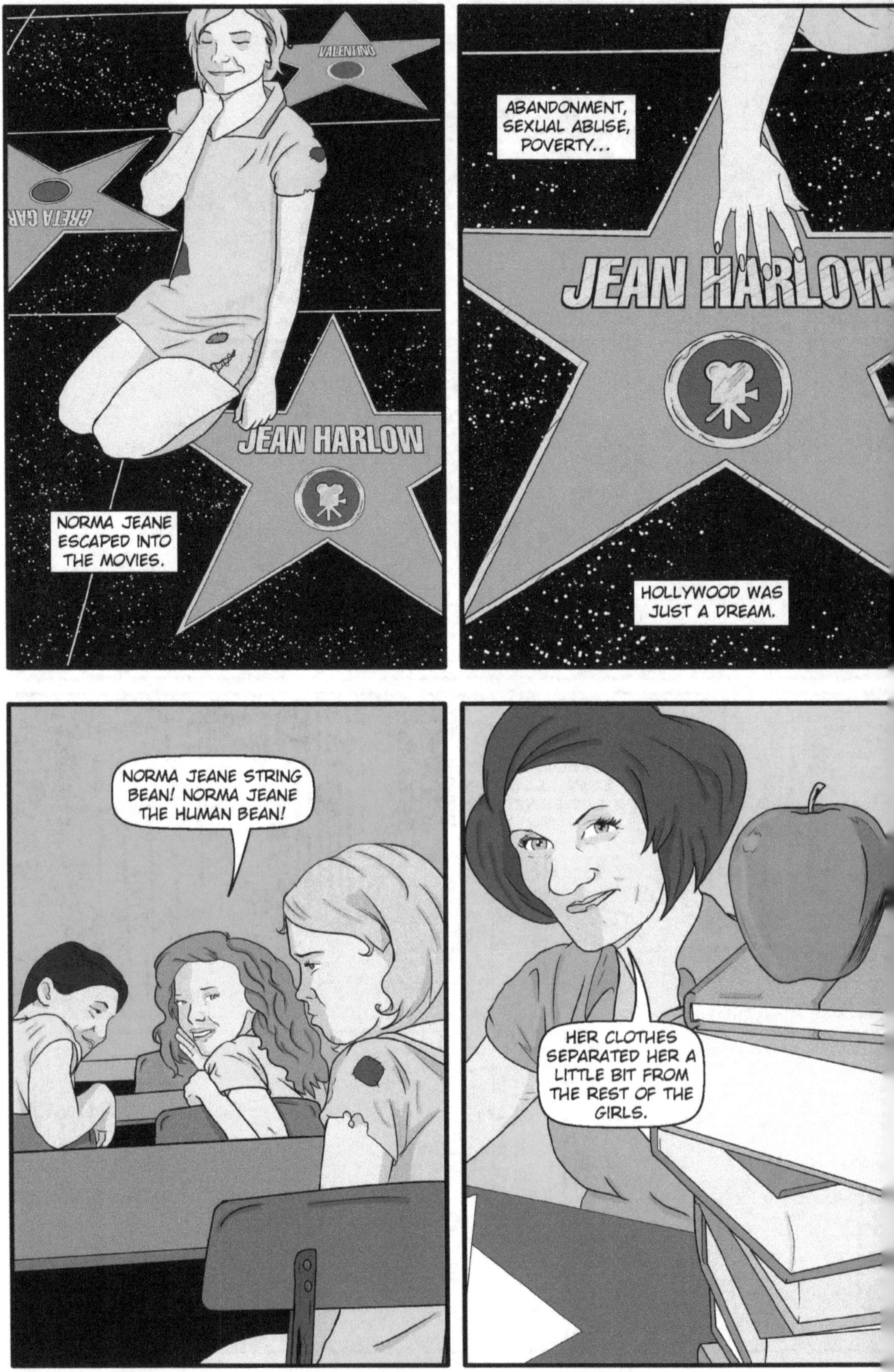
VALENTINO
GRETA GAR
JEAN HARLOW
NORMA JEANE ESCAPED INTO THE MOVIES.
ABANDONMENT, SEXUAL ABUSE, POVERTY...
JEAN HARLOW
HOLLYWOOD WAS JUST A DREAM.
NORMA JEANE STRING BEAN! NORMA JEANE THE HUMAN BEAN!
HER CLOTHES SEPARATED HER A LITTLE BIT FROM THE REST OF THE GIRLS.

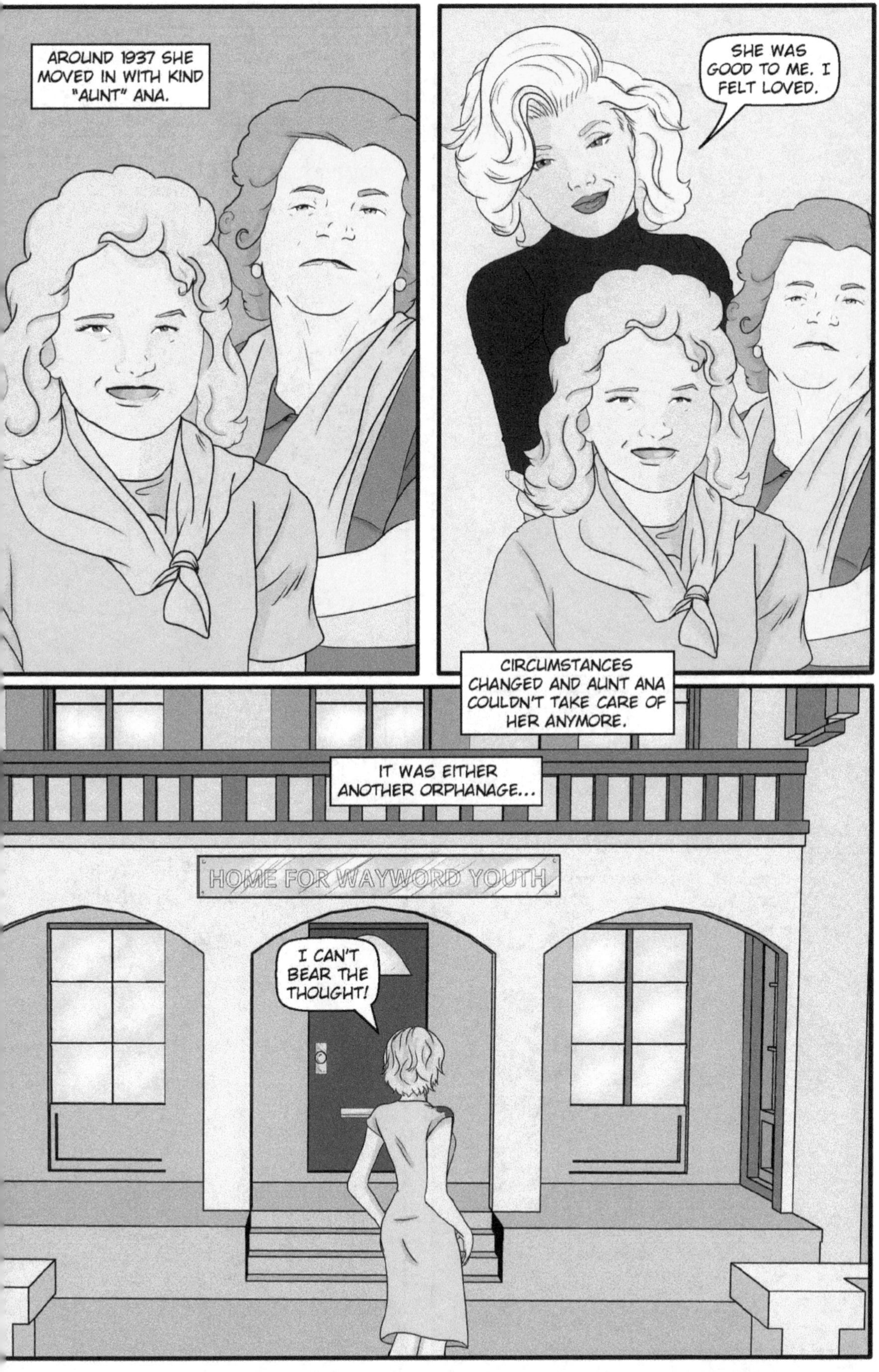
AROUND 1937 SHE MOVED IN WITH KIND "AUNT" ANA.
SHE WAS GOOD TO ME. I FELT LOVED.
CIRCUMSTANCES CHANGED AND AUNT ANA COULDN'T TAKE CARE OF HER ANYMORE.
IT WAS EITHER ANOTHER ORPHANAGE...
HOME FOR WAYWORD YOUTH
I CAN'T BEAR THE THOUGHT!

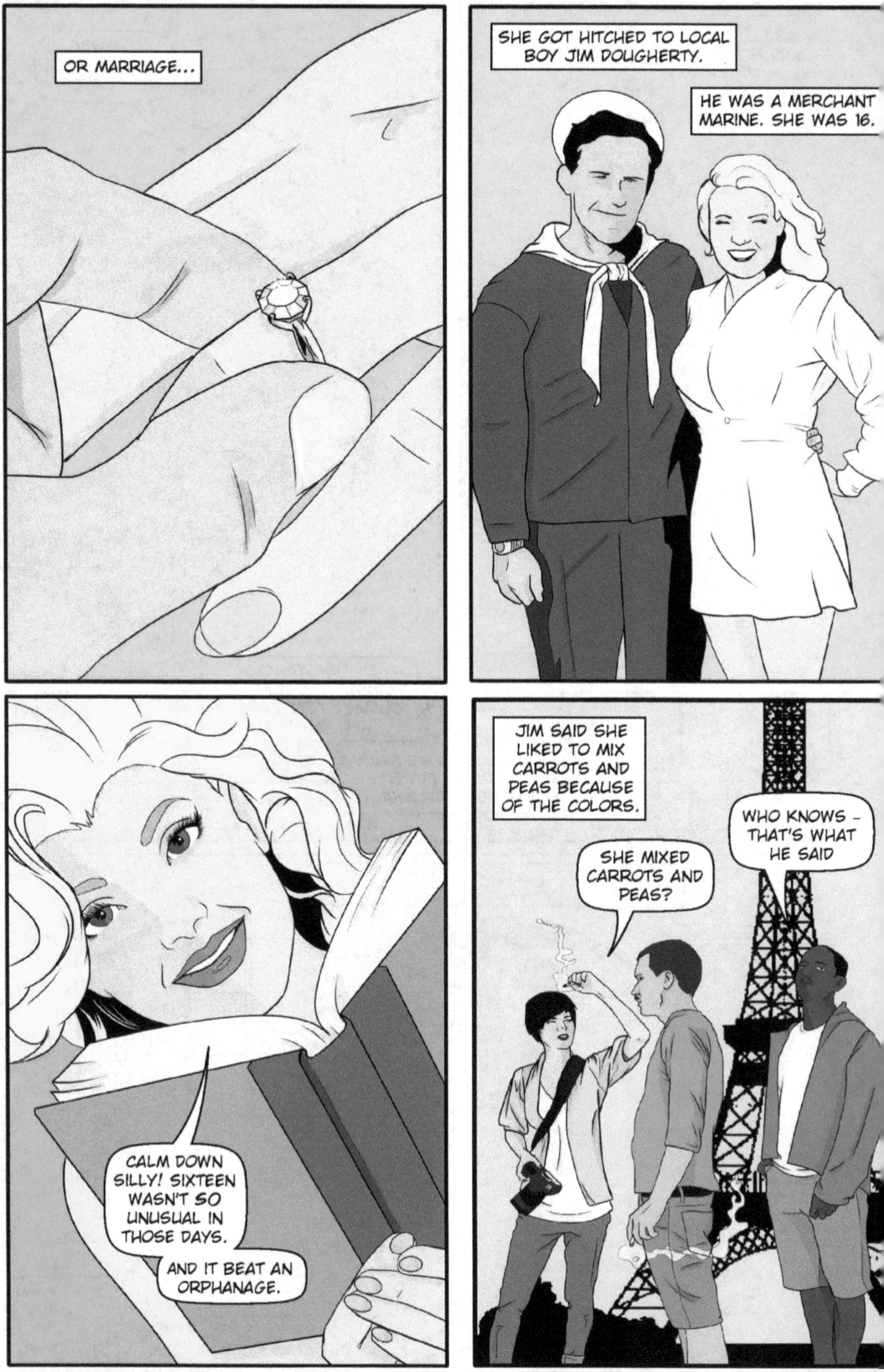
OR MARRIAGE...
SHE GOT HITCHED TO LOCAL BOY JIM DOUGHERTY.
HE WAS A MERCHANT MARINE. SHE WAS 16.
CALM DOWN SILLY! SIXTEEN WASN'T SO UNUSUAL IN THOSE DAYS.
AND IT BEAT AN ORPHANAGE.
JIM SAID SHE LIKED TO MIX CARROTS AND PEAS BECAUSE OF THE COLORS.
SHE MIXED CARROTS AND PEAS?
WHO KNOWS - THAT'S WHAT HE SAID

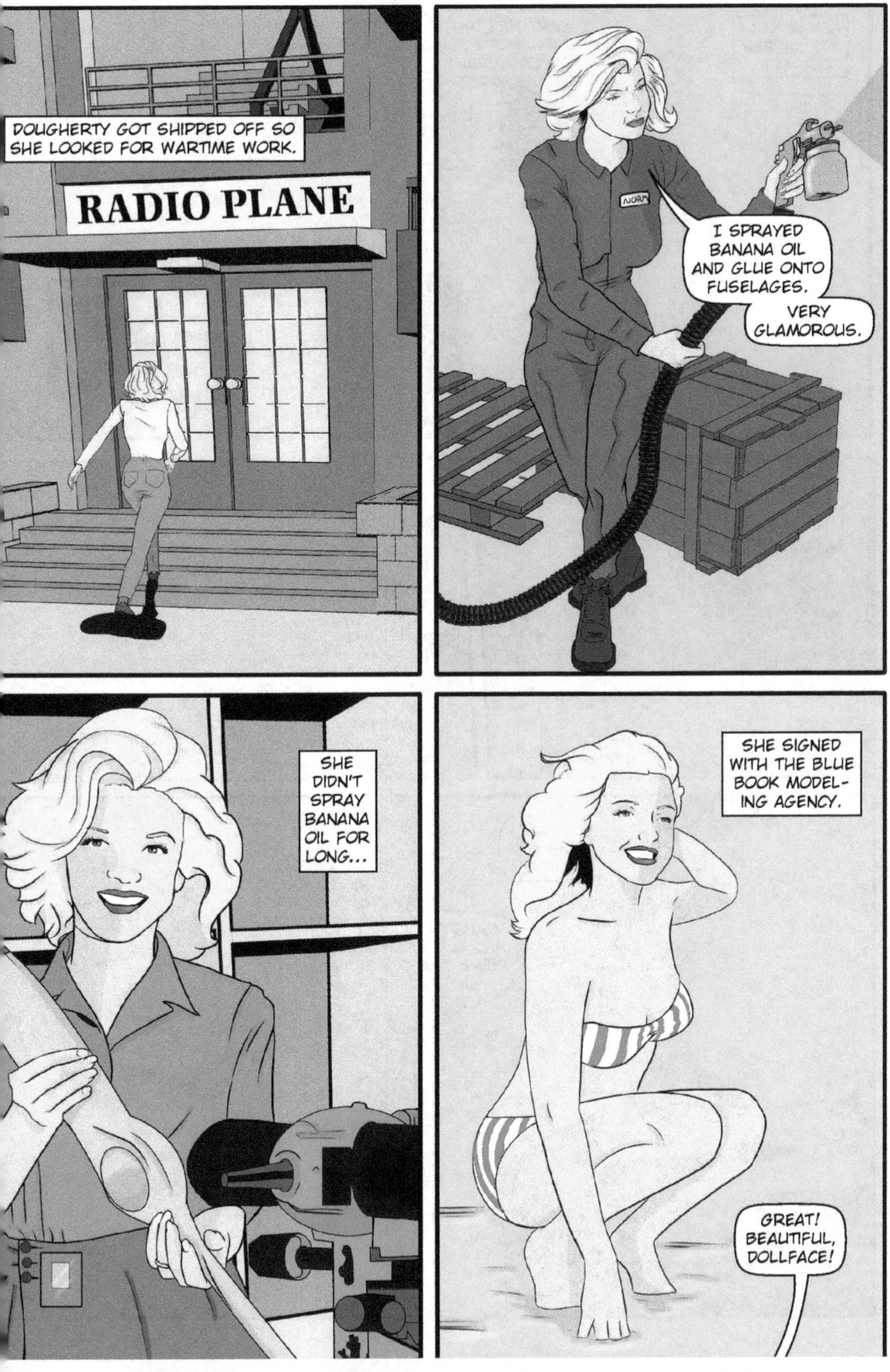
DOUGHERTY GOT SHIPPED OFF SO SHE LOOKED FOR WARTIME WORK.
RADIO PLANE
I SPRAYED BANANA OIL AND GLUE ONTO FUSELAGES.
VERY GLAMOROUS.
SHE DIDN'T SPRAY BANANA OIL FOR LONG...
SHE SIGNED WITH THE BLUE BOOK MODEL-ING AGENCY.
GREAT! BEAUTIFUL, DOLLFACE!

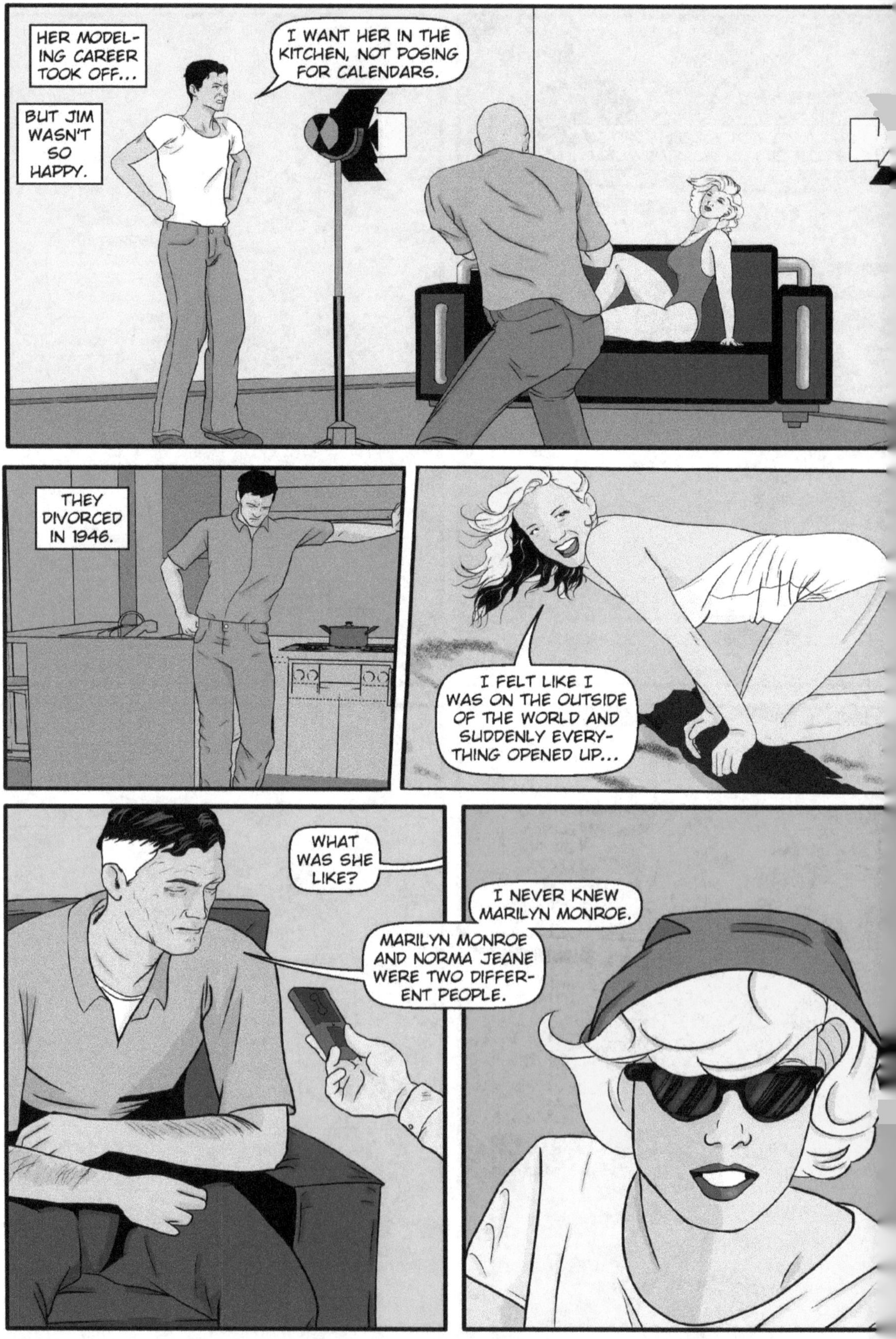
HER MODELING CAREER TOOK OFF...
BUT JIM WASN'T SO HAPPY.
I WANT HER IN THE KITCHEN, NOT POSING FOR CALENDARS.
THEY DIVORCED IN 1946.
I FELT LIKE I WAS ON THE OUTSIDE OF THE WORLD AND SUDDENLY EVERYTHING OPENED UP...
WHAT WAS SHE LIKE?
MARILYN MONROE AND NORMA JEANE WERE TWO DIFFERENT PEOPLE.
I NEVER KNEW MARILYN MONROE.

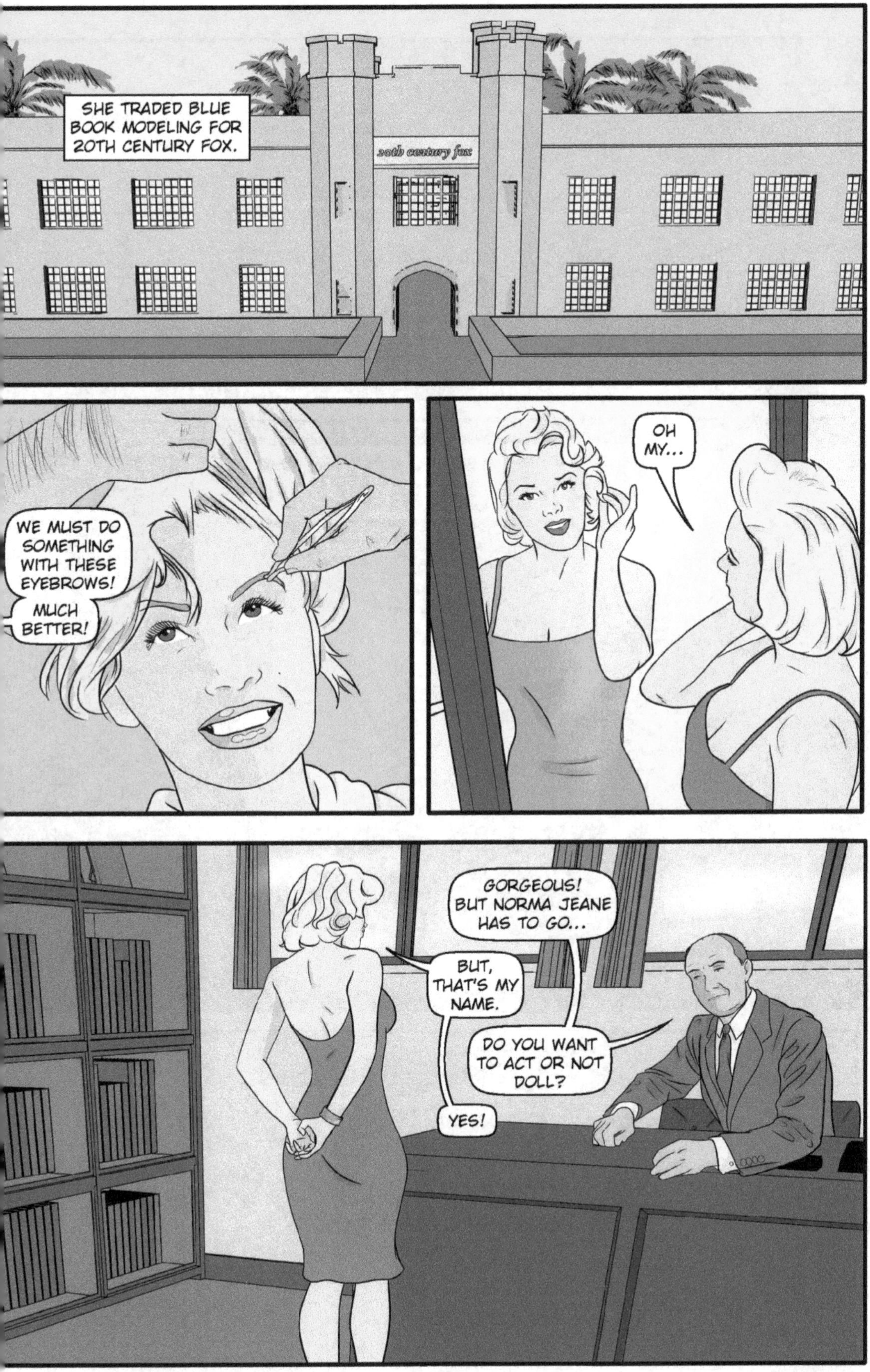
SHE TRADED BLUE BOOK MODELING FOR 20TH CENTURY FOX.
20th century fox
WE MUST DO SOMETHING WITH THESE EYEBROWS!
MUCH BETTER!
OH MY...
GORGEOUS! BUT NORMA JEANE HAS TO GO...
BUT, THAT'S MY NAME.
DO YOU WANT TO ACT OR NOT DOLL?
YES!

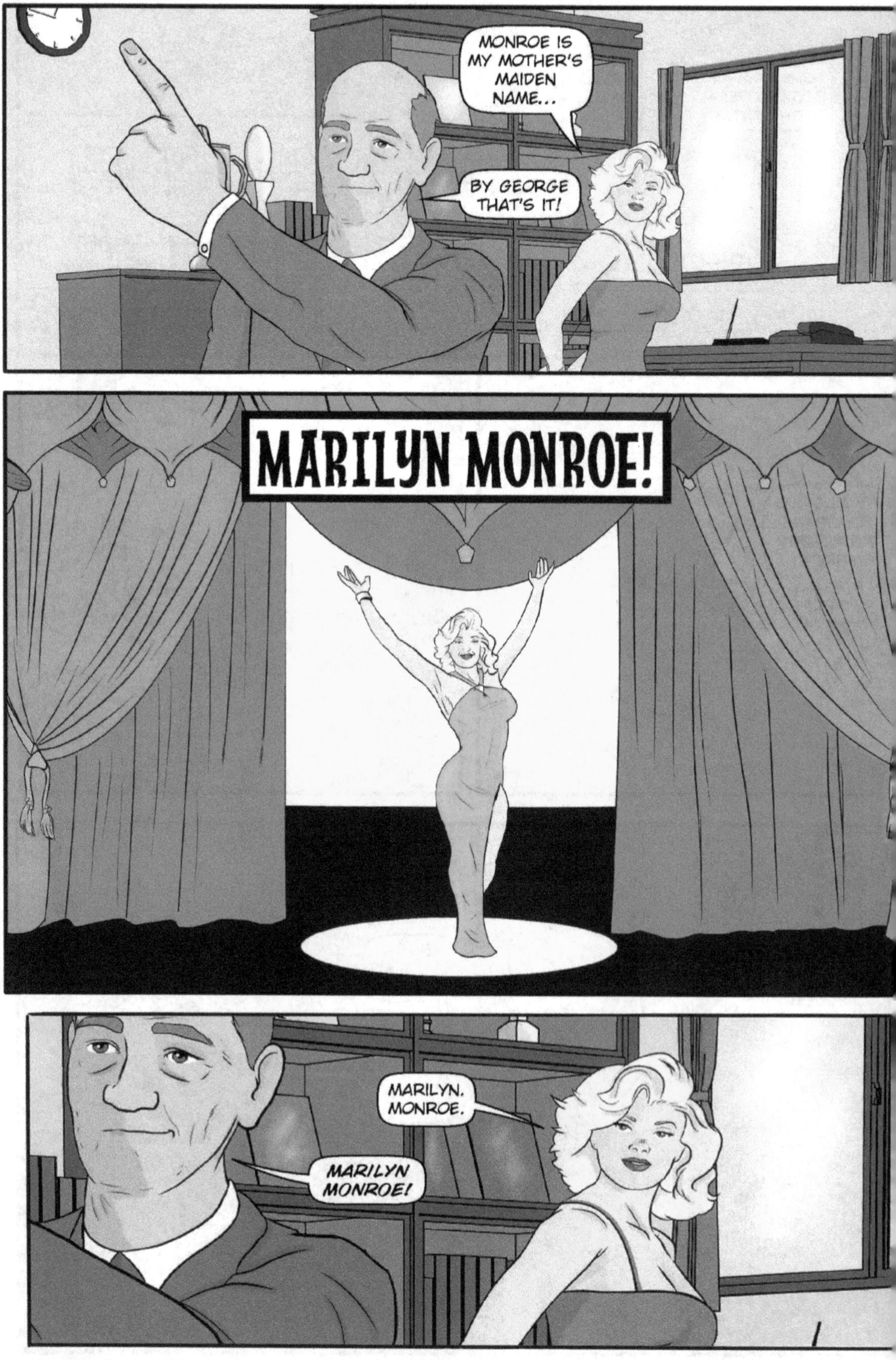

MONROE IS MY MOTHER'S MAIDEN NAME...
BY GEORGE THAT'S IT!
MARILYN MONROE!
MARILYN. MONROE.
MARILYN MONROE!

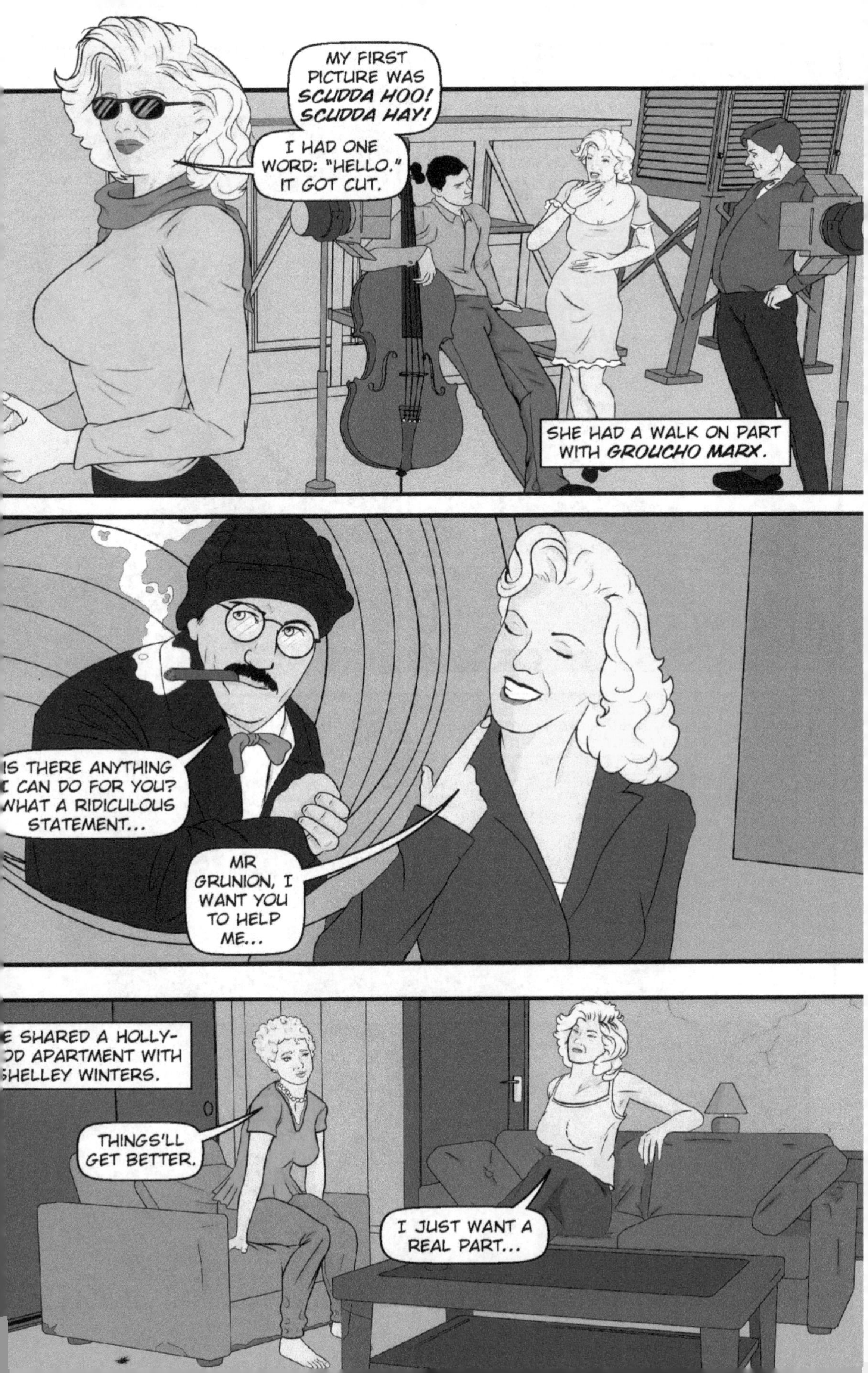

MY FIRST PICTURE WAS SCUDDA HOO! SCUDDA HAY!
I HAD ONE WORD: "HELLO." IT GOT CUT.
SHE HAD A WALK ON PART WITH GROUCHO MARX.
IS THERE ANYTHING I CAN DO FOR YOU? WHAT A RIDICULOUS STATEMENT...
MR GRUNION, I WANT YOU TO HELP ME...
E SHARED A HOLLY-
OD APARTMENT WITH
SHELLEY WINTERS.
THINGS'LL GET BETTER.
I JUST WANT A REAL PART...

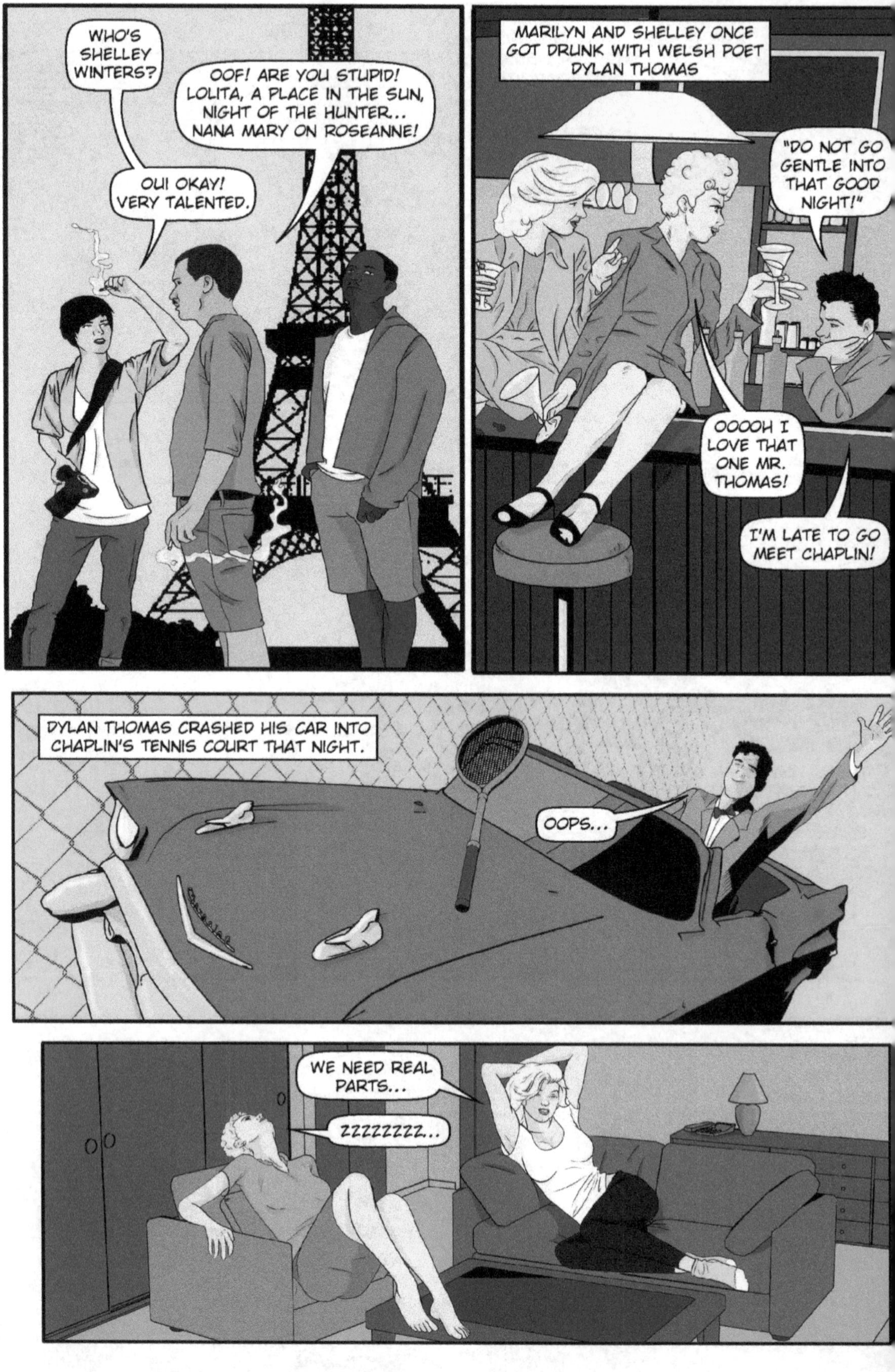
WHO'S SHELLEY WINTERS?
OOF! ARE YOU STUPID! LOLITA, A PLACE IN THE SUN, NIGHT OF THE HUNTER... NANA MARY ON ROSEANNE!
OUI OKAY! VERY TALENTED.
MARILYN AND SHELLEY ONCE GOT DRUNK WITH WELSH POET DYLAN THOMAS
"DO NOT GO GENTLE INTO THAT GOOD NIGHT!"
OOOOH I LOVE THAT ONE MR. THOMAS!
I'M LATE TO GO MEET CHAPLIN!
DYLAN THOMAS CRASHED HIS CAR INTO CHAPLIN'S TENNIS COURT THAT NIGHT.
OOPS...
WE NEED REAL PARTS...
ZZZZZZZZ...

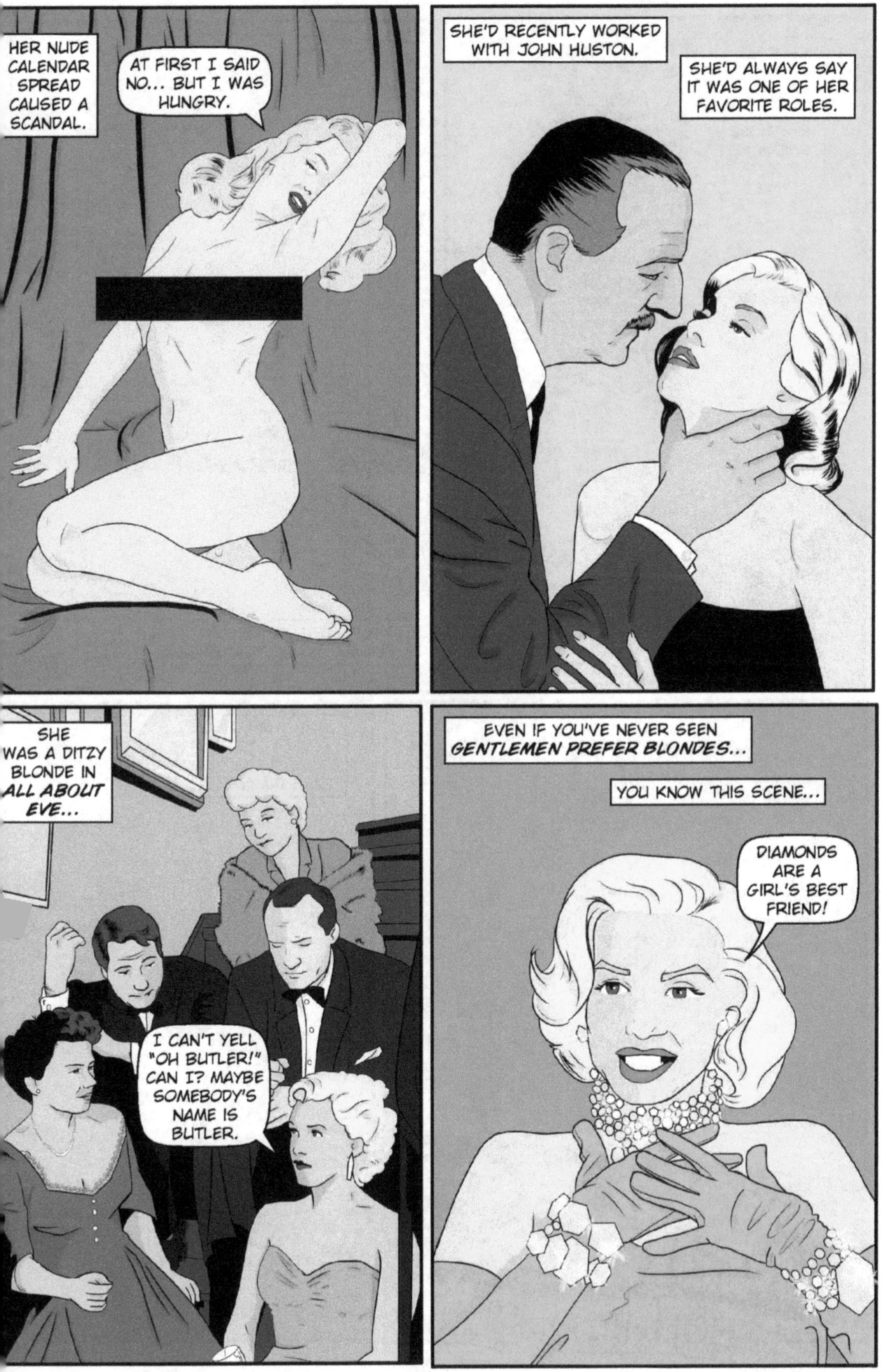
HER NUDE CALENDAR SPREAD CAUSED A SCANDAL.
AT FIRST I SAID NO... BUT I WAS HUNGRY.
SHE'D RECENTLY WORKED WITH JOHN HUSTON.
SHE'D ALWAYS SAY IT WAS ONE OF HER FAVORITE ROLES.
SHE WAS A DITZY BLONDE IN ***ALL ABOUT EVE...***
I CAN'T YELL "OH BUTLER!" CAN I? MAYBE SOMEBODY'S NAME IS BUTLER.
EVEN IF YOU'VE NEVER SEEN ***GENTLEMEN PREFER BLONDES...***
YOU KNOW THIS SCENE...
DIAMONDS ARE A GIRL'S BEST FRIEND!

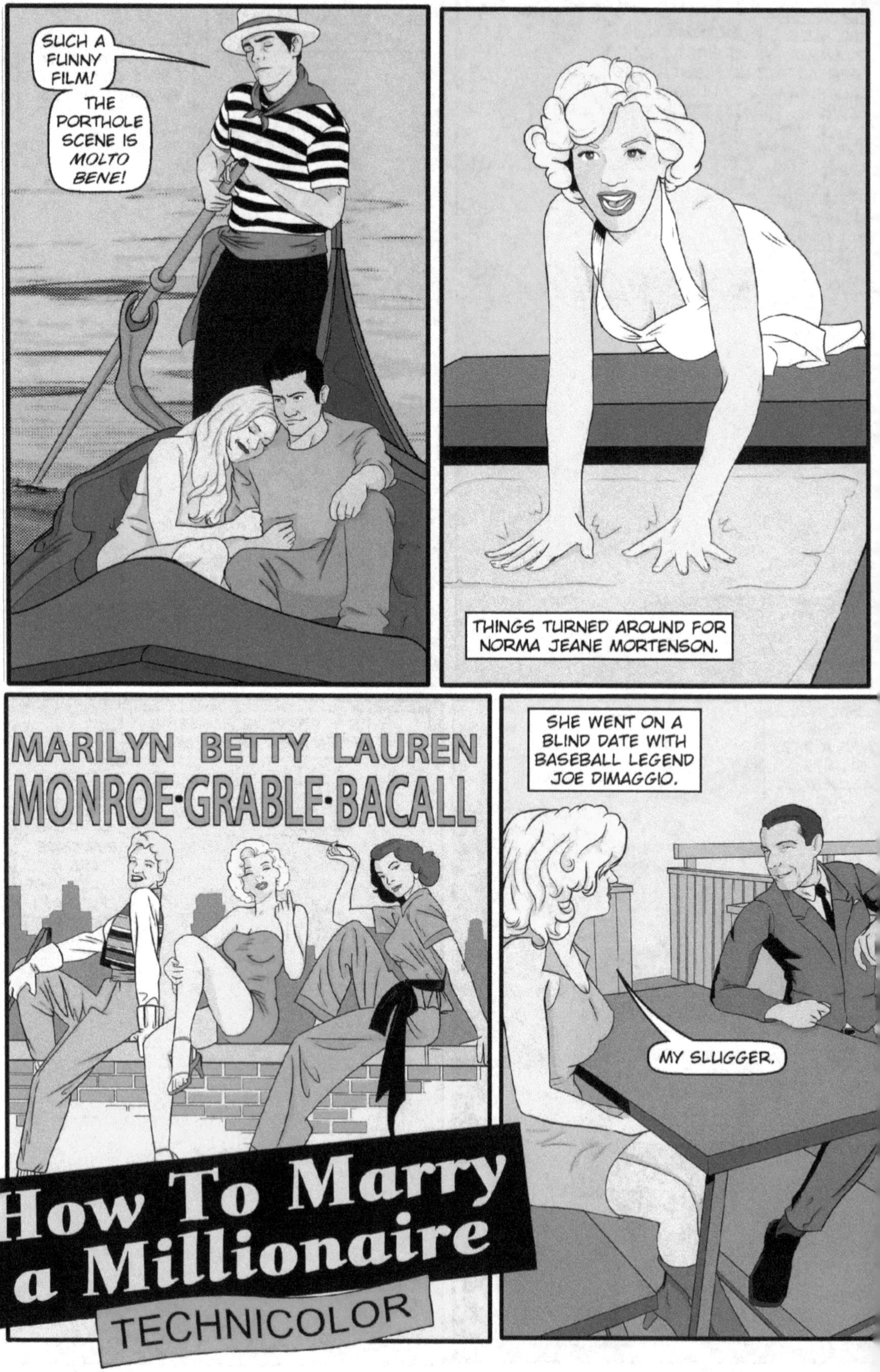
SUCH A FUNNY FILM!
THE PORTHOLE SCENE IS *MOLTO BENE!*
THINGS TURNED AROUND FOR NORMA JEANE MORTENSON.
MARILYN BETTY LAUREN
MONROE·GRABLE·BACALL
How To Marry a Millionaire
TECHNICOLOR
SHE WENT ON A BLIND DATE WITH BASEBALL LEGEND JOE DIMAGGIO.
MY SLUGGER.

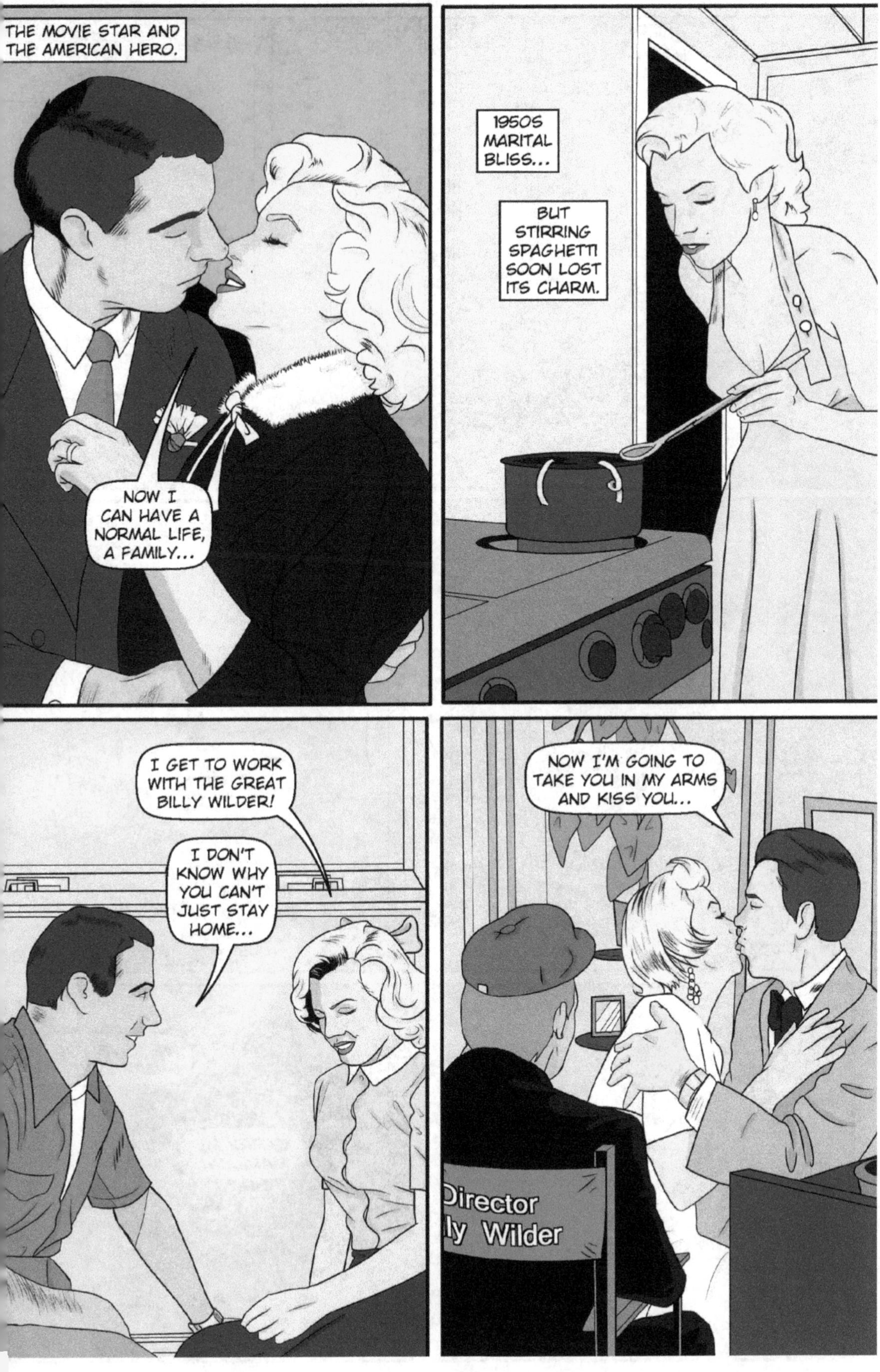
THE MOVIE STAR AND THE AMERICAN HERO.
NOW I CAN HAVE A NORMAL LIFE, A FAMILY...
1950S MARITAL BLISS...
BUT STIRRING SPAGHETTI SOON LOST ITS CHARM.
I GET TO WORK WITH THE GREAT BILLY WILDER!
I DON'T KNOW WHY YOU CAN'T JUST STAY HOME...
NOW I'M GOING TO TAKE YOU IN MY ARMS AND KISS YOU...
Director
lly Wilder

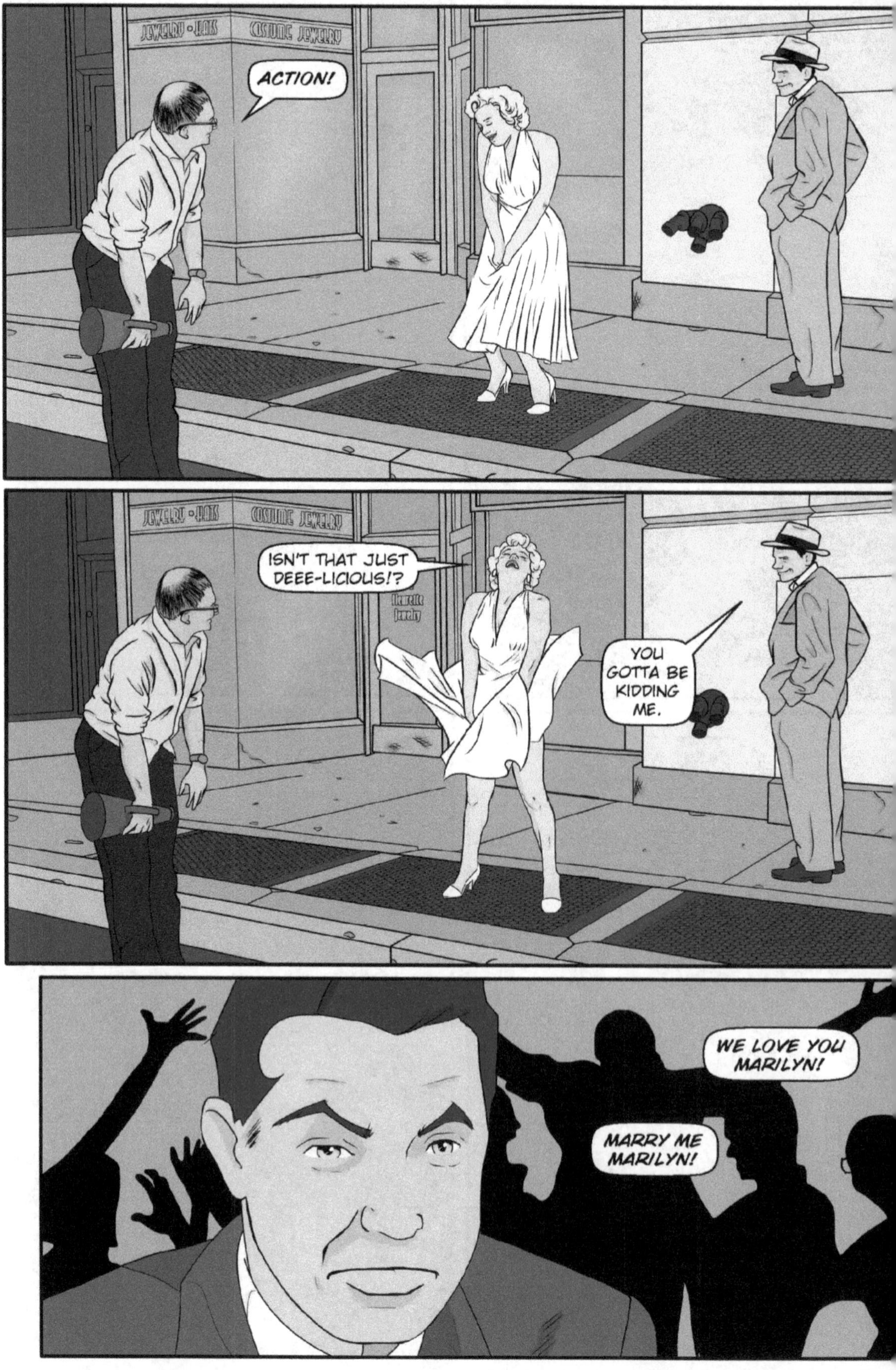
JEWELRY • HATS
COSTUME JEWELRY
ACTION!
ISN'T THAT JUST DEEE-LICIOUS!?
YOU GOTTA BE KIDDING ME.
WE LOVE YOU MARILYN!
MARRY ME MARILYN!

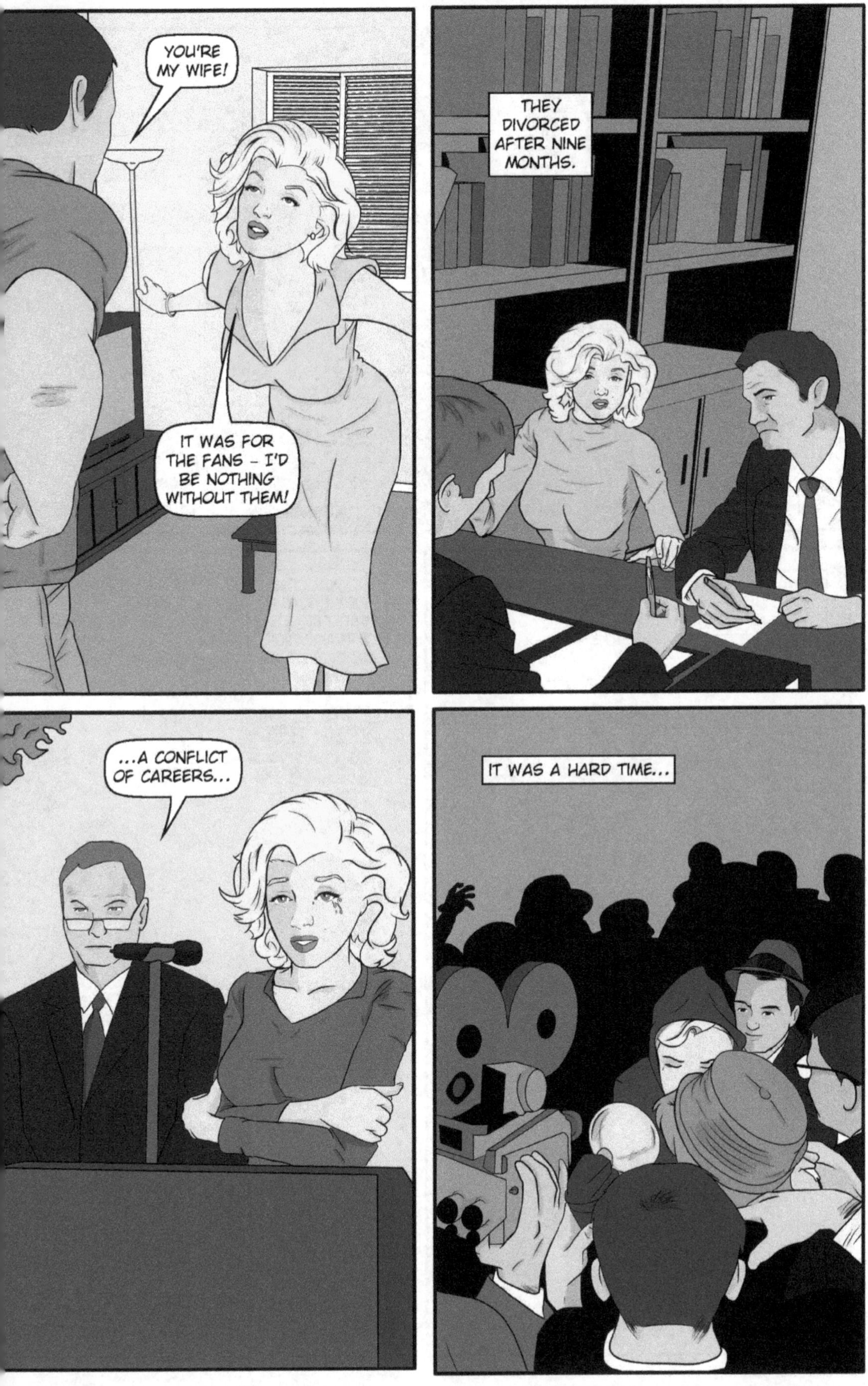
YOU'RE MY WIFE!
IT WAS FOR THE FANS – I'D BE NOTHING WITHOUT THEM!
THEY DIVORCED AFTER NINE MONTHS.
...A CONFLICT OF CAREERS...
IT WAS A HARD TIME...

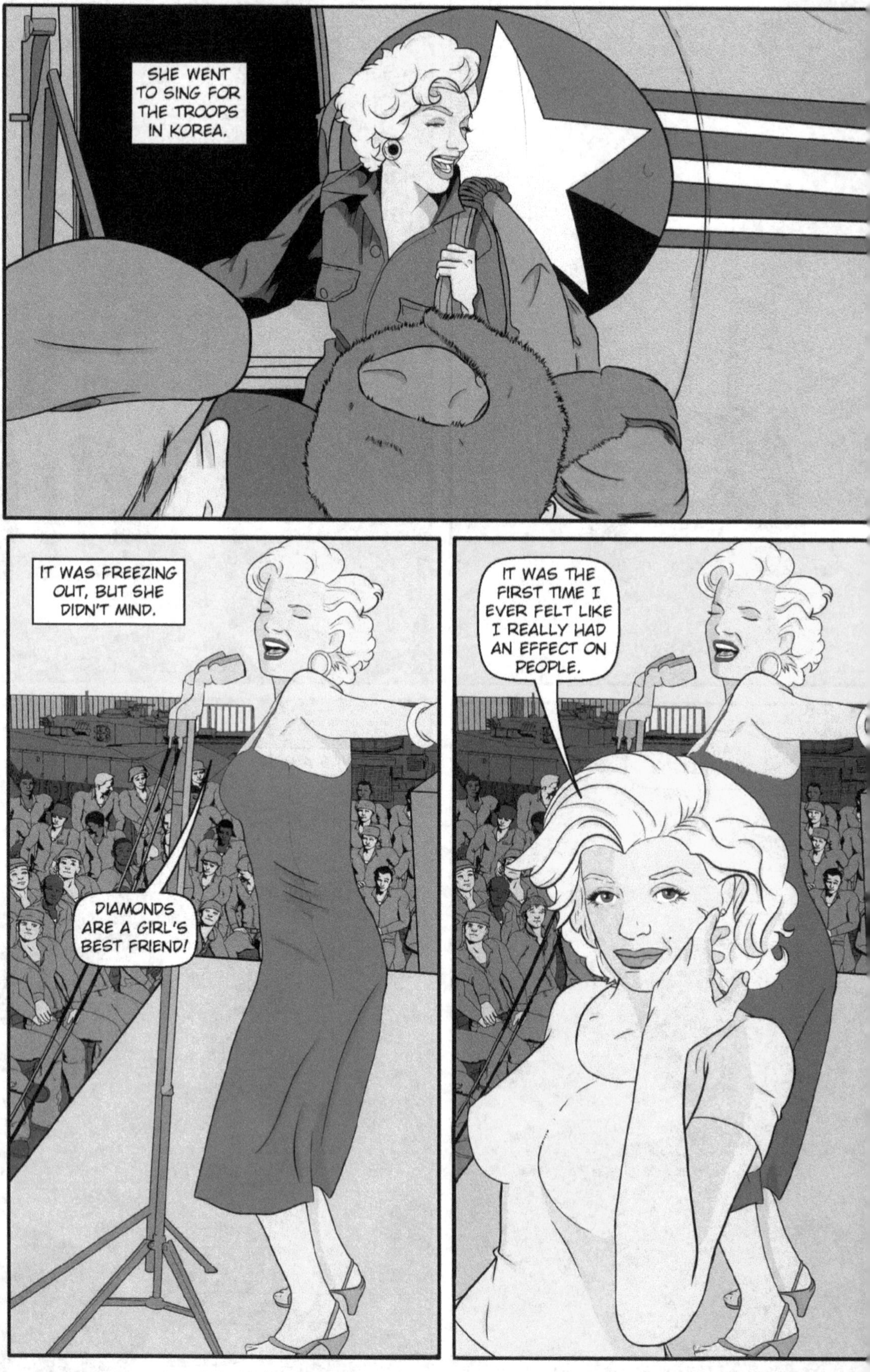
SHE WENT TO SING FOR THE TROOPS IN KOREA.
IT WAS FREEZING OUT, BUT SHE DIDN'T MIND.
DIAMONDS ARE A GIRL'S BEST FRIEND!
IT WAS THE FIRST TIME I EVER FELT LIKE I REALLY HAD AN EFFECT ON PEOPLE.

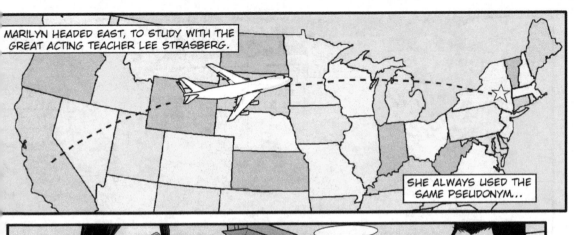

MARILYN HEADED EAST, TO STUDY WITH THE GREAT ACTING TEACHER LEE STRASBERG.

SHE ALWAYS USED THE SAME PSEUDONYM...

I'M *ZELDA ZONK.*

ZONK?

THAT'S RIGHT. *ZONK.*

THE ACTORS STUDIO

EVEN THOUGH SHE WAS AN INTERNATIONAL STAR, MARILYN CRAVED RESPECT.

THE ACTORS STUDIO

IF I SAY I WANT TO BE AN ACTRESS, THEY LOOK AT MY FIGURE...

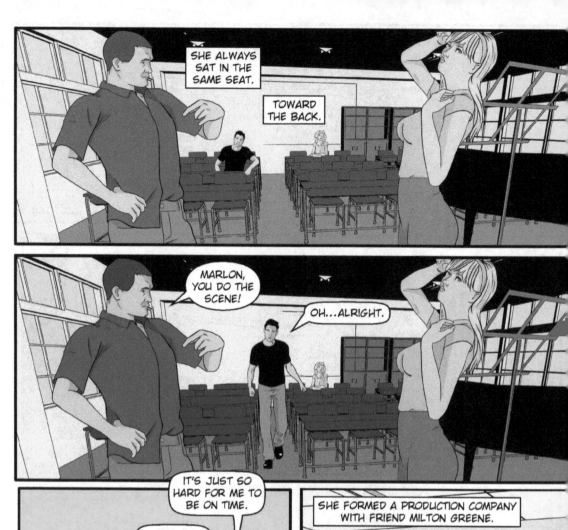

SHE ALWAYS SAT IN THE SAME SEAT.

TOWARD THE BACK.

MARLON, YOU DO THE SCENE!

OH...ALRIGHT.

IT'S JUST SO HARD FOR ME TO BE ON TIME.

WELL BE EARLY THEN!

SHE FORMED A PRODUCTION COMPANY WITH FRIEND MILTON GREENE.

NOW I CAN FIND BETTER PARTS.

MAYBE WE CAN BRING MARLON IN TOO.

Ms. Monroe

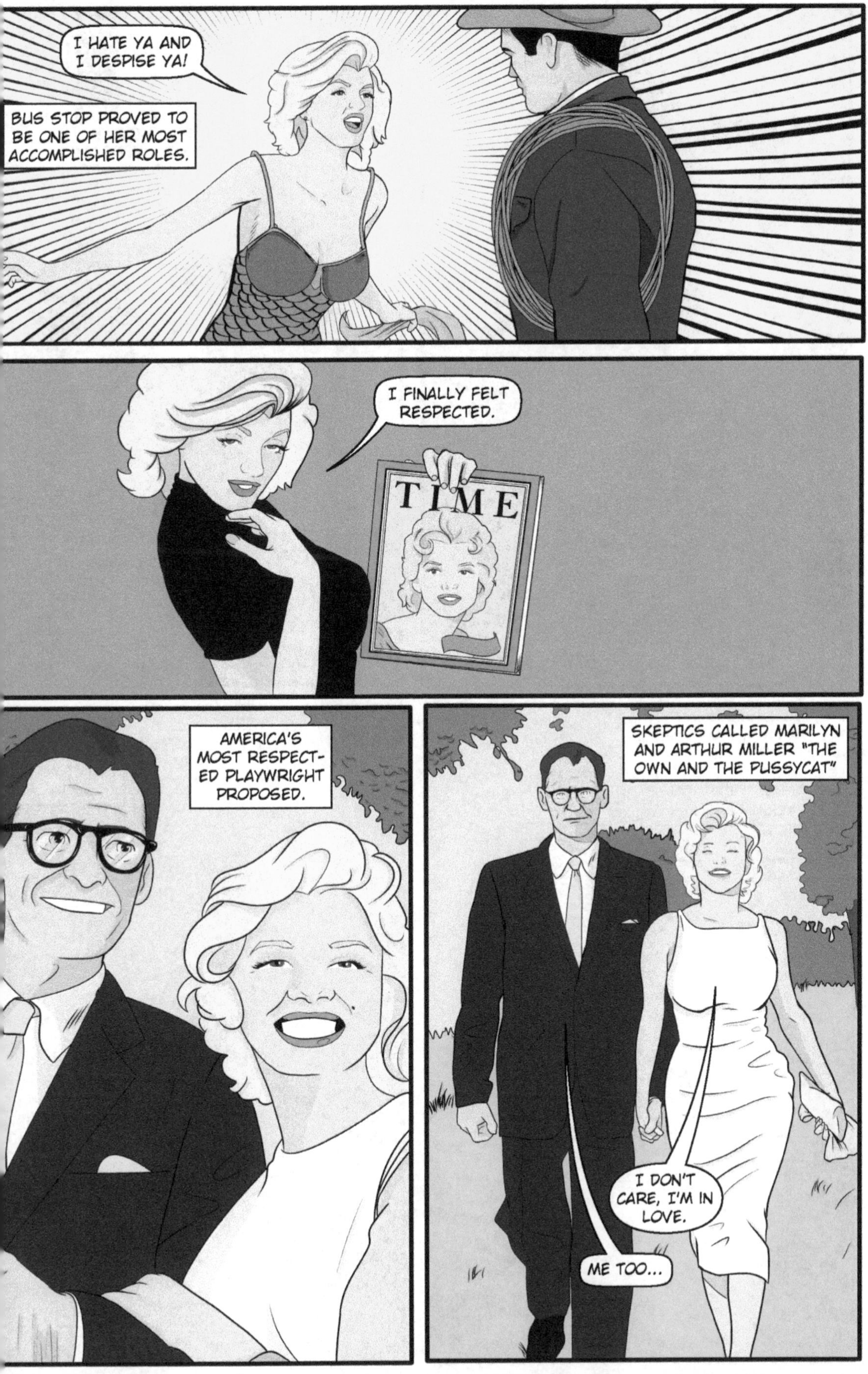
I HATE YA AND I DESPISE YA!
BUS STOP PROVED TO BE ONE OF HER MOST ACCOMPLISHED ROLES.
I FINALLY FELT RESPECTED.
TIME
AMERICA'S MOST RESPECT-ED PLAYWRIGHT PROPOSED.
SKEPTICS CALLED MARILYN AND ARTHUR MILLER "THE OWN AND THE PUSSYCAT"
I DON'T CARE, I'M IN LOVE.
ME TOO...

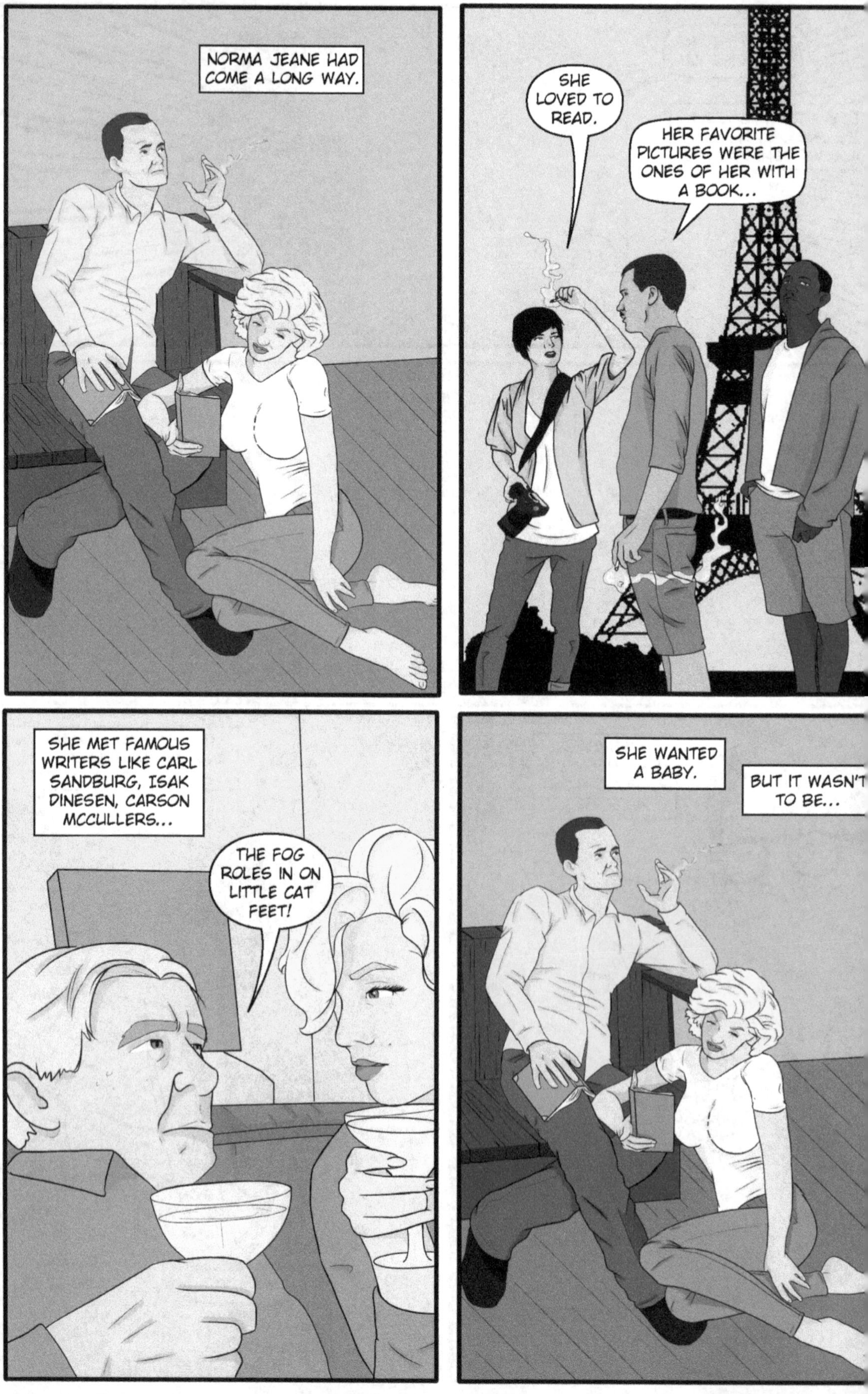
NORMA JEANE HAD COME A LONG WAY.
SHE LOVED TO READ.
HER FAVORITE PICTURES WERE THE ONES OF HER WITH A BOOK...
SHE MET FAMOUS WRITERS LIKE CARL SANDBURG, ISAK DINESEN, CARSON MCCULLERS...
THE FOG ROLES IN ON LITTLE CAT FEET!
SHE WANTED A BABY.
BUT IT WASN'T TO BE...

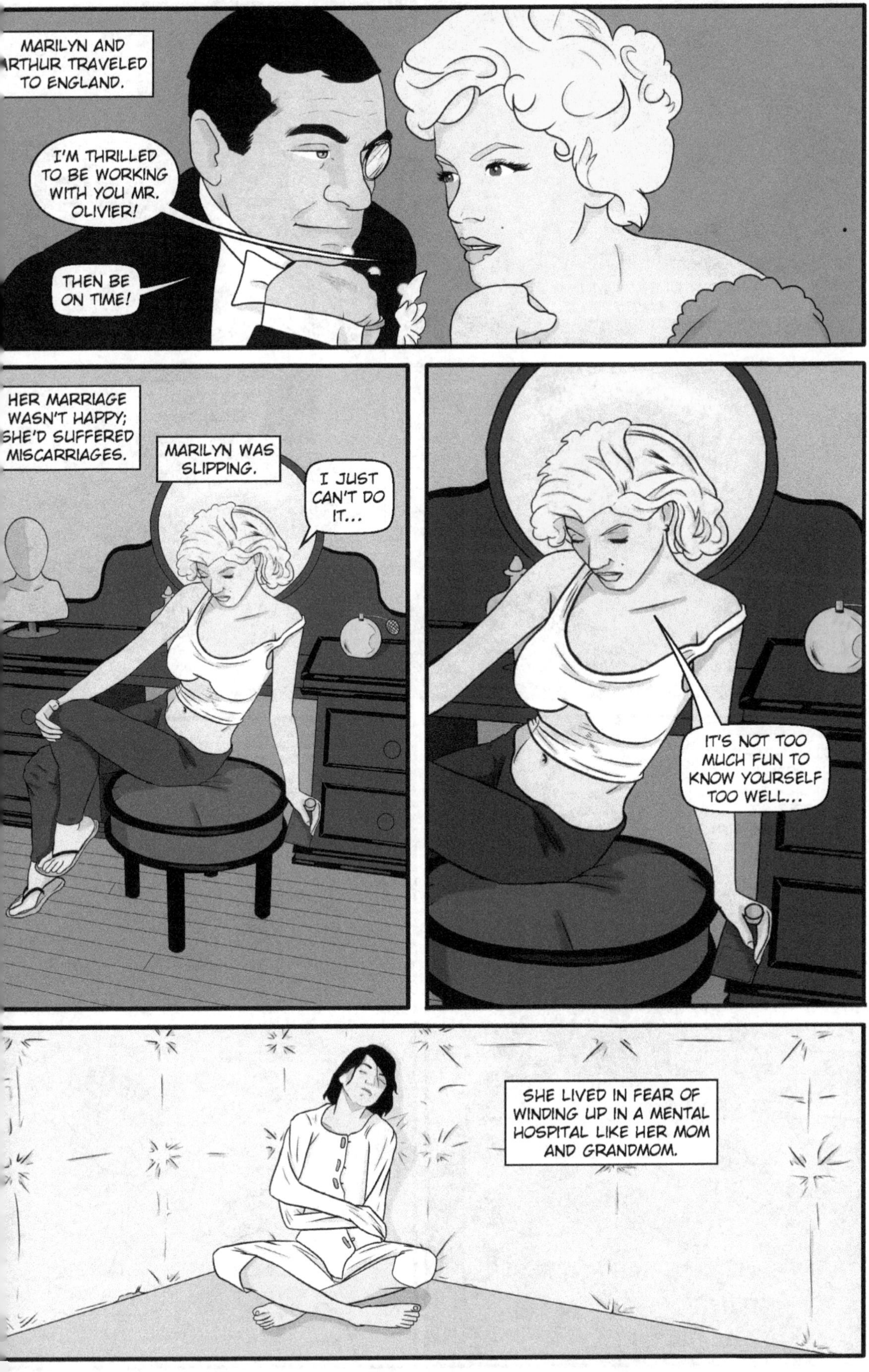
MARILYN AND ARTHUR TRAVELED TO ENGLAND.
I'M THRILLED TO BE WORKING WITH YOU MR. OLIVIER!
THEN BE ON TIME!
HER MARRIAGE WASN'T HAPPY; SHE'D SUFFERED MISCARRIAGES.
MARILYN WAS SLIPPING.
I JUST CAN'T DO IT...
IT'S NOT TOO MUCH FUN TO KNOW YOURSELF TOO WELL...
SHE LIVED IN FEAR OF WINDING UP IN A MENTAL HOSPITAL LIKE HER MOM AND GRANDMOM.

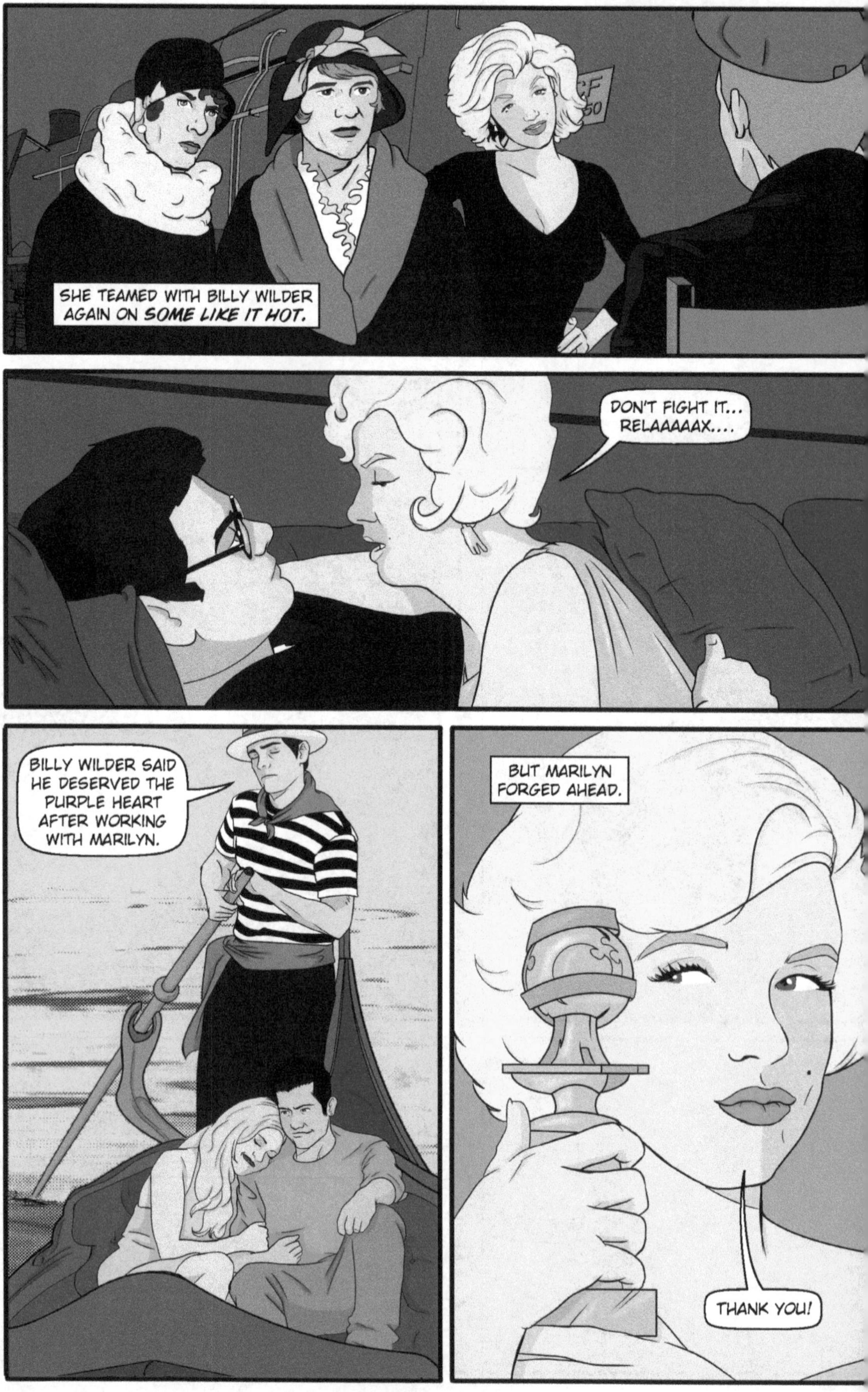
SHE TEAMED WITH BILLY WILDER AGAIN ON *SOME LIKE IT HOT.*
DON'T FIGHT IT... RELAAAAAX....
BILLY WILDER SAID HE DESERVED THE PURPLE HEART AFTER WORKING WITH MARILYN.
BUT MARILYN FORGED AHEAD.
THANK YOU!

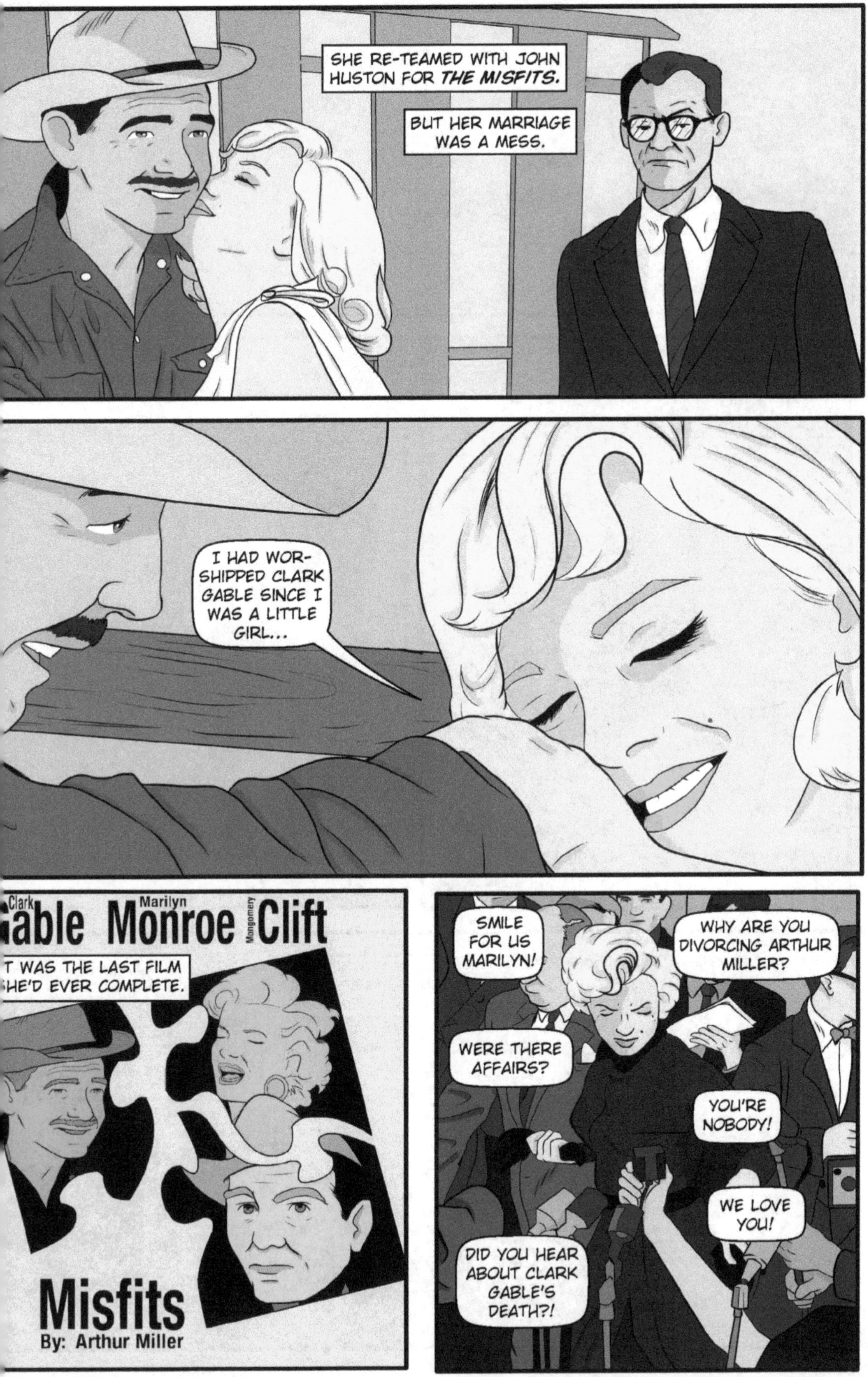

SHE RE-TEAMED WITH JOHN HUSTON FOR *THE MISFITS.*
BUT HER MARRIAGE WAS A MESS.
I HAD WOR-SHIPPED CLARK GABLE SINCE I WAS A LITTLE GIRL...
Clark Gable Marilyn Monroe Montgomery Clift
T WAS THE LAST FILM SHE'D EVER COMPLETE.
Misfits
By: Arthur Miller
SMILE FOR US MARILYN!
WHY ARE YOU DIVORCING ARTHUR MILLER?
WERE THERE AFFAIRS?
YOU'RE NOBODY!
WE LOVE YOU!
DID YOU HEAR ABOUT CLARK GABLE'S DEATH?!

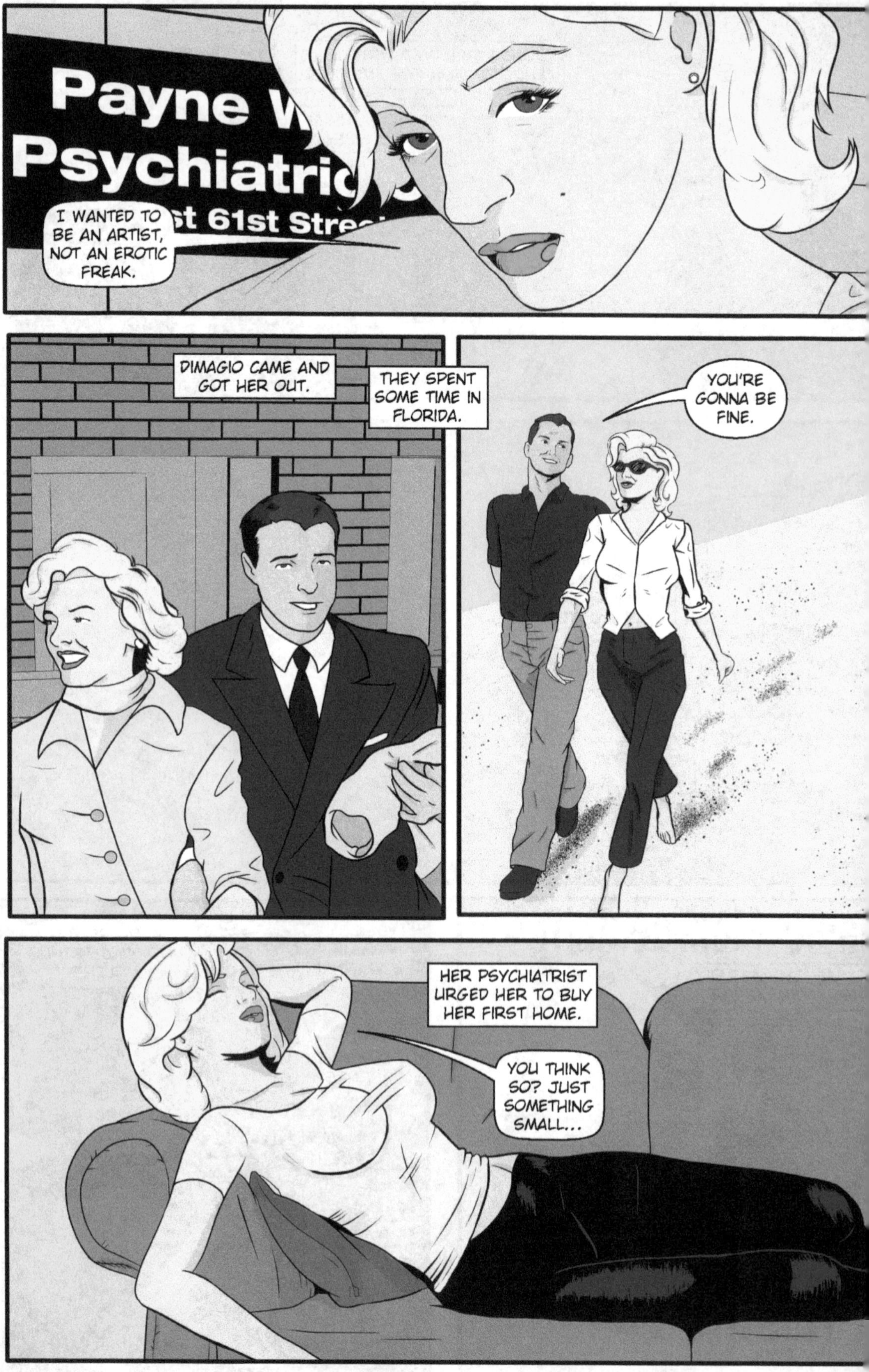
Payne W
Psychiatric
st 61st Stre
I WANTED TO BE AN ARTIST, NOT AN EROTIC FREAK.
DIMAGIO CAME AND GOT HER OUT.
THEY SPENT SOME TIME IN FLORIDA.
YOU'RE GONNA BE FINE.
HER PSYCHIATRIST URGED HER TO BUY HER FIRST HOME.
YOU THINK SO? JUST SOMETHING SMALL...

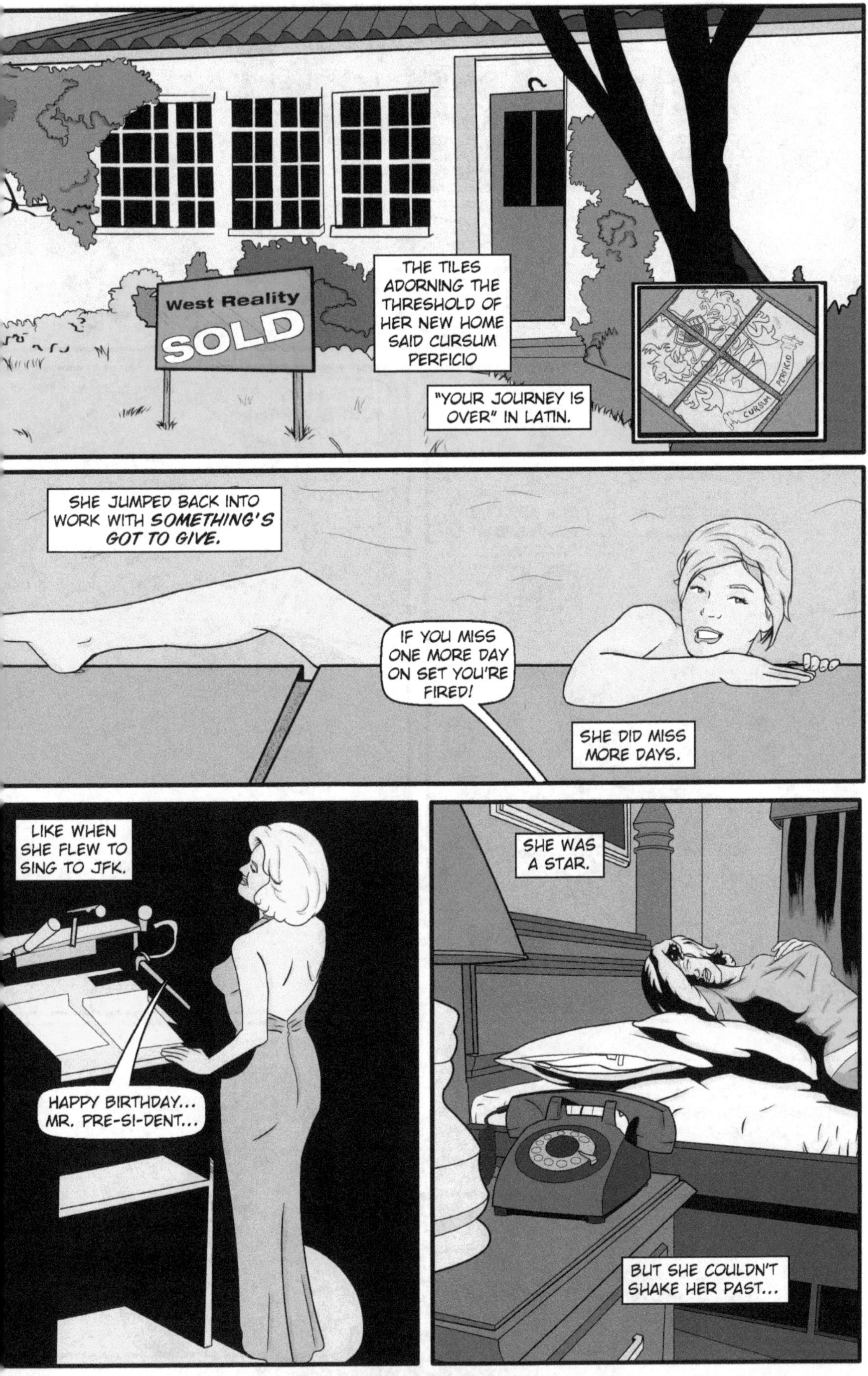
West Reality
SOLD
THE TILES ADORNING THE THRESHOLD OF HER NEW HOME SAID CURSUM PERFICIO
"YOUR JOURNEY IS OVER" IN LATIN.
CURSUM PERFICIO
SHE JUMPED BACK INTO WORK WITH *SOMETHING'S GOT TO GIVE.*
IF YOU MISS ONE MORE DAY ON SET YOU'RE FIRED!
SHE DID MISS MORE DAYS.
LIKE WHEN SHE FLEW TO SING TO JFK.
HAPPY BIRTHDAY... MR. PRE-SI-DENT...
SHE WAS A STAR.
BUT SHE COULDN'T SHAKE HER PAST...

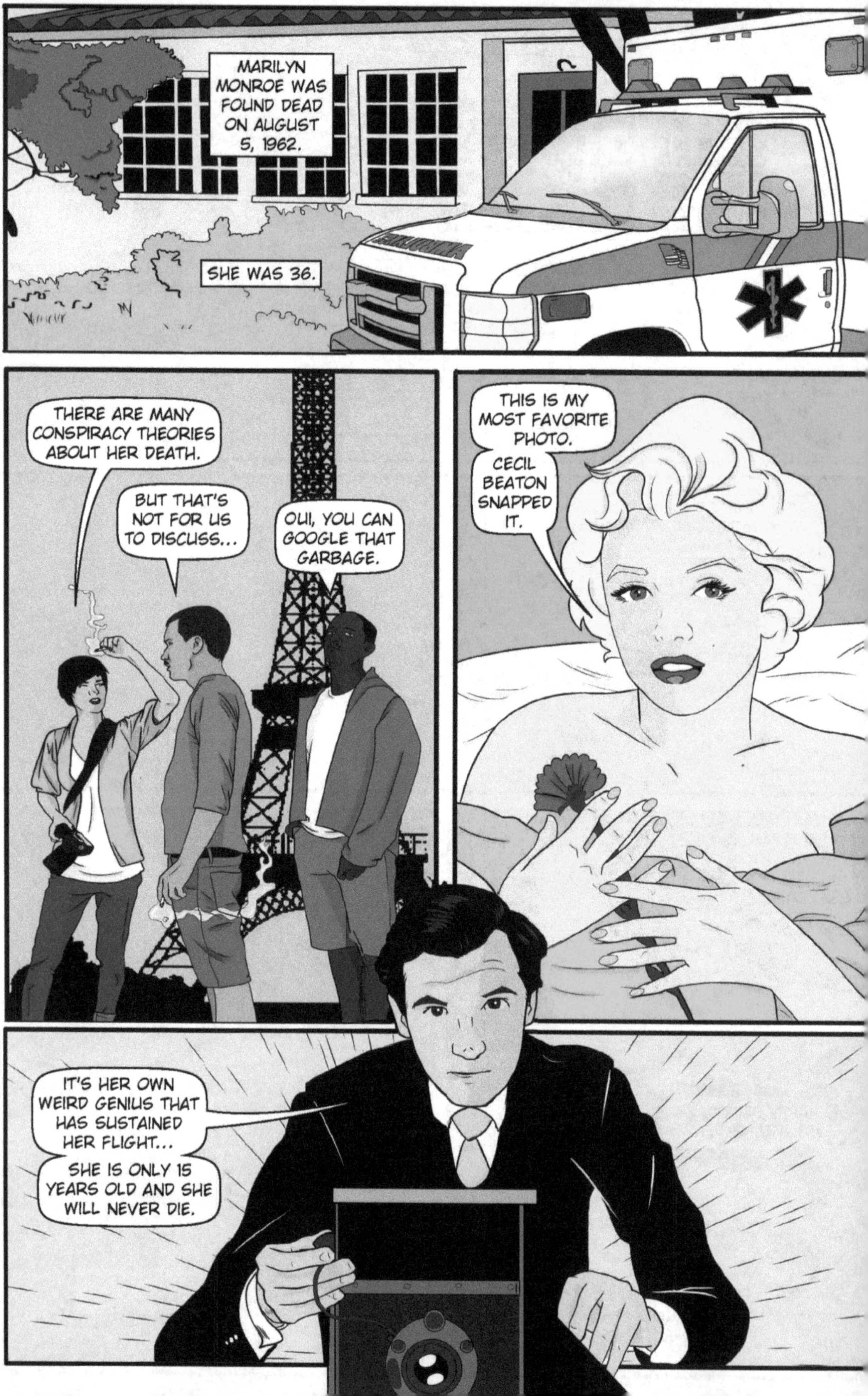
MARILYN MONROE WAS FOUND DEAD ON AUGUST 5, 1962.
SHE WAS 36.
THERE ARE MANY CONSPIRACY THEORIES ABOUT HER DEATH.
BUT THAT'S NOT FOR US TO DISCUSS...
OUI, YOU CAN GOOGLE THAT GARBAGE.
THIS IS MY MOST FAVORITE PHOTO.
CECIL BEATON SNAPPED IT.
IT'S HER OWN WEIRD GENIUS THAT HAS SUSTAINED HER FLIGHT...
SHE IS ONLY 15 YEARS OLD AND SHE WILL NEVER DIE.

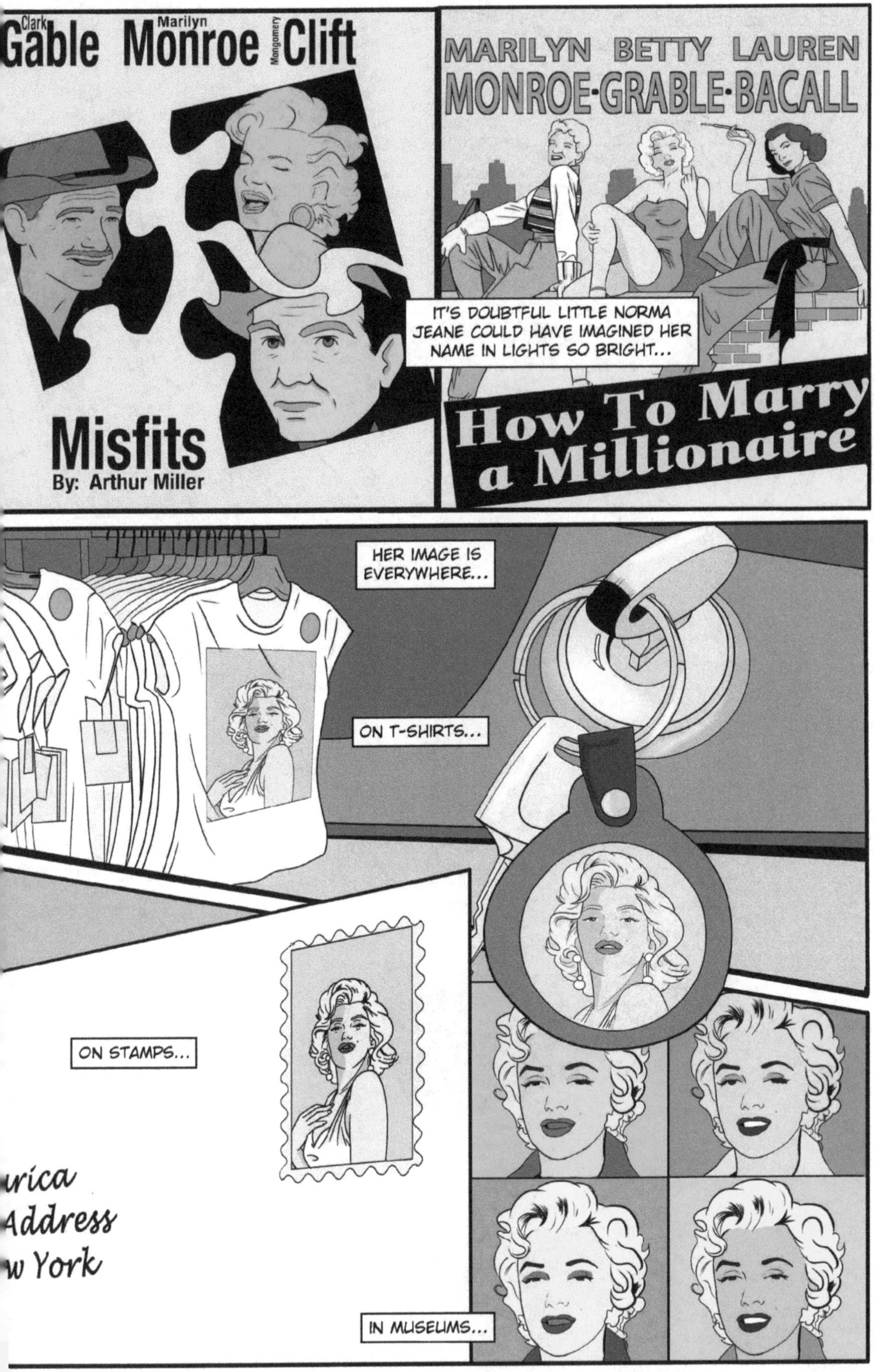

Clark Gable Marilyn Monroe Mongomery Clift
Misfits
By: Arthur Miller
MARILYN BETTY LAUREN
MONROE·GRABLE·BACALL
IT'S DOUBTFUL LITTLE NORMA JEANE COULD HAVE IMAGINED HER NAME IN LIGHTS SO BRIGHT...
How To Marry a Millionaire
HER IMAGE IS EVERYWHERE...
ON T-SHIRTS...
ON STAMPS...
urica
Address
w York
IN MUSEUMS...

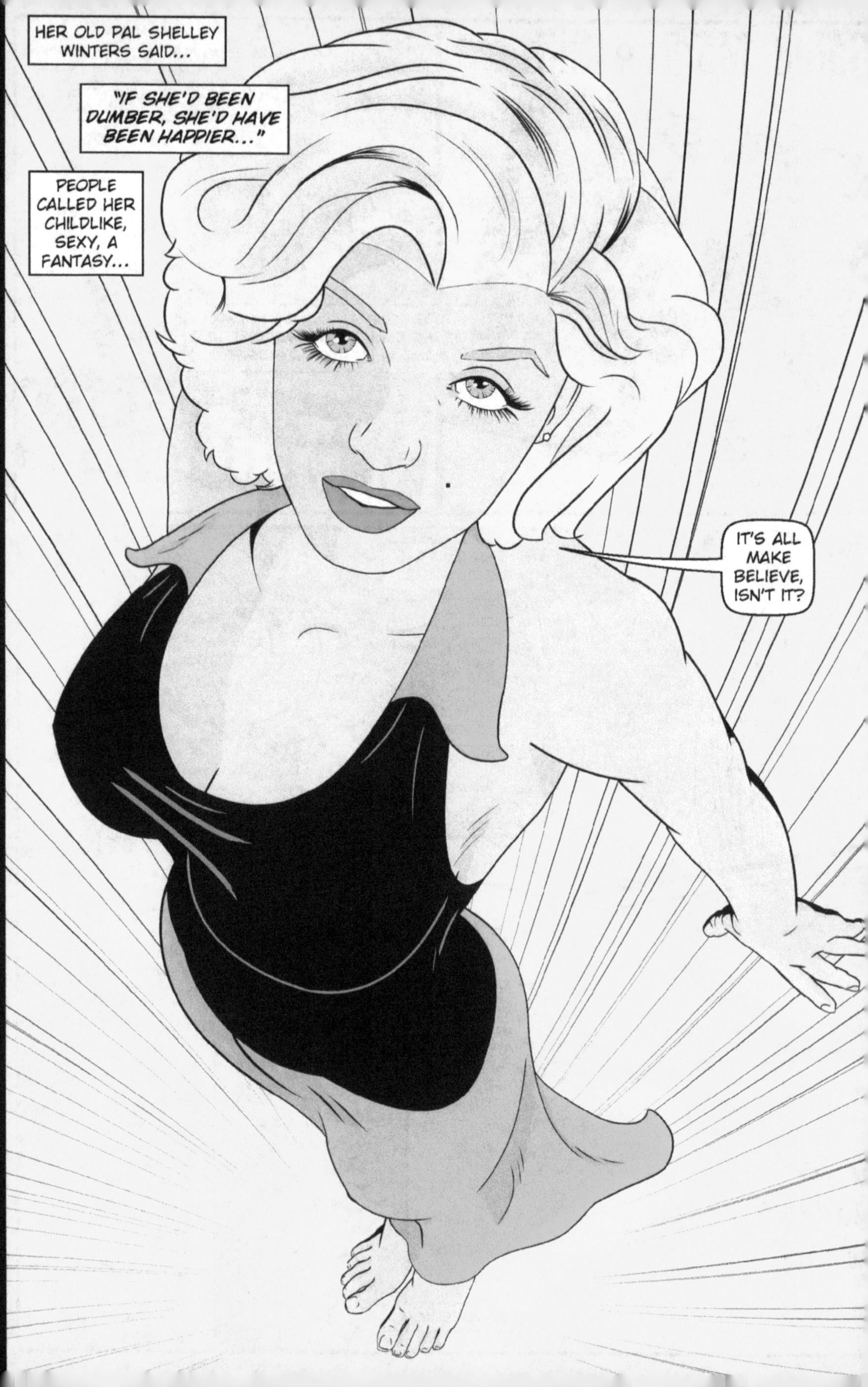
HER OLD PAL SHELLEY WINTERS SAID...
"IF SHE'D BEEN DUMBER, SHE'D HAVE BEEN HAPPIER..."
PEOPLE CALLED HER CHILDLIKE, SEXY, A FANTASY...
IT'S ALL MAKE BELIEVE, ISN'T IT?

TIDALWAVE COMICS

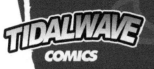

Michael L. Frizell, Melissa Seymour, J. Reed, Dina Gachman — Writer

Rafael Cordeiro, Manuel Díaz, Patricio Carbajal, Nathan Girten, Nicholas Justus — Penciler

Darren G. Davis — Editor

David Hopkins, Gary Scott Beatty, Warren Montgomery — Letterer

Rob Aragon — Cover

Darren G. Davis
Publisher

Maggie Jessup
Publicity

Susan Ferris
ntertainment Manager

TIDALWAVE PRODUCTIONS

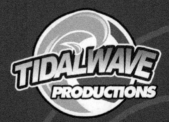